# Contemporary POETRY in America

# Contemporary POETRY in America

EDITED BY

## MILLER WILLIAMS

UNIVERSITY OF ARKANSAS

RANDOM HOUSE

NEW YORK

Library of Congress Cataloging in Publication Data
Williams, Miller, comp.
Contemporary poetry in America.

Bibliography: p.
1. American poetry—20th century. I. Title.
PS613.W5          811'.5'408          76–38587
ISBN 0–394–31625–8

Manufactured in the United States of America

Designed by Jack Ribik
Cover illustration by Kathleen Anderson

First Edition
9 8 7 6 5 4 3 2 1

# Acknowledgments

RALPH ADAMO, "Easter Sunday: Not the Artist" and "Low Along the River." © Ralph Adamo. Reprinted by permission of the author.

DICK ALLEN, "Podunk, 1941" and "To a Woman Half a World Away" from *Anon and Various Time Machine Poems* by Dick Allen. Copyright © 1971 by Dick Allen. Reprinted by permission of the publisher, Delacorte Press.

A.R. AMMONS, "Cascadilla Falls" from *Uplands, New Poems* by A.R. Ammons. Copyright © 1970 by A.R. Ammons. Reprinted by permission of W.W. Norton & Company, Inc. "Hymn" from *Expressions of Sea Level* by A.R. Ammons. Copyright © 1957, 1964 by A.R. Ammons. Originally appeared in the *Hudson Review*. Reprinted by permission of Ohio State University Press. "Identity" from *Impetus*. Reprinted by permission of the publisher.

ALVIN AUBERT, "Nat Turner in the Clearing," "Bessie Smith's Funeral," "Last Will and Testament," and "Codicil." Copyright © 1970 by Alvin Aubert. Reprinted by permission of the author.

JOHN BERRYMAN, "Winter Landscape," "Parting as Descent," "Venice, 182-," and "A Poem for Bhain" from *Short Poems* by John Berryman. Copyright 1940 by New Directions, copyright © 1948, 1958 by John Berryman. Reprinted by permission of Farrar, Straws & Giroux, Inc.

JOHN BIGUENET, "One-Day Diary" and "Everyone Begs for Mercy." Reprinted by permission of the author.

ELIZABETH BISHOP, "The Prodigal," "The Fish," "Roosters," and "House Guest" from *The Complete Poems* by Elizabeth Bishop. Copyright renewed 1968 by Elizabeth Bishop. Reprinted by permission of Farrar, Straus & Giroux, Inc.

ROBERT BLY, "Come with Me" from *The Light Around the Body* by Robert Bly. Copyright © 1964 by Robert Bly. "Written in Dejection Near Rome" from *The Light Around the Body* by Robert Bly. Copyright © 1966 by Robert Bly. "Hurrying Away from the Earth" and "The Fire of Despair Has Been Our Savior" from *The Light Around the Body* by Robert Bly. Copyright © 1967 by Robert Bly. Reprinted by permission of Harper & Row, Publishers, Inc.

GWENDOLYN BROOKS, "We Real Cool," "The Bean Eaters," and "Old Mary" from *Selected Poems* by Gwendolyn Brooks. Copyright © 1959 by Gwendolyn Brooks. "Sadie and Maud" from *Selected Poems* by Gwendolyn Brooks. Copyright, 1945 by Gwendolyn Brooks Blakely. Reprinted by permission of Harper & Row, Publishers, Inc.

CHARLES BUKOWSKI, "Footnote Upon the Construction of the Masses:" and "For Jane" from *The Days Run Away Like Wild Horses Over the Hills* by Charles Bukowski. Reprinted by permission of Black Sparrow Press. "The Tragedy of the Leaves" and "The Singular Self." Copyright Charles Bukowski. Reprinted by permission of the author.

ROBERT CANZONERI, "One Lion, Once" from *Watch Us Pass* by Robert Canzoneri. Copyright © 1963, 1968 by the Ohio State University Press. Originally appeared in the *Saturday Review*. Reprinted by permission of the Ohio State University Press. "The Unloved" from *New Campus Writing* edited by Judson Jerome. Reprinted by permission of Judson Jerome.

JOHN CIARDI, "The Evil Eye" from *As If: Poems New & Selected* by John Ciardi. © 1955 by The Trustees of Rutgers College in New Jersey. "A Magus" from *This Strangest Everything* by John Ciardi. © 1966 by Rutgers, The State University. "The Benefits of an Education: Boston, 1931" from *Lives of X* by John Ciardi. © 1971 by Rutgers, The State University. "On a Photo of Sgt. Ciardi a Year Later" from *Other Skies* by John Ciardi. ©

**PHOTO CREDITS**

photo by S. S. Gardons; Gary Snyder, photo by Diana Hadley; Barry Spacks, photo by David Fanger; William Stafford, photo by Kit Stafford; David Steingass, photo by Susan Cohen; John Stone, photo by Robert B. Beveridge; Mark Strand, photo by LaVerne H. Clark; Dabney Stuart, photo by John Hughes, Washington and Lee University; Hollis Summers, photo by Larry McConkey; Diane Wakoski, photo by Thomas Victor; Robert Wallace, photo by Janeen Wallace; Robert Penn Warren, photo by Michael V. Carlisle; James Whitehead, photo by Gustavo A. Nelson; Richard Wilbur, photo by Rollie McKenna; John Williams, photo by Ed Curda; Charles Wright, photo by Holly Wright; James Wright, photo by Galway Kinnell.

# Preface

The term "contemporary," as we use it in the titles of anthologies, is a contemporary invention and has never been tied down to a specific number of years. We take it to describe a period more recent than *modern,* but exactly how recent depends on the time and the critical context in which it's used. There is no intent to set a definition here, and there is no rigid cut-off date for the poems included in this collection. Nothing important flips over on New Year's Day. But it does seem that *contemporary* can fairly describe the poetry written in the context of that world known to those writing now and those who would be writing, had they lived out their lives.

With this in mind, the anthology has been limited to those poets born in the twentieth century and who earned their full reputation after the beginning of World War II. Some were born after the war was over, which covers the near end of *contemporary.*

This is the place to say, as has to be said of every anthology, that there are good poets, and considerably more good poems, not included. And this is the place to say, as has to be said by every anthologist, that choices have to be made, and that there is no way to defend the choices except to say, "Here is the sum total of them." Any anthology is its own defense, or there isn't any.

If the editor can't offer any defense, however, he can offer some explanation along the way.

*On the biographies:* Each of the poets living at the time the anthology got under way was invited to write an autobiographical note, either in the first or third person. Some accepted the invitation; some chose not to, which is why some of the biographies are in the words of the editor, and some are in the words of the poets. If the editor has sometimes summed up a poet's life flatly, the failing is in the editor and not the life.

*On the photographs:* The poets were also invited to send their own pictures and were urged to make them as casual as they liked, even to shots from a Woolworth's photo booth. Some, and generally the same poets as before, accepted the invitation; some chose to leave it to the editor to search out a picture. A publisher's promotional shot is not very interesting, and often it is not very believable, but in some cases that's what it came down to. Here the editor disclaims responsibility.

*On the good help the editor had:* A dozen roses and a new blue pencil for June Fischbein of Random House, a superb editor, who has made this one appear much better than he is.

Miller Williams
Fayetteville, Arkansas
1972

# Contents

# Introduction

The outbreak of World War II did more than bring an awful end to the economic and spiritual depression of the 1930s. It brought an end also– for a while– to the proletarian, anti-establishment writing of the thirties and introduced the English-speaking world to a new generation of American poets.

The poets whose works had filled the anthologies and the journals since the so-called "little renaissance" associated with Harriet Monroe's *Poetry* magazine in Chicago were now just old enough to be ineligible for military service. At a time when the entire nation was oriented toward war, the attention of the publishers and the poetry-reading public naturally turned to those poets who were young enough to be directly involved in the war.

Unlike the English poets associated with World War I, the American poets of World War II did not, even at first, send back poems about the glory of war or the honor of death in battle. And so, unlike the majority of those earlier English poets, they were not writing deeply bitter poems at the end of the war. Instead, they approached the fight with what was almost a bemused detachment; if not quite cynical, they seemed resigned to what most of them felt was an ugly job that had to be done. Hence, the poems they wrote tended to be not so much about the war as about themselves, about people they would not have known except for the war, and they wrote of—and out of—whatever insights came to them out of the war.

Among the poets often thought of in connection with the war are John Ciardi, Richard Eberhart, Randall Jarrell, Karl Shapiro, Louis Simpson, and Peter Viereck. Perhaps four poets who were writing at the time ought to be mentioned for their absence from the list. There is Kenneth Patchen, who had established himself, even before the war broke out, as a poet of peace and reverence for life, so that although he was not thought of as one of the "war poets"–and certainly would not have wanted to be–he was writing poems profoundly concerned with the fact of the war. Another exception is Robert Lowell, who refused military service and was sent to prison as a conscientious objector, so that technically he is not one of the war poets either. But his too was certainly a war experience, and his poems which have come out of it have to be read in this context. Finally, there are Howard Nemerov and Theodore Roethke, both of whom seem to have passed into and out of military service without paying much attention to it, if we are to judge from their poetry.

These poets, whatever their perspective, knew the same world, and their poems came out of it. After 1945, with such others as John Nims and Richard Wilbur (and excepting especially Kenneth Patchen), they formed that accidental grouping of professor-poets often referred to as the "academics." Their poems and their attitudes were primarily responsible for the tone of American poetry for the next decade. They were called "academics" not only because most of them came home from the war to the college campus, where they took degrees and stayed on to teach, but also because their work often reflected their erudition in scholarly references, intricate metaphors, and ingenious forms. According to some who read them—and surely did not read them well enough—they had simply moved poetry from the Victorian drawing room to the mid-twentieth-century classroom and had brought it no whit closer to the streets, where, these critics claimed, poetry began and ought to be.

This attitude has since spread and taken root in the schools, so that by now "academic" has become almost a pejorative term, as "Victorian" had come to be earlier. Both cases reflect a serious misconception. The Victorians and the academics have given us some of the best, and some of the toughest and most realistic, poetry in the language. Browning's "The Bishop Orders His Tomb at Saint Praxed's Church," for example, and George Meredith's "Dirge in Woods" are not for greeting cards or gift books. And it is not easy to understand how any reader could dismiss the academic poets as inhabitants of an ivory tower, out of touch with the "real world," after reading such poems as Richard Wilbur's "Still, Citizen Sparrow," Peter Viereck's "Poet," Karl Shapiro's "The Fly," or John Ciardi's "The Evil Eye," unless we are to believe that verse forms in themselves are somehow decadent.

Such a view did, as a matter of fact, gain some currency in the fifties. The poems coming from the professor-poets were not raw enough for some who read them, and the academics were often accused of not coming to grips with the world as it is. This objection, however justified it may or may not have been, took artistic shape and found wide public attention in 1956 when Allen Ginsberg, in the long poem entitled "Howl," showed America something of what he believed poetry ought to be (in 1956, anyway). This poem eventually came to be thought of as the manifesto of the "Beat Movement" of the late fifties and early sixties, a movement which was more than literary, and whose adherents loudly rejected the values of the commercially oriented society in which they felt themselves innocently trapped. The Beats expressed their rebellion against that society, or their withdrawal from it, in often lengthy, sometimes imaginative and exciting, poems, not infrequently read to the accompaniment of a jazz group in out-of-the-way coffee houses, first in San Francisco and then throughout the country. This suggests, certainly, that the poetry being written during the previous decade was objected to only in part for its own failings; the poetry stood trial as a part of and product of the educational and cultural structure to which the Beats objected. Among those in whom it found a sympathetic chord, Beat poetry was taken as a cry for freedom of thought and expression, for the rejection of the hypocritical societies of J. Alfred Prufrock and Babbitt and for the release of the democratic spirit dreamed of a century earlier by Walt Whitman, whose poetry the new movement echoed in technique as well as in theme.

"Howl" was not by any means Ginsberg's first poem nor were the Beats the first group of poets to build their poetry on a rejection of the qualities of academic verse. Shortly after the war, and during the period of the eminence of the academics, there was a group in San Francisco giving readings, publishing in small journals and broadsides, and writing very much of, for, and sometimes in, the streets. This group, which included Lawrence Ferlinghetti, attracted enough notice (at least in retrospect) to claim for its activity the name of the San Francisco Renaissance.

At about the same time, and running on for some time later, important things were happening at Black Mountain College, an experimental school in North Carolina. Charles Olson and Robert Creeley were among several poets of like mind teaching at the college and publishing in the *Black Mountain Review*. Denise Levertov also published her poems in the magazine and is generally associated with the Black Mountain poets. This group, under the strong influence of Olson, set forth a poetry which showed a suspicion of rhyme and meter, adjective and simile—that is, those aspects of poetry considered by the Black Mountain poets to be most "literary"—and which showed a special respect for the syllable, the natural rhythms of the breath, and the typewriter's topographical precision. All this was before the Beat Generation (Ginsberg, Gregory Corso, and others, joined by Ferlinghetti) attracted public attention with their readings and publications and took their name.

In the sixties a poetry arose which incorporates to a striking degree the characteristic qualities of the several attitudes which preceded it and on which it builds. The terrible perception of life as a function of death and of death as a function of life that the war poets brought back home with them; the exquisite joy in craftsmanship that the same poets learned and taught a decade later; the insistent concreteness of the Beats, sharpening our senses to the smell of a drunkard's breath or the sound of a garbage can being knocked over in the night—all this is a part of the best poetry written in the sixties and still being written today. This synthesis may be found not only in the younger poets, those who began writing in the sixties and were thus the heirs to the previous traditions, but also in the older poets, the ones who helped create those traditions. Young and old, they have picked up sounds and rhythms and ideas from one another. Such cross-pollination takes place, of course, in any age, but it seems particularly the case now, in a time of consolidation after periods of specialized writing.

This is not to suggest that a "new poetry" is upon us, or even that a synthesis of the most desirable qualities of earlier poetry amounts to a new direction at all. On the contrary, what we have now is actually a return to the main current of English literary history. In a recent essay, "Poetry and the Mind of Modern Man," Conrad Aiken commented on his 1917 review of Eliot's *Prufrock and Other Observations:*

> I was opposed to the extremes of fragmentation advocated by the Imagists and the Others, and argued . . . that Eliot's rhymed free verse, which was not really free verse at all, but a highly controlled and very subtly modulated medium, was probably the best signpost available as to the direction in which the form and tone of poetry might most adventurously go.

Mr. Aiken was right. Many qualities that we still speak of as modern—irony, conversational tone, the strong metaphor, the mixing of ambiguity and telling-it-like-it-is—all were a part of the poetry of Eliot, and of Wallace Stevens, for that matter, and of Robert Browning and John Donne. All were masters of the same controlled freedom which Eliot's poems exemplified. What is most notable about the poetry of today is not that it is new in a way that would interest most graduate students. We may be pleased, or surely ought to be, that it is not generally a poetry of extremes, as extremes tend to become tedious and are soon and properly forgotten. What matters about contemporary poetry is that in the process of gathering to itself the strengths of earlier styles, it has created its own unique strength. In short, what matters is that some of it is very good poetry and thus matters in the way good poetry has always mattered.

The historical lines drawn here—the progression from proletarian poetry through war poetry and then, through the antitheses presented by the anti-academic styles, to a present synthesis of styles—must, of course, not be taken as an explanation of the changes, or even as comprehensive. Neither the lives nor the poems of some of the older and much respected poets included here—poets such as Robert Penn Warren, Elizabeth Bishop, and Kenneth Patchen—will allow them to wear any of the labels we have discussed. Some others—Hollis Summers, Robert Huff, William Meredith, William Stafford, George Garrett, James Dickey, to name a few—might have been thought of as war poets and/or might have been grouped with the academics after the war except that they did not become known as poets until later.

Further exception must be made for the black poets, who are a group unto themselves, in part because white society has always preferred to see them that way, and in part because now many of the black poets want to see themselves that way. It seems hardly profitable, though, either for the black poet or for the reader of poetry to continue to set the work of blacks apart. Certainly the experience of the black poet in America is uniquely his own, and the poetry is different for that, but no one writes from any but his own roots, from what he perceives as his own most compelling difference, whether that difference be racial, religious, sexual, regional, or personal. After the agony of self-discovery and the rebirth of pride and the release of rage and the celebration of difference, the poetry called "Black" is coming to be made up more and more of poems as different one from the other, as any of them are different from the poems of those who are not black.

The texture of its own, the tone of voice at once recognizable in the best contemporary black poetry, comes to some degree out of the nature of the black experience in America, but it also comes from the poet's reaching back toward the beginnings of black history for his own movement and his own sounds. Even so, in the poems of the black poets represented here, the most important common denominator is poetry. There is as much poetry as protest, often at the same time (not an easy thing to achieve, for any poet), and the work is important for reasons that are not sociological at all.

It is also worth noting that while America has been involved in two wars since the war poets came home in 1945, we have not had a significant body of new war poetry. This is in part because those educated to poetry and of fighting age were to a large degree indifferent to the Korean War and opposed to the war in Vietnam, and it is in great part because most of those who would have been writing the war poetry managed, through student exemptions and other measures, such as going to Canada, to stay home from the war.

What we have instead of war poetry is a poetry of war, poetry written not at the firebase or in the jungles but at home, by those who protest against the war and against the systems which they believe have brought it about. This is not new; even Rudyard Kipling did it, and so did Kenneth Patchen—but it is new to most of us.

It is through such exceptions that we learn to modify our rules and qualify statements, but we would be wise to refrain, in any event, from drawing straight lines between poets. In setting up historical categories, we are, after all, discussing people, not mathematics, and in any discussion about people the drawing of such lines is at best a convenience, a help in gaining a perspective, a long view. Such a scheme is no better than a road map, but also no worse if the traveler realizes that it is only a rough representation of the countryside. Nothing very much worth seeing is shown on the map. You have to go yourself.

# Langston Hughes

## JAZZONIA

Oh, silver tree!
Oh, shining rivers of the soul!

In a Harlem cabaret
Six long-headed jazzers play.
A dancing girl whose eyes are bold
Lifts high a dress of silken gold.

Oh, singing tree!
Oh, shining rivers of the soul!

Were Eve's eyes
In the first garden
Just a bit too bold?
Was Cleopatra gorgeous
In a gown of gold?

Oh, shining tree!
Oh, silver rivers of the soul!

In a whirling cabaret
Six long-headed jazzers play.

## CROSS

My old man's a white old man
And my old mother's black.
If ever I cursed my white old man
I take my curses back.

If ever I cursed my black old mother
And wished she were in hell,
I'm sorry for that evil wish
And now I wish her well.

My old man died in a fine big house.
My ma died in a shack.
I wonder where I'm gonna die,
Being neither white nor black?

## THE NEGRO SPEAKS OF RIVERS

I've known rivers:
I've known rivers ancient as the world and
    older than the flow of human blood in
    human veins.

My soul has grown deep like the rivers.

I bathed in the Euphrates when dawns
    were young.

I built my hut near the Congo and it lulled
    me to sleep.
I looked upon the Nile and raised the
    pyramids above it.
I heard the singing of the Mississippi when
    Abe Lincoln went down to New Orleans,
    and I've seen its muddy bosom turn all
    golden in the sunset.
I've known rivers:
Ancient, dusky rivers.

My soul has grown deep like the rivers.

## LENOX AVENUE MURAL

### Harlem

What happens to a dream deferred?

> Does it dry up
> like a raisin in the sun?
> Or fester like a sore—
> And then run?
> Does it stink like rotten meat?
> Or crust and sugar over—
> like a syrupy sweet?

> Maybe it just sags
> like a heavy load.

*Or does it explode?*

### Good Morning

Good morning, daddy!
I was born here, he said,
watched Harlem grow
until colored folks spread
from river to river
across the middle of Manhattan
out of Penn Station
dark tenth of a nation,
planes from Puerto Rico,
and holds of boats, chico,
up from Cuba Haiti Jamaica,
in buses marked New York
from Georgia Florida Louisiana
to Harlem Brooklyn the Bronx
but most of all to Harlem
dusky sash across Manhattan
I've seen them come dark

**LANGSTON HUGHES**

Langston Hughes was born February 1, 1902, in Joplin, Missouri, and was raised in the Midwest. Immediately after high school graduation he left for Mexico, later returning to the United States to spend some time as a student at Columbia. Then, after a short stint on shipboard as an able-bodied seaman, he made his way to Paris and, after nearly a year there, on to Italy and Spain and then back to New York and finally to Washington, D.C. A job as a busboy in Washington supported him while he developed his highly individual poetic style. His poetry, pervaded by the rhythms and tones of the blues and sometimes of jazz, is as close to the voices of Bessie Smith and Robert Johnson as it is to the voice of any other poet. "The Weary Blues," which was the title poem of his first book, won the First Prize for Poetry offered by *Opportunity* magazine in 1925. His alma mater, Lincoln University in Pennsylvania, honored him with a Litt.D. in 1943, and he received a Guggenheim Fellowship in 1935, a Rosenwald Fellowship in 1940, and an American Academy of Arts and Letters Grant in 1947. Langston Hughes died in 1967.

wondering
wide-eyed
dreaming
out of Penn Station—
but the trains are late.
The gates open—
but there're bars
at each gate.

What happens
to a dream deferred?

Daddy, ain't you heard?

### Same in Blues

I said to my baby,
Baby, take it slow.
I can't, she said, I can't!
I got to go!

*There's a certain*
*amount of traveling*
*in a dream deferred.*

Lulu said to Leonard,
I want a diamond ring.
Leonard said to Lulu,
You won't get a goddamn thing!

*A certain*
*amount of nothing*
*in a dream deferred.*

Daddy, daddy, daddy,
All I want is you.
You can have me, baby—
but my lovin' days is through.

*A certain*
*amount of impotence*
*in a dream deferred.*

Three parties
On my party line—
But that third party,
Lord, ain't mine!

*There's liable*
*to be confusion*
*in a dream deferred.*

From river to river
Uptown and down,
There's liable to be confusion
When a dream gets kicked around.

### Comment on Curb

You talk like
they don't kick
dreams around
downtown.

*I expect they do—*
*But I'm talking about*
*Harlem to you!*

### Letter

*Dear Mama,*
    *Time I pay rent and get my food*
*and laundry I don't have much left*
*but here is five dollars for you*
*to show you I still appreciates you.*
*My girl-friend send her love and say*
*she hopes to lay eyes on you sometime*
    *in life.*
*Mama, it has been raining cats and*
    *dogs up*
*here. Well, that is all so I will close.*
    *Your son baby*
        *Respectably as ever,*
            *Joe*

### Island

Between two rivers,
North of the park,
Like darker rivers
The streets are dark.

Black and white,
Gold and brown—
Chocolate-custard
Pie of a town.

*Dream within a dream,*
*Our dream deferred.*

Good morning, daddy!

Ain't you heard?

# Richard Eberhart

## THE FURY OF AERIAL BOMBARDMENT

You would think the fury of aerial
  bombardment
Would rouse God to relent; the infinite
  spaces
Are still silent. He looks on shock-pried
  faces.
History, even, does not know what is
  meant.

You would feel that after so many
  centuries
God would give man to repent; yet he
  can kill
As Cain could, but with multitudinous will,
No farther advanced than in his ancient
  furies.

Was man made stupid to see his own
  stupidity?
Is God by definition indifferent, beyond us
  all?
Is the eternal truth man's fighting soul
Wherein the Beast ravens in its own
  avidity?

Of Van Wettering I speak, and Averill,
Names on a list, whose faces I do not recall
But they are gone to early death, who late
  in school
Distinguished the belt feed lever from the
  belt holding pawl.

## 'COVER ME OVER'

Cover me over, clover;
Cover me over, grass.
The mellow day is over
And there is night to pass.

Green arms about my head,
Green fingers on my hands.
Earth has no quieter bed
In all her quiet lands.

## THE GROUNDHOG

In June, amid the golden fields,
I saw a groundhog lying dead.
Dead lay he; my senses shook,
And mind outshot our naked frailty.
There lowly in the vigorous summer
His form began its senseless change,
And made my senses waver dim
Seeing nature ferocious in him.
Inspecting close his maggots' might
And seething cauldron of his being,
Half with loathing, half with a strange love,
I poked him with an angry stick.
The fever arose, became a flame
And Vigour circumscribed the skies,
Immense energy in the sun,
And through my frame a sunless trembling.
My stick had done nor good nor harm.
Then stood I silent in the day
Watching the object, as before;
And kept my reverence for knowledge
Trying for control, to be still,
To quell the passion of the blood;
Until I had bent down on my knees
Praying for joy in the sight of decay.
And so I left; and I returned
In Autumn strict of eye, to see
The sap gone out of the groundhog,
But the bony sodden hulk remained.
But the year had lost its meaning,
And in intellectual chains
I lost both love and loathing,
Mured up in the wall of wisdom.
Another summer took the fields again
Massive and burning, full of life,
But when I chanced upon the spot
There was only a little hair left,
And bones bleaching in the sunlight
Beautiful as architecture;
I watched them like a geometer,
And cut a walking stick from a birch.
It has been three years, now.
There is no sign of the groundhog.
I stood there in the whirling summer,
My hand capped a withered heart,
And thought of China and of Greece,
Of Alexander in his tent;
Of Montaigne in his tower,
Of Saint Theresa in her wild lament.

**RICHARD EBERHART**
Born in Austin, Minnesota, on
April 5, 1904, Richard Eberhart
graduated from Dartmouth Col-
lege in 1926, took a master's de-
gree from St. John's College,
Cambridge, in 1933, and then at-
tended Harvard for a year. In the
early thirties he served as tutor
to the son of the King of Siam.
Then, after serving in the Navy
during World War II, he became
associated with the Butcher Pol-
ish Company of Boston, where he
now holds a position on the
board of directors. In 1950 he
founded and was named first
president of the Poets' Theatre
in Cambridge, Massachusetts. He
has since taught at a number of
schools, including the University
of Washington, the University of
Connecticut, and Princeton, and
is now professor of English and
poet-in-residence at Dartmouth.
He has received many of the
prizes given for poetry in this
country, including both the Harriet
Monroe Memorial Prize and the
Shelley Memorial Prize in 1950,
the Bollingen Prize in 1962, and
the Pulitzer Prize in 1966. He was
Consultant in Poetry at the Li-
brary of Congress from 1959 to
1961. He married Helen Butcher
in 1941; they now have two grown
children.

**ROBERT PENN WARREN**

Born on April 24, 1905, in Guthrie, Kentucky, Robert Penn Warren earned his B.A. from Vanderbilt in 1925, his M.A. from the University of California at Berkeley in 1927, and his B.Litt. from Oxford University in 1930, while in attendance as a Rhodes Scholar. During his student days at Vanderbilt he became associated with John Crowe Ransom and the Fugitive Group during the last days of the publication of *Fugitive* magazine; later he joined most of the same group in the publication of a book of essays on the South entitled *I'll Take My Stand*. In 1935, with Cleanth Brooks, he founded the *Southern Review* and remained one of its editors until it ceased publication in 1942. He has won many of the awards offered in this country both for poetry and for fiction, including the Pulitzer Prize in 1947 for the novel *All the King's Men* and both the National Book Award and the Pulitzer Prize in 1958 for *Promises: Poems 1954– 1956*. He lives in Fairfield, Connecticut, and is currently professor of English at Yale University.

## RUMINATION

When I can hold a stone within my hand
And feel time make it sand and soil, and see
The roots of living things grow in this land,
Pushing between my fingers flower and tree,
Then I shall be as wise as death,
For death has done this and he will
Do this to me, and blow his breath
To fire my clay, when I am still.

## FLUX

The old Penobscot Indian
Sells me a pair of moccasins
That stain my feet yellow.

The gods of this world
Have taken the daughter of my neighbor,
Who died this day of encephalitis.

The absentee landlord has taken over Tree
    Island

Where one now hesitates to go for picnics,
Off the wide beach to see Fiddle Head.

The fogs are as unpredictable as the winds.
The next generation comes surely on,
Their nonchalance baffles my intelligence.

Some are gone for folly, some by
    mischance,
Cruelty broods over the inexpressible,
The inexorable is ever believable.

The boy, in his first hour on his motorbike,
Met death in a head-on collision.
His dog stood silent by the young corpse.

Last week, the sea farmer off Stonington
Was tripped in the wake of a cruiser.
He went down in the cold waters of the
    summer.

Life is stranger than any of us expected,
There is a somber, imponderable fate.
Enigma rules, and the heart has no
    certainty.

# Robert Penn Warren

## ORIGINAL SIN: A SHORT STORY

Nodding, its great head rattling like a gourd,
And locks like seaweed strung on the stinking stone,
The nightmare stumbles past, and you have heard
It fumble your door before it whimpers and is gone:
It acts like the old hound that used to snuffle your door and moan.

You thought you had lost it when you left Omaha,
For it seemed connected then with your grandpa, who
Had a wen on his forehead and sat on the veranda
To finger the precious protuberance, as was his habit to do,
Which glinted in sun like rough garnet or the rich old brain bulging through.

But you met it in Harvard Yard as the historic steeple
Was confirming the midnight with its hideous racket,
And you wondered how it had come, for it stood so imbecile,
With empty hands, humble, and surely nothing in pocket:
Riding the rods, perhaps—or Grandpa's will paid the ticket.

You were almost kindly then, in your first homesickness,
As it tortured its stiff face to speak, but scarcely mewed.
Since then you have outlived all your homesickness,
But have met it in many another distempered latitude:
Oh, nothing is lost, ever lost! at last you understood.

It never came in the quantum glare of sun
To shame you before your friends, and had nothing to do
With your public experience or private reformation:
But it thought no bed too narrow—it stood with lips askew
And shook its great head sadly like the abstract Jew.

Never met you in the lyric arsenical meadow
When children call and your heart goes stone in the bosom—
At the orchard anguish never, nor ovoid horror,
Which is furred like a peach or avid like the delicious plum.
It takes no part in your classic prudence or fondled axiom.

Not there when you exclaimed: "Hope is betrayed by
Disastrous glory of sea-capes, sun-torment of whitecaps
—There must be a new innocence for us to be stayed by."
But there it stood, after all the timetables, all the maps,
In the crepuscular clutter of *always, always,* or *perhaps.*

You have moved often and rarely left an address,
And hear of the deaths of friends with a sly pleasure,
A sense of cleansing and hope which blooms from distress;
But it has not died, it comes, its hand childish, unsure,
Clutching the bribe of chocolate or a toy you used to treasure.

It tries the lock; you hear, but simply drowse:
There is nothing remarkable in that sound at the door.
Later you hear it wander the dark house
Like a mother who rises at night to seek a childhood picture;
Or it goes to the backyard and stands like an old horse cold in the pasture.


## BEARDED OAKS

The oaks, how subtle and marine,
Bearded, and all the layered light
Above them swims; and thus the scene,
Recessed, awaits the positive night.

So, waiting, we in the grass now lie
Beneath the languorous tread of light:
The grasses, kelp-like, satisfy
The nameless motions of the air.

Upon the floor of light, and time,
Unmurmuring, of polyp made,
We rest; we are, as light withdraws,
Twin atolls on a shelf of shade.

Ages to our construction went,
Dim architecture, hour by hour:
And violence, forgot now, lent
The present stillness all its power.

The storm of noon above us rolled,
Of light the fury, furious gold,
The long drag troubling us, the depth:
Dark is unrocking, unrippling, still.

Passion and slaughter, ruth, decay
Descend, minutely whispering down,
Silted through swaying streams, to lay
Foundation for our voicelessness.

All our debate is voiceless here,
As all our rage, the rage of stone;
If hope is hopeless, then fearless fear,
And history is thus undone.

Our feet once wrought the hollow street
With echo when the lamps were dead
At windows; once our headlight glare
Disturbed the doe that, leaping, fled.

I do not love you less that now
The caged heart makes iron stroke,
Or less that all that light once gave
The graduate dark should now revoke.

We live in time so little time
And we learn all so painfully,
That we may spare this hour's term
To practice for eternity.

7

## PURSUIT

The hunchback on the corner, with gum and shoelaces,
Has his own wisdom and pleasures, and may not be lured
To divulge them to you, for he has merely endured
Your appeal for his sympathy and your kind purchases;
And wears infirmity but as the general who turns
Apart, in his famous old greatcoat there on the hill
At dusk when the rapture and cannonade are still,
To muse withdrawn from the dead, from his gorgeous subalterns;
Or stares from the thicket of his familiar pain, like a fawn
That meets you a moment, wheels, in imperious innocence is gone.

Go to the clinic. Wait in the outer room
Where like an old possum the snag-nailed hand will hump
On its knee in murderous patience, and the pomp
Of pain swells like the Indies, or a plum.
And there you will stand, as on the Roman hill,
Stunned by each withdrawn gaze and severe shape,
The first barbarian victor stood to gape
At the sacrificial fathers, white-robed, still;
And even the feverish old Jew stares stern with authority
Till you feel like one who has come too late, or improperly clothed, to a party.

The doctor will take you now. He is burly and clean;
Listening, like lover or worshiper, bends at your heart;
But cannot make out just what it tries to impart;
So smiles; says you simply need a change of scene.
Of scene, of solace: therefore Florida,
Where Ponce de Leon clanked among the lilies,
Where white sails skit on blue and cavort like fillies,
And the shoulder gleams in the moonlit corridor.
A change of love: if love is a groping Godward, though blind,
No matter what crevice, cranny, chink, bright in dark, the pale tentacle find.

In Florida consider the flamingo,
Its color passion but its neck a question;
Consider even that girl the other guests shun
On beach, at bar, in bed, for she may know
The secret you are seeking, after all;
Or the child you humbly sit by, excited and curly,
That screams on the shore at the sea's sunlit hurlyburly,
Till the mother calls its name, toward nightfall.
Till you sit alone: in the dire meridians, off Ireland, in fury
Of spume-tooth and dawnless sea-heave, salt rimes the lookout's devout eye.

Till you sit alone—which is the beginning of error—
Behind you the music and the lights of the great hotel:
Solution, perhaps, is public, despair personal,
But history held to your breath clouds like a mirror.
There are many states, and towns in them, and faces,
But meanwhile, the little old lady in black, by the wall,
Who admires all the dancers, and tells you how just last fall
Her husband died in Ohio, and damp mists her glasses;
She blinks and croaks, like a toad or a Norn, in the horrible light,
And rattles her crutch, which may put forth a small bloom, perhaps white.

## THE OWL

Here was the sound of water falling only,
Which is not sound but silence musical
Tumbling forever down the gorge's wall.
Like late milkweed that blooms beside the lonely
And sunlit stone, peace bloomed all afternoon.
Where time is not is peace; and here the shadow,
That crept to him across the Western meadow
And climbed the hill to mark the dropping sun,
Seemed held a space, washed downward by the water
Whose music flowed against the flow of time.

It could not be. Dark fell along the stream,
And like a child grown suddenly afraid,
With shaking knees, hands bloody on the stone,
Toward the upland gleaming fields he fled.
Light burned against their rim, was quickly gone.

Later he would remember this, and start.
And once or twice again his tough old heart
Knew sickness that the rabbit's heart must know,
When star by star the great wings float,
And down the moonlit track below
Their mortal silken shadow sweeps the snow.
O scaled bent claw, infatuate deep throat!

## THE JET MUST BE HUNTING FOR SOMETHING

One cop holds the spic delicately between thumb and forefinger.
It is as though he did not want to get a white glove dirty.

The jet prowls the sky and Penn Station looks bombed-out.

The spic has blood over one eye. He had tried to run away.
He will not try again, and in that knowledge, his face is
                              as calm as congealing bacon grease.

Three construction workers come out from behind the hoarding.

The two cops are not even talking to each other, and in spite of
The disturbance you are so metronomically creating, ignore
                              you. They are doing their duty.

The jet prowls. I do not know what it is hunting for.

The three construction workers are looking at you like a technical
Problem. I look at them. One looks at his watch. For everything
                                  there is a season.

How long since last I heard birdsong in the flowery hedgerows of France?

Just now, when I looked at you, I had the distinct impression
                         that you were staring me straight in the eye, and
Who wants to be a piece of white paper filed for eternity on
                        the sharp point of a filing spindle?

The orange-colored helmets of the construction workers
                         bloom brilliant as zinnias.

When you were a child in Georgia, a lard-can of zinnias
                     bloomed by the little cabin door.
Your mother had planted them in the lard-can. People
                      call zinnias nigger-flowers.

Nobody wants to be a piece of white paper filed in the dark
                  on the point of a black-enameled spindle forever.

The jet is so far off there is no sound, not even the sizzle
                  it makes as it sears the utmost edges of air.
It prowls the edge of distance like the raw edge of experience.
                                 Oh, reality!

I do not know what the jet is hunting for. It must
                  be hunting for something.

# Theodore Roethke

**THEODORE ROETHKE**

Theodore Roethke was born in Saginaw, Michigan, on May 25, 1908, and was educated at the University of Michigan and at Harvard. He taught English at Harvard, at Bennington, and at Lafayette College in Pennsylvania and also coached the tennis teams at these schools. He remained a fiercely competitive athlete all his life—especially on the tennis court—and died in 1963 of a heart attack suffered while swimming. There are few major awards in American poetry that did not come to Roethke. In 1953 he won the Pulitzer Prize for *The Waking,* and in 1958 he won both the Edna St. Vincent Millay Award and the Bollingen Prize for his collected verse, *Words for the Wind.* Also, in 1958, *Words for the Wind* won him the National Book Award. In 1965 he won posthumously the National Book Award for *The Far Field.* He spent the last years of his life in Washington with his wife, Beatrice Heath O'Connell, a former student of his at Bennington. Since his death his reputation as a poet, already outstanding during his later years, has grown steadily, and several of his younger colleagues name him as the major influence on their work.

## DOLOR

I have known the inexorable sadness of pencils,
Neat in their boxes, dolor of pad and paper-weight,
All the misery of manilla folders and mucilage,
Desolation in immaculate public places,
Lonely reception room, lavatory, switchboard,
The unalterable pathos of basin and pitcher,
Ritual of multigraph, paper-clip, comma,
Endless duplication of lives and objects.
And I have seen dust from the walls of institutions,
Finer than flour, alive, more dangerous than silica,
Sift, almost invisible, through long afternoons of tedium,
Dropping a fine film on nails and delicate eyebrows,
Glazing the pale hair, the duplicate gray standard faces.

## I KNEW A WOMAN

I knew a woman, lovely in her bones,
When small birds sighed, she would sigh back at them;
Ah, when she moved, she moved more ways than one:
The shapes a bright container can contain!
Of her choice virtues only gods should speak,
Or English poets who grew up on Greek
(I'd have them sing in chorus, cheek to cheek).

How well her wishes went! She stroked my chin,
She taught me Turn, and Counter-turn, and Stand;
She taught me Touch, that undulant white skin;
I nibbled meekly from her proffered hand;
She was the sickle; I, poor I, the rake,
Coming behind her for her pretty sake
(But what prodigious mowing we did make).

Love likes a gander, and adores a goose:
Her full lips pursed, the errant note to seize;
She played it quick, she played it light and loose;
My eyes, they dazzled at her flowing knees;
Her several parts could keep a pure repose,
Or one hip quiver with a mobile nose
(She moved in circles, and those circles moved).

Let seed be grass, and grass turn into hay:
I'm martyr to a motion not my own;
What's freedom for? To know eternity.
I swear she cast a shadow white as stone.
But who would count eternity in days?
These old bones live to learn her wanton ways:
(I measure time by how a body sways).

ELEGY FOR JANE

*My Student, Thrown by a Horse*

I remember the neckcurls, limp and damp as tendrils;
And her quick look, a sidelong pickerel smile;
And how, once startled into talk, the light syllables leaped for her,
And she balanced in the delight of her thought,
A wren, happy, tail into the wind,
Her song trembling the twigs and small branches.
The shade sang with her;
The leaves, their whispers turned to kissing;
And the mold sang in the bleached valleys under the rose.

Oh, when she was sad, she cast herself down into such a pure depth,
Even a father could not find her:
Scraping her cheek against straw;
Stirring the clearest water.

My sparrow, you are not here,
Waiting like a fern, making a spiny shadow.
The sides of wet stones cannot console me,
Nor the moss, wound with the last light.

If only I could nudge you from this sleep,
My maimed darling, my skittery pigeon.
Over this damp grave I speak the words of my love:
I, with no rights in this matter,
Neither father nor lover.

**CHARLES OLSON**

Charles Olson was born on December 27, 1910, in Worchester, Massachusetts. After attending Wesleyan, Yale, and Harvard, he taught at Clark College and at Harvard before going to Black Mountain College in 1951 as teacher and rector. He won two Guggenheim Fellowships, and in 1952 he received a grant from the Wenner-Gren Foundation to support his study of Mayan picture-writing in the Yucatan peninsula. Most of the last years of his life were spent working on the *Maximus Poems* in his home town of Gloucester. He is looked on by many as one of the guiding spirits behind the experimental movement that began at almost the same time in San Francisco and at Black Mountain, gained attention as the Beat phenomenon of the early and middle fifties, and still survives in the work of individual and individualist poets throughout the country. Charles Olson died in 1970.

NIGHT CROW

When I saw that clumsy crow
Flap from a wasted tree,
A shape in the mind rose up:
Over the gulfs of dream
Flew a tremendous bird
Further and further away
Into a moonless black,
Deep in the brain, far back.

# Charles Olson

THE SONGS OF MAXIMUS

**Song 1**

      colored pictures
of all things to eat: dirty
postcards
    And words, words, words
all over everything
      No eyes or ears left
to do their own doings (all

invaded, appropriated, outraged, all senses

including the mind, that worker on what is

          And that other sense
made to give even the most wretched, or any of us, wretched,
that consolation (greased
        lulled
even the street-cars

    song

**Song 2**

      all
wrong
      And I am asked—ask myself (I, too, covered
with the gurry of it) where
shall we go from here, what can we do
when even the public conveyances
sing?
      how can we go anywhere,
even cross-town
               how get out of anywhere (the bodies
all buried
in shallow graves?

**Song 3**

      This morning of the small snow
I count the blessings, the leak in the faucet
which makes of the sink time, the drop
of the water on water as sweet
as the Seth Thomas
in the old kitchen
my father stood in his drawers to wind (always
he forgot the 30th day, as I don't want to remember
the rent

      a house these days
so much somebody else's,
especially,
Congoleum's

         Or the plumbing,
that it doesn't work, this I like, have even used paper clips
as well as string to hold the ball up  And flush it
with my hand
         But that the car doesn't, that no moving
            things moves
without that song I'd void my ear of, the musickracket
of all ownership . . .

        Holes
in my shoes, that's all right, my fly
gaping, me out
at the elbows, the blessing
          that difficulties are once more

        "In the midst of plenty, walk
        as close to
        bare
          In the face of sweetness,
        piss
          In the time of goodness,
        go side, go
        smashing, beat them, go as
        (as near as you can

        tear

In the land of plenty, have
nothing to do with it

               take the way of

      the lowest,
including your legs, go
contrary, go

      sing

**Song 4**

I know a house made of mud & wattles,
I know a dress just sewed

               (saw the wind

blow its cotton
against her body
from the ankle

         so!

it was Nike

        And her feet: such bones
I could have had the tears
that lovely pedant had
who couldn't unwrap it himself, had to ask them to, on the
  schooner's deck

and he looked,
the first human eyes to look again
at the start of human motion (just last week
300,000,000 years ago

          She
was going fast
across the square, the water
this time of year, that
scarce

And the fish

**Song 5**

I have seen faces of want,
and have not wanted the FAO: Appleseed
's gone back to
what any of us
New England

**Song 6**

you sing, you

who also

wants

## MAXIMUS, TO HIMSELF

I have had to learn the simplest things
last. Which made for difficulties.
Even at sea I was slow, to get the hand out, or to cross
a wet deck.
       The sea was not, finally, my trade.
But even my trade, at it, I stood estranged
from that which was most familiar. Was delayed,
and not content with the man's argument
that such postponement
is now the nature of
obedience,

        that we are all late
        in a slow time,
        that we grow up many
        And the single
        is not easily
        known

It could be, though the sharpness (the *achiote)*
I note in others,
makes more sense
than my own distances. The agilities

        they show daily
        who do the world's
        businesses
        And who do nature's
        as I have no sense
        I have done either

I have made dialogues,
have discussed ancient texts,
have thrown what light I could, offered
what pleasures
doceat allows

        But the known?
This, I have had to be given,
a life, love, and from one man
the world.

        Tokens.
        But sitting here
        I look out as a wind
        and water man, testing
        And missing
        some proof

I know the quarters
of the weather, where it comes from,
where it goes. But the stem of me,
this I took from their welcome,
or their rejection, of me

        And my arrogance
        was neither diminished
        nor increased,
        by the communication

        2
It is undone business
I speak of, this morning,
with the sea
stetching out
from my feet

---

## A NEWLY DISCOVERED 'HOMERIC' HYMN

*(for Jane Harrison, if she were alive)*

Hail and beware the dead who will talk life until you are blue
in the face. And you will not understand what is wrong,
they will not be blue, they will have tears in their eyes,
they will seem to you so much more full of life
than the rest of us, and they will ask so much, not of you no
but of life, they will cry, isn't it this way, if it isn't
I don't care for it, and you will feel the blackmail, you will not know
what to answer, it will all have become one mass

Hail and beware them, for they come from where you have not been,
they come from where you cannot have come, they come into life
by a different gate. They come from a place which is not easily known,
it is known only to those who have died. They carry seeds
you must not touch, you must not touch the pot they taste of,
no one must touch the pot, no one must, in their season.

Hail and beware them, in their season. Take care. Prepare
to receive them, they carry what the living cannot do without,

13

but take the proper precautions, do the prescribed things, let
down the thread from the right shoulder. And from the forehead.
And listen to what they say, listen to the talk, hear
every word of it—they are drunk from the pot, they speak
like no living man may speak, they have the seeds in their mouth—
listen, and beware

Hail them solely that they have the seeds in their mouth, they
are drunk, you cannot do without a drunkenness, seeds can't,
they must be soaked in the contents of the pot, they must be all one mass.
But you who live cannot know what else the seeds must be. Hail
and beware the earth, where the dead come from. Life
is not of the earth. The dead are of the earth. Hail and beware
the earth, where the pot is buried.

Greet the dead in the dead man's time. He is drunk of the pot.
He speaks like spring does. He will deceive you. You are meant
to be deceived. You must observe the drunkenness. You are not to
drink. But you must hear, and see. You must beware.

Hail them, and fall off. Fall off! The drink is not yours,
it is not yours! You do not come
from the same place, you do not suffer as the dead do,
they do not suffer, they need, because they have drunk of the pot,
they need. Do not drink of the pot, do not touch it. Do not touch
them.

   Beware the dead. And hail them. They teach you drunkenness.
You have your own place to drink. Hail and beware them, when they come.

**ELIZABETH BISHOP**

Born in 1911, in Worchester, Mas-
sachusetts, Elizabeth Bishop grad-
uated from Vassar College in
1934. She lived for some years in
Brazil and now divides her time
between that country and the
United States. In 1949 and 1950
she was Consultant in Poetry at
the Library of Congress; in 1955
she was awarded the Pulitzer
Prize for *Poems: North & South*
and in 1970 the National Book
Award for *Complete Poems*. A
biography of Miss Bishop, written
by Ann Stevenson, has been pub-
lished in the Twayne Series on
American Writers.

# Elizabeth Bishop

## THE PRODIGAL

The brown enormous odor he lived by
was too close, with its breathing and thick hair,
for him to judge. The floor was rotten; the sty
was plastered halfway up with glass-smooth dung.
Light-lashed, self-righteous, above moving snouts,
the pigs' eyes followed him, a cheerful stare—
even to the sow that always ate her young—
till, sickening, he leaned to scratch her head.
But sometimes mornings after drinking bouts
(he hid the pints behind a two-by-four),
the sunrise glazed the barnyard mud with red;
the burning puddles seemed to reassure.
And then he thought he almost might endure
his exile yet another year or more.

But evenings the first star came to warn.
The farmer whom he worked for came at dark
to shut the cows and horses in the barn
beneath their overhanging clouds of hay,

with pitchforks, faint forked lightnings, catching light,
safe and companionable as in the Ark.
The pigs stuck out their little feet and snored.
The lantern—like the sun, going away—
laid on the mud a pacing aureole.
Carrying a bucket along a slimy board,
he felt the bats' uncertain staggering flight,
his shuddering insights, beyond his control,
touching him. But it took him a long time
finally to make his mind up to go home.

---

## THE FISH

I caught a tremendous fish
and held him beside the boat
half out of water, with my hook
fast in a corner of his mouth.
He didn't fight.
He hadn't fought at all.
He hung a grunting weight,
battered and venerable
and homely. Here and there
his brown skin hung in strips
like ancient wallpaper,
and its pattern of darker brown
was like wallpaper:
shapes like full-blown roses
stained and lost through age.
He was speckled with barnacles,
fine rosettes of lime,
and infested
with tiny white sea-lice,
and underneath two or three
rags of green weed hung down.
While his gills were breathing in
the terrible oxygen
—the frightening gills,
fresh and crisp with blood,
that can cut so badly—
I thought of the coarse white flesh
packed in like feathers,
the big bones and the little bones,
the dramatic reds and blacks
of his shiny entrails,
and the pink swim-bladder
like a big peony.
I looked into his eyes
which were far larger than mine
but shallower, and yellowed,
the irises backed and packed
with tarnished tinfoil
seen through the lenses
of old scratched isinglass.
They shifted a little, but not
to return my stare.
—It was more like the tipping
of an object toward the light.
I admired his sullen face,
the mechanism of his jaw,
and then I saw
that from his lower lip
—if you could call it a lip—
grim, wet, and weaponlike,
hung five old pieces of fish-line,
or four and a wire leader
with the swivel still attached,
with all their five big hooks
grown firmly in his mouth.
A green line, frayed at the end
where he broke it, two heavier lines,
and a fine black thread
still crimped from the strain and snap
when it broke and he got away.
Like medals with their ribbons
frayed and wavering,
a five-haired beard of wisdom
trailing from his aching jaw.
I stared and stared
and victory filled up
the little rented boat,
from the pool of bilge
where oil had spread a rainbow
around the rusted engine
to the bailer rusted orange,
the sun-cracked thwarts,
the oarlocks on their strings,
the gunnels—until everything
was rainbow, rainbow, rainbow!
And I let the fish go.

---

## ROOSTERS

At four o'clock
in the gun-metal blue dark
we hear the first crow of the first cock

just below
the gun-metal blue window
and immediately there is an echo

off in the distance,
then one from the backyard fence,
then one, with horrible insistence,

grates like a wet match
from the broccoli patch,
flares, and all over town begins to catch.

Cries galore
come from the water-closet door,
from the dropping-plastered henhouse floor,

where in the blue blurr
their rustling wives admire,
the roosters brace their cruel feet and glare

with stupid eyes
while from their beaks there rise
the uncontrolled, traditional cries.

Deep from protruding chests
in green-gold medals dressed,
planned to command and terrorize the rest,

the many wives
who lead hens' lives
of being courted and despised;

deep from raw throats
a senseless order floats
all over town. A rooster gloats

over our beds
from rusty iron sheds
and fences made from old bedsteads,

over our churches
where the tin rooster perches,
over our little wooden northern houses,

making sallies
from all the muddy alleys,
marking out maps like Rand McNally's:

glass-headed pins,
oil-golds and copper greens,
anthracite blues, alizarins,

each one an active
displacement in perspective;
each screaming, "This is where I live!"

Each screaming
"Get up! Stop dreaming!"
Roosters, what are you projecting?

You, whom the Greeks elected
to shoot at on a post, who struggled
when sacrificed, you whom they labelled

"Very combative . . ."
what right have you to give
commands and tell us how to live,

cry "Here!" and "Here!"
and wake us here where are
unwanted love, conceit and war?

The crown of red
set on your little head
is charged with all your fighting blood.

Yes, that excrescence
makes a most virile presence,
plus all that vulgar beauty of iridescence.

Now in mid-air
by twos they fight each other.
Down comes a first flame-feather,

and one is flying,
with raging heroism defying
even the sensation of dying.

And one has fallen,
but still above the town

his torn-out, bloodied feathers drift down;

and what he sung
no matter. He is flung
on the gray ash-heap, lies in dung

with his dead wives
with open, bloody eyes,
while those metallic feathers oxidize.

St. Peter's sin
was worse than that of Magdalen
whose sin was of the flesh alone;

of spirit, Peter's,
falling, beneath the flares,
among the "servants and officers."

Old holy sculpture
could set it all together
in one small scene, past and future:

Christ stands amazed,
Peter, two fingers raised
to surprised lips, both as if dazed.

But in between
a little cock is seen
carved on a dim column in the travertine,

explained by *Gallus Canit;*
*Flet Petrus* underneath it.
There is inescapable hope, the pivot;

yes, and there Peter's tears
run down our chanticleer's
sides and gem his spurs.

Tear-encrusted thick
as a medieval relic
he waits. Poor Peter, heart-sick,

still cannot guess
those cock-a-doodles yet might bless,
his dreadful rooster come to mean
    forgiveness,

a new weathervane
on basilica and barn,
and that outside the Lateran

there would always be
a bronze cock on a porphyry
pillar so the people and the Pope might see

that even the Prince
of the Apostles long since
had been forgiven, and to convince

all the assembly
that "Deny deny deny"
is not all the roosters cry.

In the morning
a low light is floating
in the backyard, and gilding

from underneath
the broccoli, leaf by leaf;
how could the night have come to grief?

gilding the tiny
floating swallow's belly
and lines of pink cloud in the sky,

the day's preamble
like wandering lines in marble.
The cocks are now almost inaudible.

The sun climbs in,
following "to see the end,"
faithful as enemy, or friend.

## HOUSE GUEST

The sad seamstress
who stays with us this month
is small and thin and bitter.
No one can cheer her up.
Give her a dress, a drink,
roast chicken, or fried fish—
it's all the same to her.

She sits and watches TV.
No, she watches zigzags.
"Can you adjust the TV?"
"No," she says. No hope.
She watches on and on,
without hope, without air.

Her own clothes give us pause,
but she's not a poor orphan.
She has a father, a mother,
and all that, and she's earning
quite well, and we're stuffing
her with fattening foods.

We invite her to use the binoculars.
We say, "Come see the jets!"
We say, "Come see the baby!"
Or the knife grinder who cleverly
plays the National Anthem
on his wheel so shrilly.
Nothing helps.

She speaks: "I need a little
money to buy buttons."
She seems to think it's useless
to ask. Heavens, buy buttons,
if they'll do any good,
the biggest in the world—
by the dozen, by the gross!
Buy yourself an ice cream,
a comic book, a car!

Her face is closed as a nut,
closed as a careful snail
or a thousand-year-old seed.
Does she dream of marriage?
Of getting rich? Her sewing
is decidedly mediocre.

Please! Take our money! Smile!
What on earth have we done?
What has everyone done
and when did it all begin?
Than one day she confides
that she wanted to be a nun
and her family opposed her.

Perhaps we should let her go,
or deliver her straight off
to the nearest convent—and wasn't
her month up last week, anyway?
Can it be that we nourish
one of the Fates in our bosoms?
Clotho, sewing our lives
with a bony little foot
on a borrowed sewing machine,
and our fates will be like hers,
and our hems crooked forever?

**JOSEPHINE MILES**

**Josephine Miles was born on June 11, 1911, in Chicago. She writes: For a poet, a poetical biography seems most sensible. Mine in my childhood years in Los Angeles begins with the ballads in *Poems Every Child Should Know,* moves to the *St. Nicholas League,* and then, big high school jump, to *The Bookman.* I still remember the poems I liked there, Lynn Rigg's for example, pre-*Oklahoma* and pre-*Green Grow the Lilacs* at the Pasadena Playhouse. Plays, too, O'Neill and Dunsany as I heard them read aloud in a neighborhood reading group. The "new" poetry of Sandburg and Lowell in the 1920's seemed too free and sentimental to me, so that the literary rediscovery of Yeats and Donne, and the growth of *Southern* and *Kenyon Reviews* in the thirties and forties when I was a graduate student and beginning to teach at Berkeley, seemed a great liberation into the sound of sense I admired. My poem "Poetry South" makes a little fun of this sequence. Lately with the faithful persistence of Bay poets I've grown fond of the Whitman tradition even though I can't write in it. My chief admiration in poetry now goes back to where I began —the beauty of the ballad tradition, of language spoken and heard.**

# Josephine Miles

"When the sun came, the rooster expanded to meet it"

When the sun came, the rooster expanded to meet it,
    Stood up, stirred his wings,
    Raised his red comb and sentence
    Rendered imperative utterance
    Saying, Awake. Nothing answered.

He took in a beakful of air; yes, first it was he,
And engendered a number of hard-shelled cacklers,
One for each day in the week.
They grew in their yard, the dust in their feathers,
Who heard them praise him? An egg.

In the night, in the barn, the eggs wakened and cried,
Saying, We have been wakened,
And cried, saying Father, so named him,
His feathers and beak from the white and the yolk.
Father, who newly can ring out the welkin,
And crow, we will listen to hear.
As toward him we move, and the wings of our feathers
    grow bright,
And we spring from the dust into flame
He will call us his chickens.
But that was already their name.

---

## "After I come home from the meeting with friends"

After I come home from the meeting with friends
    I lie to sleep on the turn of the earth as it spins
    Toward the sun, toward the rising light as the day begins
    And think of those I love as the day ends.

    They are clearing the dishes, sweeping the ashes away,
    They are threading the traffic, moving toward distances,
    Disposing their hearts as the dark midnight spins,
    Gathering toward the light of the new day.

    Spent and regained, their strength for a cause, for a
        plain
    Defeat or delight, strengthens my heart as it moves
    Into sleep, and my sleep as it runs in the grooves
    Toward the east where a waking heart is more than
        mine.

---

## "The doctor who sits at the bedside of a rat"

The doctor who sits at the bedside of a rat
    Obtains real answers—a paw twitch,
    An ear tremor, a gain or loss of weight,
    No problem as to which
    Is temper and which is true.
    What a rat feels, he will do.

    Concomitantly then, the doctor who sits
    At the bedside of a rat
    Asks real questions, as befits
    The place, like where did that potassium go, not what
    Do you think of Willie Mays or the weather?
    So rat and doctor may converse together.

---

## "In the town where every man is king"

In the town where every man is king,
    Every man has one subject,
    Every man bends to his own foot.
    Bring on the mirror that he may properly bend.
    But who will bring it on?

    In the castle where is no hunger and no need,
    Every man gives gifts and receives
    Gifts. But of these only his own
    Enhance him, the ring giver.
    He must wear his ring.

    Gradually, as he resolves the oppression of his edicts,
    Losing his fellow lords to dim perspectives,
    Monoliths of rock and stone, even
    Of reinforced concrete, become before him
    Mirrors. He licks the glass.

---

# J. V. Cunningham

**J. V. CUNNINGHAM**

J. V. Cunningham was born in Cumberland, Maryland, on August 23, 1911. He writes: I grew up in Montana and Denver, worked some years after high school, and spent fourteen years at Stanford. I have taught at various universities, the last eighteen years at Brandeis. I am an academic pro, an historical scholar, and a poet. I am married, have a daughter and four grandchildren. I sit on West Beach in Santa Barbara for a few weeks in January.

## FOR MY CONTEMPORARIES

How time reverses
The proud in heart!
I now make verses
Who aimed at art.

But I sleep well.
Ambitious boys
Whose big lines swell
With spiritual noise,

Despise me not!
And be not queasy
To praise somewhat:
Verse is not easy.

But rage who will.
Time that procured me
Good sense and skill
Of madness cured me.

## MONTANA PASTORAL

I am no shepherd of a child's surmises.
I have seen fear where the coiled serpent rises,

Thirst where the grasses burn in early May
And thistle, mustard, and the wild oat stay.

There is dust in this air. I saw in the heat
Grasshoppers busy in the threshing wheat.

So to this hour. Through the warm dusk I drove
To blizzards sifting on the hissing stove,

And found no images of pastoral will,
But fear, thirst, hunger, and this huddled chill.

## "Lady, of anonymous flesh and face"

Lady, of anonymous flesh and face
In the half-light, in the rising embrace
Of my losses, in the dark dress and booth,
The stripper of the gawking of my youth,
Lady, I see not, care not, what you are.
I sit with beer and bourbon at this bar.

## "And what is love? Misunderstanding, pain"

And what is love? Misunderstanding, pain,
Delusion, or retreat? It is in truth
Like an old brandy after a long rain,
Distinguished, and familiar, and aloof.

# Kenneth Patchen

**KENNETH PATCHEN**

Kenneth Patchen was born in Niles, Ohio, on December 13, 1911. At seventeen he went to work in the steel mills, soon leaving to drift about the country for several years. His formal education was gained at the Experimental College of the University of Wisconsin in 1928 and 1929. One of the most prolific of poets, whether in spite of or because of a debilitating spinal condition from which he suffered increasingly since 1937, he published more than twenty books of poetry and four novels since he first became disabled. A Guggenheim Memorial Award in 1936 was followed by the Shelley Award in 1954 and an award from the National Foundation for the Arts and Humanities in 1967. In his later years he devoted a great deal of his time to the integration of the verbal and graphic arts and published several books of poem-drawings, in which, for instance, the words of a poem are scattered apparently at random through what white space is available between a bird's legs or a tree's limbs. Others of his poems are accompanied by pictures of animals drawn from the bestiary of his imagination. In 1969 his paintings-and-poetry were exhibited at the Corcoran Gallery in Washington, D.C. Patchen lived with his wife, Miriam, in Palo Alto, California, until his death January 8, 1972.

## DO THE DEAD KNOW WHAT TIME IT IS?

The old guy put down his beer.
Son, he said,
    (and a girl came over to the table where we were:
    asked us by Jack Christ to buy her a drink.)
Son, I am going to tell you something
The like of which nobody ever was told.
    (and the girl said, I've got nothing on tonight;
    how about you and me going to your place?)
I am going to tell you the story of my mother's
Meeting with God.
    (and I whispered to the girl: I don't have a room,
    but maybe. . .)
She walked up to where the top of the world is
And He came right up to her and said
So at last you've come home.
    (but maybe what?
    I thought I'd like to stay here and talk to you.)
My mother started to cry and God
Put His arms around her.
    (about what?
    Oh, just talk . . . we'll find something.)
She said it was like a fog coming over her face
And light was everywhere and a soft voice saying
You can stop crying now.
    (what can we talk about that will take all night?
    and I said that I didn't know.)
*You can stop crying now.*

## THE FOX

Because the snow is deep
Without spot that white falling through white air

Because she limps a little—bleeds
Where they shot her

Because hunters have guns
And dogs have hangmen's legs

Because I'd like to take her in my arms
And tend her wound

Because she can't afford to die
Killing the young in her belly

I don't know what to say of a soldier's dying
Because there are no proportions in death.

## BECAUSE HE LIKED TO BE AT HOME

He usually managed to be there when
He arrived. A horse, his name was
Hunry Fencewaver Walkins—he'd sometimes
Be almost too tired to make it;
Because, since he also hated being alone,
He was always on the alert to pop forth
At a full run whenever the door opened.
Than one day it happened—
*He didn't get there in time!*
Of course he couldn't risk opening the door—
So, panting, he just stood there in the hall—
And listened to the terrible sound of himself weeping
In that room he could never, never enter again.

ELE PHA NTS

ESK IM OS

are the sort of inventions makes me sure that God has a couple three-four kids of His own

WHO ASKED FOR A POEM ABOUT THREE
WOLFHOUNDS, A BEAUTIFUL YOUNG
WOMAN, AND A BLIND OLD BOXER,
STANDING UNDER A STREETLIGHT
IN THE RAIN?

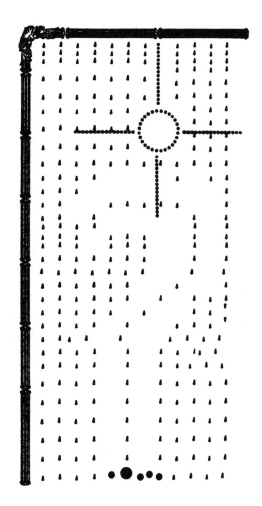

(and now the words 'May God have mercy upon them'
should be repeated very slowly until there is a Sign)

**WILLIAM EVERSON**

Son of a farm girl from Minnesota and a musician-composer who had immigrated to this country from Norway, William Everson was born in Sacramento, California, on September 10, 1912. He grew up in Selma, California, where his father was a bandmaster, and from there he went to Fresno State College but left before graduating. After the war, most of which he spent in a work camp as a conscientious objector, he came into contact with the San Francisco poets, and, through his second wife, Mary Fabilli, he became interested in Roman Catholicism. He and his wife separated, as he puts it, "to enter the Roman Catholic Church," and, after several years of troubled spiritual questioning, Everson joined the Dominican lay brotherhood and took the name of Brother Antoninus. It was under this name that he was associated with the Beat Generation in the fifties. He left the brotherhood in 1970 and is now writing again under the name of William Everson.

## MAY I ASK YOU A QUESTION, MR. YOUNGSTOWN SHEET & TUBE?

Mean grimy houses, shades drawn
Against the yellow-brown smoke
That blows in
Every minute of every day. And
Every minute of every night. To bake a cake or have a
 baby,
With the taste of tar in your mouth. To wash clothes or fix
 supper,
With the taste of tar in your mouth. Ah, but the grand
 funerals . . .
Rain hitting down
On the shiny hearses. "And it's a fine man he was, such a
 comfort
To his old ma.— Struck cold in the flower of his youth."
 Bedrooms
Gray-dim with the rumor of old sweat and urine. Pot roasts
And boiled spuds; *Ranch Romances* and The Bleeding Heart
Of Our Dear Lord— "Be a good lad . . . run down to Tim's
And get this wee pail filled for your old father now." The
 kids
Come on like the green leaves in the spring, but I'm not
 spry
Anymore and the missus do lose the bloom from her soft
 cheek.
(And of a Saturday night then, in Tim O'Sullivan's Elite
 Tavern itself:
"It is a world of sadness we live in, Micky boy."
"Aye, that it is. And better we drink to that."
"This one more, for home is where I should be now."
"Aye, but where's the home for the soul of a man!"
"It's a frail woman ye act like, my Micky."
"And it be a dumb goose who hasn't a tear to shed this night.")

Rain dripping down from a rusty evespout
Into the gray-fat cinders of the millyard . . .
The dayshift goes on in four minutes.

# William Everson

## SAN JOAQUIN

This valley after the storms can be beautiful beyond the
 telling,
Though our city-folk scorn it, cursing heat in the summer
 and drabness in winter,
And flee it—Yosemite and the sea.
They seek splendor, who would touch them must stun
 them;
The nerve that is dying needs thunder to rouse it.

I in the vineyard, in green-time and dead-time, come to it
 dearly,
And take nature neither freaked nor amazing,
But the secret shining, the soft indeterminate wonder.
I watch it morning and noon, the unutterable sundowns;
And love as the leaf does the bough.

## TRIFLES

The man laughing on the steep hill tripped on a stone,
Fell broken among boulders, suffered his life out under the
    noon sun.
The young wife, when the tire blew on the Trimmer road,
Took that long crash screaming into the rocks.
By sand slipping, by the shoe splitting on the narrow street,
By the parting of atoms,
By the shaping of all those enormous trifles we plunge to
    that border,
Writhing under the long dark in the agony of destruction,
The great sky and the flaming west riding our eyes,
Gathering in from the heavy hills, and the tides of the sea.

O poets! sleepers forever under the soil!
You have spoken it out of the bitter mouths hundreds of
    times;
Your anguish beats from the pages, beats on our bored and
    indolent sight!
But earth yields and a man is smothered,
Wood splits and a man is broken—
Simply, the mute and terrible ease of the function—
And you and your shouting burst up before us;
We taste that wry and sterile bitterness,
And pound with our hands on the dark.

**ROBERT HAYDEN**

Robert Hayden was born in Detroit, Michigan, on August 4, 1913. He received his bachelor's degree from Wayne State University and his master's from the University of Michigan, where he is now a professor of English. Before returning to Michigan he taught at Fisk University for more than twenty years and was visiting professor at the University of Louisville and the University of Washington. In 1965 his collection *A Ballad of Remembrance* was awarded the Grand Prize for Poetry at the First World Festival of Negro Arts in Dakar. He has also received the Hopwood Award from the University of Michigan and the Russell Loines Award from the American Institute of Arts and Letters. He is the editor of *Kaleidoscope: Poems by American Negro Poets* (1967) and poetry editor of the Baha'i quarterly, *World Order*. He lives with his wife and daughter in Ann Arbor.

## THE STRANGER

Pity this girl.
At callow sixteen,
Glib in the press of rapt companions,
She bruits her smatter,
Her bed-lore brag.
She prattles the lip-learned, light-love list.
In the new itch and squirm of sex,
How can she foresee?

How can she foresee the thick stranger,
Over the hills from Omaha,
Who will break her across a hired bed,
Open the loins,
Rive the breach,
And set the foetus wailing within the
    womb,
To hunch toward the knowledge of its
    disease,
And shamble down time to doomsday?

# Robert Hayden

## FREDERICK DOUGLASS

When it is finally ours, this freedom, this liberty, this
    beautiful
and terrible thing, needful to man as air,
usable as earth; when it belongs at last to all,
when it is truly instinct, brain matter, diastole, systole,
reflex action; when it is finally won; when it is more

than the gaudy mumbo jumbo of politicians:
this man, this Douglass, this former slave, this Negro
beaten to his knees, exiled, visioning a world
where none is lonely, none hunted, alien,
this man, superb in love and logic, this man
shall be remembered. Oh, not with statues' rhetoric,
not with legends and poems and wreaths of bronze alone,
but with the lives grown out of his life, the lives
fleshing his dream of the beautiful, needful thing.

# MIDDLE PASSAGE

## I

*Jesús, Estrella, Esperanza, Mercy:*

> Sails flashing to the wind like weapons,
> sharks following the moans the fever and the dying;
> horror the corposant and compass rose.

Middle Passage:
> voyage through death
> to life upon these shores.

"10 April 1800—
Blacks rebellious. Crew uneasy. Our linguist says
their moaning is a prayer for death,
ours and their own. Some try to starve themselves.
Lost three this morning leaped with crazy laughter
to the waiting sharks, sang as they went under."

*Desire, Adventure, Tartar, Ann:*

> Standing to America, bringing home
> black gold, black ivory, black seed.

> *Deep in the festering hold thy father lies,*
> *of his bones New England pews are made,*
> *those are altar lights that were his eyes.*

Jesus Saviour Pilot Me
Over Life's Tempestuous Sea

We pray that Thou wilt grant, O Lord,
safe passage to our vessels bringing
heathen souls unto Thy chastening.

Jesus Saviour

> "8 bells. I cannot sleep, for I am sick
> with fear, but writing eases fear a little
> since still my eyes can see these words take shape
> upon the page & so I write, as one
> would turn to exorcism. 4 days scudding,
> but now the sea is calm again. Misfortune
> follows in our wake like sharks (our grinning
> tutelary gods). Which one of us
> has killed an albatross? A plague among
> our blacks—Ophthalmia: blindness—& we
> have jettisoned the blind to no avail.
> It spreads, the terrifying sickness spreads.
> Its claws have scratched sight from the Capt.'s eyes
> & there is blindness in the fo'c'sle
> & we must sail 3 weeks before we come
> to port."

> *What port awaits us, Davy Jones'*
> *or home? I've heard of slavers drifting, drifting,*
> *playthings of wind and storm and chance, their*
> *crews*
> *gone blind, the jungle hatred*
> *crawling up on deck.*

Thou Who Walked On Galilee

"Deponent further sayeth *The Bella J*
left the Guinea Coast
with cargo of five hundred blacks and odd
for the barracoons of Florida:

"That there was hardly room 'tween-decks for half
the sweltering cattle stowed spoon-fashion there;
that some went mad of thirst and tore their flesh
and sucked the blood:

"That Crew and Captain lusted with the comeliest
of the savage girls kept naked in the cabins;
that there was one they called The Guinea Rose
and they cast lots and fought to lie with her:

"That when the Bo's'n piped all hands, the flames
spreading from starboard already were beyond
control, the negroes howling and their chains
entangled with flames:

"That the burning blacks could not be reached,
that the Crew abandoned ship,
leaving their shrieking negresses behind,
that the Captain perished drunken with the wenches:

"Further Deponent sayeth not."

Pilot Oh Pilot Me

## II

Aye, lad, and I have seen those factories,
Gambia, Rio Pongo, Calabar;
have watched the artful mongos baiting traps
of war wherein the victor and the vanquished

Were caught as prizes for our barracoons.
Have seen the nigger kings whose vanity
and greed turned wild black hides of Fellatah,
Mandingo, Ibo, Kru to gold for us.

And there was one—King Anthracite we named him—
fetish face beneath French parasols
of brass and orange velvet, impudent mouth
whose cups were carven skulls of enemies:

He'd honor us with drum and feast and conjo
and palm-oil-glistening wenches deft in love,
and for tin crowns that shone with paste,
red calico and German-silver trinkets

Would have the drums talk war and send
his warriors to burn the sleeping villages
and kill the sick and old and lead the young
in coffles to our factories.

Twenty years a trader, twenty years,
for there was wealth aplenty to be harvested
from those black fields, and I'd be trading still
but for the fevers melting down my bones.

**III**

Shuttles in the rocking loom of history,
the dark ships move, the dark ships move,
their bright ironical names
like jests of kindness on a murderer's mouth;
plough through thrashing glister toward
fata morgana's lucent melting shore,
weave toward New World littorals that are
mirage and myth and actual shore.

Voyage through death,
                    voyage whose chartings are unlove.

A charnel stench, effluvium of living death
spreads outward from the hold,
where the living and the dead, the horribly dying,
lie interlocked, lie foul with blood and excrement.

*Deep in the festering hold thy father lies,*
*the corpse of mercy rots with him,*
*rats eat love's rotten gelid eyes.*

*But, oh, the living look at you*
*with human eyes whose suffering accuses you,*
*whose hatred reaches through the swill of dark*
*to strike you like a leper's claw.*

*You cannot stare that hatred down*
*or chain the fear that stalks the watches*
*and breathes on you its fetid scorching breath;*
*cannot kill the deep immortal human wish,*
*the timeless will.*

"But for the storm that flung up barriers
of wind and wave, *The Amistad,* señores,
would have reached the port of Principe in two,
three days at most; but for the storm we should
have been prepared for what befell.
Swift as the puma's leap it came. There was
that interval of moonless calm filled only
with the water's and the rigging's usual sounds,
then sudden movement, blows and snarling cries
and they had fallen on us with machete
and marlinspike. It was as though the very
air, the night itself were striking us.
Exhausted by the rigors of the storm,
we were no match for them. Our men went down
before the murderous Africans. Our loyal
Celestino ran from below with gun
and lantern and I saw, before the cane-
knife's wounding flash, Cinquez,
that surly brute who calls himself a prince,
directing, urging on the ghastly work.
He hacked the poor mulatto down, and then
he turned on me. The decks were slippery
when daylight finally came. It sickens me
to think of what I saw, of how these apes
threw overboard the butchered bodies of

our men, true Christians all, like so much jetsam.
Enough, enough. The rest is quickly told:
Cinquez was forced to spare the two of us
you see to steer the ship to Africa,
and we like phantoms doomed to rove the sea
voyaged east by day and west by night,
deceiving them, hoping for rescue,
prisoners on our own vessel, till
at length we drifted to the shores of this
your land, America, where we were freed
from our unspeakable misery. Now we
demand, good sirs, the extradition of
Cinquez and his accomplices to La
Havana. And it distresses us to know
there are so many here who seem inclined
to justify the mutiny of these blacks.
We find it paradoxical indeed
that you whose wealth, whose tree of liberty
are rooted in the labor of your slaves
should suffer the august John Quincy Adams
to speak with so much passion of the right
of chattel slaves to kill their lawful masters
and with his Roman rhetoric weave a hero's
garland for Cinquez. I tell you that
we are determined to return to Cuba
with our slaves and there see justice done.
    Cinquez—
or let us say 'the Prince'—Cinquez shall die."

The deep immortal human wish,
the timeless will:

Cinquez its deathless primaveral image,
life that transfigures many lives.

Voyage through death
                    to life upon these shores.

---

## HOMAGE TO THE EMPRESS OF THE BLUES

Because there was a man somewhere in a candystripe silk
    shirt,
gracile and dangerous as a jaguar and because a woman
    moaned
for him in sixty-watt gloom and mourned him Faithless
    Love
Twotiming Love Oh Love Oh Careless Aggravating Love,

She came out on the stage in yards of pearls,
    emerging like
a favorite scenic view, flashed her golden smile
    and sang.

Because gray laths began somewhere to show from
    underneath
torn hurdygurdy lithographs of dollfaced heaven;

and because there were those who feared alarming fists of
  snow
on the door and those who feared the riot-squad of
  statistics,

    She came out on the stage in ostrich feathers, beaded
  satin,
    and shone that smile on us and sang.

---

## THOSE WINTER SUNDAYS

Sundays too my father got up early
and put his clothes on in the blueblack cold,
then with cracked hands that ached
from labor in the weekday weather made
banked fires blaze. No one ever thanked him.

I'd wake and hear the cold splintering, breaking.
When the rooms were warm, he'd call,

and slowly I would rise and dress,
fearing the chronic angers of that house,

Speaking indifferently to him,
who had driven out the cold
and polished my good shoes as well.
What did I know, what did I know
of love's austere and lonely offices?

---

**KARL SHAPIRO**

Karl Shapiro was born on November 10, 1913, in Baltimore, Maryland. He was educated at the University of Virginia and Johns Hopkins University. During his service in the Army from 1941 to 1945, he published four books of poems, including the remarkable *Essay on Rime,* an examination of the state of poetry in English. He has served as Consultant in Poetry at the Library of Congress (1947–1948), as editor of *Poetry* (1950–1956), and as editor of *Prairie Schooner* (1956–1963). Among the awards he has received are two of the prizes offered by *Poetry,* an American Academy of Arts and Letters Grant, two Guggenheim Fellowships, and the Pulitzer Prize in 1945 for *V-Letter and Other Poems,* one of the volumes written while he was overseas during the war. In addition to his poetry, he has also written an opera libretto entitled *The Tenor,* four books of criticism, and a textbook on prosody. He lives in California with his wife, Teri, and teaches at the University of California at Davis.

# Karl Shapiro

## THE FLY

O hideous little bat, the size of snot,
With polyhedral eye and shabby clothes,
To populate the stinking cat you walk
The promontory of the dead man's nose,
Climb with the fine leg of a Duncan-Phyfe
  The smoking mountains of my food
    And in a comic mood
  In mid-air take to bed a wife.

Riding and riding with your filth of hair
On gluey foot or wing, forever coy,
Hot from the compost and green sweet
  decay,
Sounding your buzzer like an urchin toy—
You dot all whiteness with diminutive
  stool,
  In the tight belly of the dead
    Burrow with hungry head
  And inlay maggots like a jewel.

At your approach the great horse stomps
  and paws
Bringing the hurricane of his heavy tail;
Shod in disease you dare to kiss my hand
Which sweeps against you like an angry
  flail;
Still you return, return, trusting your wing
  To draw you from the hunter's reach
    That learns to kill to teach
  Disorder to the tinier thing.

My peace is your disaster. For your death
Children like spiders cup their pretty hands
And wives resort to chemistry of war.
In fens of sticky paper and quicksands
You glue yourself to death. Where you are
  stuck
  You struggle hideously and beg
    You amputate your leg
  Imbedded in the amber muck.

But I, a man, must swat you with my hate,
Slap you across the air and crush your
  flight,
Must mangle with my shoe and smear your
  blood,
Expose your little guts pasty and white,
Knock your head sidewise like a drunk-
  ard's hat,
  Pin your wings under like a crow's,
    Tear off your flimsy clothes
  And beat you as one beats a rat.

Then like Gargantua I stride among
The corpses strewn like raisins in the dust,
The broken bodies of the narrow dead
That catch the throat with fingers of
  disgust.
I sweep. One gyrates like a top and falls
  And stunned, stone blind, and deaf
    Buzzes its frightful F
  And dies between three cannibals.

## AUTO WRECK

Its quick soft silver bell beating, beating,
And down the dark one ruby flare
Pulsing out red light like an artery,
The ambulance at top speed floating down
Past beacons and illuminated clocks
Wings in a heavy curve, dips down,
And brakes speed, entering the crowd.
The doors leap open, emptying light;
Stretchers are laid out, the mangled lifted
And stowed into the little hospital.
Then the bell, breaking the hush, tolls once,
And the ambulance with its terrible cargo
Rocking, slightly rocking, moves away,
As the doors, an afterthought, are closed.

We are deranged, walking among the cops
Who sweep glass and are large and
    composed.
One is still making notes under the light.
One with a bucket douches ponds of blood

Into the street and gutter.
One hangs lanterns on the wrecks that cling,
Empty husks of locusts, to iron poles.

Our throats were tight as tourniquets,
Our feet were bound with splints, but now,
Like convalescents intimate and gauche,
We speak through sickly smiles and warn
With the stubborn saw of common sense,
The grim joke and the banal resolution.
The traffic moves around with care,
But we remain, touching a wound
That opens to our richest horror.
Already old, the question Who shall die?
Becomes unspoken Who is innocent?
For death in war is done by hands;
Suicide has cause and stillbirth, logic;
And cancer, simple as a flower, blooms.
But this invites the occult mind,
Cancels our physics with a sneer,
And spatters all we knew of denouement
Across the expedient and wicked stones.

**JOHN FREDERICK NIMS**

John Frederick Nims was born in Muskegon, Michigan, on November 20, 1913. He attended the University of Chicago, where he earned a Ph.D. in Comparative Literature in 1945, studying tragedy in Greek, Latin, French, and English. Four years residence in Italy and Spain and travel in Greece, France, Poland, and other countries heightened his interest in the translation of poetry. His translations include Euripides' *Andromache, The Poems of St. John of the Cross,* and a collection entitled *Sappho to Valéry: Poems in Translation.* In addition, he has edited Arthur Golding's sixteenth-century translation of Ovid's *Metamorphoses.* In recent years he has twice been a visiting professor at Harvard and has frequently been a member of the poetry staff at the Bread Loaf Writers' Conference since 1958. Married, with a son in college and two teen-age daughters, he lives near Chicago, and he teaches at the University of Illinois, Chicago campus.

## THE DARK EXCITING DAYS

There are also the dark exciting days of
The dark night of the soul
The sound of the phone like a pistol shot
And the mailman like a dangerous friend
And the master bedroom like a room
    redone
    in a cool museum and cordonned off
    with a silky thick and python rope
    and the great bed like a grave.
So may there be a name like the prayer OM
Name that strikes like a match in a black
    cave.

## THERE IS GRAY IN MY EYEBROWS

There is gray in my eyebrows, white all
    over my head,
Death kissing my eyes like a homosexual.
I have a fat belly from my own poetry.
Give me your full beautiful hands with
    freckles
My name in your voice like an arpeggio in
    a minor key
Your eyes glazed like those of a Mexican
    woman
And I am the Mexican movie general
With bandoliers of words in the dust in the
    eyes of cameras.

# 𝕵ohn 𝕱rederick 𝕹ims

## LOVE POEM

My clumsiest dear, whose hands shipwreck vases,
At whose quick touch all glasses chip and ring,
Whose palms are bulls in china, burs in linen,
And have no cunning with any soft thing

Except all ill at ease fidgeting people:
The refugee uncertain at the door
You make at home; deftly you steady
The drunk clambering on his undulant floor.

Unpredictable dear, the taxi drivers' terror,
Shrinking from far headlights pale as a dime
Yet leaping before red apoplectic streetcars—
Misfit in any space. And never on time.

A wrench in clocks and the solar system. Only
With words and people and love you move at ease.
In traffic of wit expertly manoeuvre
And keep us, all devotion, at your knees.

Forgetting your coffee spreading on our flannel,
Your lipstick grinning on our coat,
So gayly in love's unbreakable heaven
Our souls on glory of spilt bourbon float.

Be with me darling early and late. Smash glasses—
I will study wry music for your sake.
For should your hands drop white and empty
All the toys of the world would break.

---

## LOVE AND DEATH

And yet a kiss (like blubber) 'd blur and slip,
Without the assuring skull beneath the lip.

---

## NATURE LOVER

Some look at nature for the surface: eye
Vetch, vireo, pond with willow, wandering sky.
Dealers in scenery, no? Obscene as those
Who looking at a girl see only clothes.

---

## DECLINE AND FALL

We had a city also. Hand in hand
Wandered happy as travellers our own land.
Murmured in turn the hearsay of each stone
Or, where a legend faltered, lived our own.
The far-seen obelisk my father set
(Pinning two roads forever where they met)
Waved us in wandering circles, turned our tread
Where once morass engulfed that passionate head.

Cornice rose in ranges, rose so high
It saw no sky, that forum, but noon sky.
Marble shone like shallows; columns too
Streamed with cool light as rocks in breakers do.

O marble many-colored as reach of thought,
Tones so recollected and so distraught.
Golden: like swimmers when the August shore
Brightens their folklore poses more and more.
Or grey with silver: moon's whirling spell
Over the breathless olives we knew well;
Ivory as shoulders there that summer-dressed
Curve to come shyly naked, then find rest
(The tresses love dishevelled leaning dazed
And grateful). Or the wayward stone that blazed
As cheeks do. Or as eyes half-lowered flare.
Violet as veins are, love knows where.
Fine coral as the shy and wild tonguetip,
Undersea coral, rich as inner lip.

There was a stone to build on!

Friezes ran
In strong chorales that where they closed began;
And statues: each a wrung or ringing phrase
In the soul's passionate cadence of her days.

O stone so matched and massive, worked so well,
Who could believe it when the first brick fell?
Who could imagine the unlucky word
Would darken to the worldwide sigh we heard?
How our eyes wrenched together and held fast
Each face tightening to a chalky cast
(So poor a copy of one hour before).
Who could believe the gloom, the funnelled roar
Of cornice falling, forum falling, all
Falling? Or dream it fallen? Not a wall
With eaves to route the rain. The rivers swelled
Till roads groped in lakebottom. Nothing held
Clean edge or corner. Caking, the black flood
Left every luminous room tunnels of mud.
Earth shook: the columns walked, in midair clashed,
And the steep stone exploded as it crashed.

Soon the barbarian swarmed like locusts blown
Between the flood and spasm of our stone.
Grunted to tug their huts and marble sties
Where friezes broke like foam in the blue skies.
Blue noses poked, recoiling as they found
Our young and glad-eyed statues underground;
Singing salvation, the lewd chisel pecks
At boy and girl: one mutilated sex.
All our high moments cheapened—greed and grime
Charred them in rickety stithies to quicklime.

Murderous world. That town that seemed a star
Rose in our soul. And there the ruins are.
We'll not walk there again. Who'd wish to walk
Where the rats gather and grey tourists talk?
Who'd walk there even alive? Or bid his ghost
Trail phosphor on the melancholy coast?

---

## D.O.M., A.D. 2167

When I've outlived three plastic hearts, or four,
Another's kidneys, corneas (*beep!*), with more
Unmentionable rubber, nylon, such—
And when (*beep!*) in a steel drawer (DO NOT TOUCH!),
Mere brain cells in saline wash, I thrive
With thousands, taped to quaver out, "Alive!"—
God grant that steel two wee (*beep!*) eyes of glass
To glitter wicked when the nurses pass.

# William Stafford

## AT THE BOMB TESTING SITE

At noon in the desert a panting lizard
waited for history, its elbows tense,
watching the curve of a particular road
as if something might happen.

It was looking for something farther off
than people could see, an important scene
acted in stone for little selves
at the flute end of consequences.

There was just a continent without much
  on it
under a sky that never cared less.

Ready for a change, the elbows waited.
The hands gripped hard on the desert.

## LONG DISTANCE

Sometimes when you watch the fire
ashes glow and gray
the way the sun turned cold on spires
in winter in the town back home
so far away.

Sometimes on the telephone
the one you hear goes far
and ghostly voices whisper in.
You think they are from other wires.
You think they are.

**WILLIAM STAFFORD**

William Stafford writes: My job is teaching English at Lewis and Clark College in Oregon, with some absences (a Guggenheim grant, a Rockefeller grant, a term as Consultant in Poetry at the Library of Congress). Married, with four children, I frequent the edges of things, little towns, the country. My life is quiet, though I have ventured onto many campuses to read and lecture, and have enjoyed sociability with writers and other interesting people. My home country is the Midwest: born in Kansas, January 17, 1914, through schools there up through a Master's at the University of Kansas, then a Ph.D. at the University of Iowa. Most days, I write, at least a little. The results are scattered, some published, far and near, high and low, in periodicals, anthologies and collections. Three collections of my poems are in print. Recurrently, I have an impulse to accomplish something really good. I might. Maybe my children will.

## REPORTING BACK

By the secret that holds the forest up,
no one will escape. (We have reached this place.)

The sky will come home some day.
(We pay all mistakes our bodies make when they move.)

Is there a way to walk that living has obscured?
(Our feet are trying to remember some path we are
  walking toward.)

## MY FATHER: OCTOBER 1942

He picks up what he thinks is
a road map, and it is
his death: he holds it easily, and·
nothing can take it from his firm hand.
The pulse in his thumb on the map
says, "1:19 P.M. next Tuesday, at
this intersection." And an ambulance
begins to throb while his face looks tired.

Any time anyone may pick up something
so right that he can't put it down:
that is the problem for all who travel—they
fatally own whatever is really theirs,
and that is the inner thread, the lock,
what can hold. If it is to be, nothing breaks
it. Millions of observers guess all the
time, but each person, once, can say, "Sure."

Then he's no longer an observer. He isn't right,
or wrong. He just wins or loses.

# Barbara Howes

**BARBARA HOWES**

Barbara Howes was born on May 1, 1914, in New York City. After graduation from Bennington College, she spent some time editing the New York quarterly *Chimera*. Formerly married to the poet William Jay Smith, she has two sons, David and Gregory. For four years she lived in Florence, Italy, and at other times has lived in Oxford, England, Southern France, and Haiti. She won a Creative Arts Poetry Grant from Brandeis University in 1958, a Guggenheim Fellowship in 1955, and a National Institute of Arts and Letters Award in 1971. With her son Gregory she has edited an anthology of short stories for young adults, and she is currently at work on a collection of stories from Latin America. She lives in North Pownal, Vermont.

## DEATH OF A VERMONT FARM WOMAN

Is it time now to go away?
July is nearly over; hay
Fattens the barn, the herds are strong,
Our old fields prosper; these long
Green evenings will keep death at bay.

Last winter lingered; it was May
Before a flowering lilac spray
Barred cold for ever. I was wrong.
              Is it time now?

Six decades vanished in a day!
I bore four sons: one lives; they
Were all good men; three dying young
Was hard on us. I have looked long
For these hills to show me where peace
   lay . . .
              Is it time now?

## LIGHT AND DARK

Lady, take care; for in the diamond eyes
Of old old men is figured your undoing;
Love is turned in behind the wrinkled lids
To nurse their fear and scorn at their near
   going.
Flesh hangs like the curtains in a house
Long unused, damp as cellars without wine;
They are the future of us all, when we
Will be dried-leaf-thin, the sour whine
Of a siren's diminuendo. They have no past
But egg-husks shattered to a rubbish heap
By memory's looting. Do not follow them
To their camp pitched in a cranny, do not
   keep
To the road for them, a weary weary yard
Will bring you in; that beckoning host
   ahead,
Inn-keeper Death, has but to lift his hat
To topple the oldster in the dust. Read,
Poor old man, the sensual moral; sleep
Narrow in your bed, wear no
More so bright a rose in your lapel;
The spell of the world is loosed, it is time
   to go.

## MERCEDES

Hopscotch
    Through patches
    Of light, a greeneyed
Dominican slanted
    From palm-frond street-shadow in
To a job, to stay on, to be safer;
But by June, daubed soap on her mirror:
*Mercedes de la Rosa esta muerta*

Mercedes had
    Worked Casuarina-long days:
    "San Francisco, San Francis-
    Co, San Fran . . ." written fifty-three
    Times . . . "In my grandmother's
        garden
Tomatoes grew, red whole
Hearts, we ate them; they said
    *'Mercedes de la Rosa is dead'"*

Dream-knives
    Cut out dolls—but I'll
    Help them—that leaf,
    Falling, is a dory . . .
    Chicago, Chicago;
Men: their pants
Pressed to the coil of a whip,
    Shoot billiard
    Eyes at me . . .
*Merced es de la Rosa*

I can hide my dolls, my
    Cuckoo-clock, though his beak
    Orders me to dance;
Sequins, I glue gold pieces, I sew
Justice on chiffon,
All colors—as I whirl,
    They dance—how my body aches!
    I must nail my cuckoo . . . The
Spinning mirror splinters:
    *Mercy befits the Rose*

Next day, duck with two heads,
Her radio quacked to itself; a needle
Slanted through the cuckoo's
    Heart; lint of chiffon
Rocked in Erzulie's breeze . . . "People
    Do strange sometimes," she had said,
    And,
*Mercedes de la Rosa is dead*

# Randall Jarrell

## THE DEATH OF THE BALL TURRET GUNNER

From my mother's sleep I fell into the State,
And I hunched in its belly till my wet fur froze.
Six miles from earth, loosed from its dream of life,
I woke to black flak and the nightmare fighters.
When I died they washed me out of the turret with a hose.

**RANDALL JARRELL**

Born in Nashville, Tennessee, on May 6, 1914, Randall Jarrell was raised in California but returned to Nashville to attend Vanderbilt University. In the Air Force during World War II, he "washed out" as a flyer and spent most of the war training B-29 crews in Arizona. After the war he taught at Kenyon College, the University of Texas, Sarah Lawrence, and what was then the Women's College of the University of North Carolina, in Greensboro. At Kenyon College he came under the tutelage of John Crowe Ransom and became a close friend of Robert Lowell. He was Consultant in Poetry at the Library of Congress for two years and poetry editor of *The Nation* for one year. Aside from his poems, he has also written a novel, *Pictures from an Institution* (1954), and a widely read collection of critical essays, *Poetry and the Age* (1953), which is standard supplementary reading on many college campuses. Jarrell won the National Book Award in 1961 for his fifth book of poems, *The Woman at the Washington Zoo.* He died in October 1965, after being hit by a car.

## BURNING THE LETTERS

*(The wife of a pilot killed in the Pacific is speaking several years
after his death. She was once a Christian, a Protestant.)*

Here in my head, the home that is left for you,
You have not changed; the flames rise from the sea
And the sea changes: the carrier, torn in two,
Sinks to its planes—the corpses of the carrier
Are strewn like ashes on the star-reflecting sea;
Are gathered, sewn with weights, are sunk.
The gatherers disperse.
                                        Here to my hands
From the sea's dark, incalculable calm,
The unchanging circle of the universe,
The letters float: the set yellowing face
Looks home to me, a child's at last,
From the cut-out paper; and the licked
Lips part in their last questioning smile.
The poor labored answers, still unanswering;
The faded questions—questioning so much,
I thought then—questioning so little;
Grew younger, younger, as my eyes grew old,
As that dreamed-out and wept-for wife,
Your last unchanging country, changed
Out of your own rejecting life—a part
Of accusation and of loss, a child's eternally—
Into my troubled separate being.

A child has her own faith, a child's.
In its savage figures—worn down, now, to death—
Men's one life issues, neither out of earth
Nor from the sea, the last dissolving sea,
But out of death: by man came death
And his Life wells from death, the death of Man.
The hunting flesh, the broken blood
Glimmer within the tombs of earth, the food
Of the lives that burrow under the hunting wings
Of the light, of the darkness: dancing, dancing,
The flames grasp flesh with their last searching grace—
Grasp as the lives have grasped: the hunted
Pull down the hunter for his unused life
Parted into the blood, the dark, veined bread

Later than all law. The child shudders, aging:
The peering savior, stooping to her clutch,
His talons cramped with his own bartered flesh,
Pales, flickers, and flares out. In the darkness—darker
With the haunting after-images of light—
The dying God, the eaten Life
Are the nightmare I awaken from to night.

(The flames dance over life. The mourning slaves
In their dark secrecy, come burying
The slave bound in another's flesh, the slave
Freed once, forever, by another's flesh:
The Light flames, flushing the passive face
With its eternal life.)
                                        The lives are fed
Into the darkness of their victory;
The ships sink, forgotten; and the sea

Blazes to darkness: the unsearchable
Death of the lives lies dark upon the life
That, bought by death, the loved and tortured lives,
Stares westward, passive, to the blackening sea.
In the tables of the dead, in the unopened almanac,
The head, charred, featureless—the unknown mean—
Is thrust from the waters like a flame, is torn
From its last being with the bestial cry
Of its pure agony. O death of all my life,
Because of you, because of you, I have not died,
By your death I have lived.
                              The sea is empty.
As I am empty, stirring the charred and answered
Questions about your home, your wife, your cat
That stayed at home with me—that died at home

Gray with the years that gleam above you there
In the great green grave where you are young
And unaccepting still. Bound in your death,
I choose between myself and you, between your life
And my own life: it is finished.
                              Here in my head
There is room for your black body in its shroud,
The dog tags welded to your breastbone, and the flame
That winds above your death and my own life
And the world of my life. The letters and the face
That stir still, sometimes, with your fiery breath—
Take them, O grave! Great grave of all my years,
The unliving universe in which all life is lost,
Make yours the memory of that accepting
And accepted life whose fragments I cast here.

## THE BIRD OF NIGHT

A shadow is floating through the moonlight.
Its wings don't make a sound.
Its claws are long, its beak is bright.
Its eyes try all the corners of the night.

It calls and calls: all the air swells and heaves
And washes up and down like water.

The ear that listens to the owl believes
In death. The bat beneath the eaves,

The mouse beside the stone are still as death.
The owl's air washes them like water.
The owl goes back and forth inside the night,
And the night holds its breath.

## JONAH

As I lie here in the sun
And gaze out, a day's journey, over Nineveh,
The sailors in the dark hold cry to me:
"What meanest thou, O sleeper? Arise and call upon
Thy God; pray with us, that we perish not."

All thy billows and thy waves passed over me.
The waters compassed me, the weeds were wrapped about
   my head;
The earth with her bars was about me forever.
A naked worm, a man no longer,
I writhed beneath the dead:

But thou art merciful.
When my soul was dead within me I remembered thee,
From the depths I cried to thee. For thou art merciful:
Thou hast brought my life up from corruption,
O Lord my God. . . . When the king said, "Who can tell

But God may yet repent, and turn away
From his fierce anger, that we perish not?"
My heart fell; for I knew thy grace of old—
In my own country, Lord, did I not say
That thou art merciful?

Now take, Lord, I beseech thee,
My life from me; it is better that I die . . .
But I hear, "Doest thou well, then, to be angry?"
And I say nothing, and look bitterly
Across the city; a young gourd grows over me

And shades me—and I slumber, clean of grief.
I was glad of the gourd. But God prepared
A worm that gnawed the gourd; but God prepared
The east wind, the sun beat upon my head
Till I cried, "Let me die!" And God said, "Doest thou well

To be angry for the gourd?"
And I said in my anger, "I do well
To be angry, even unto death." But the Lord God
Said to me, "Thou hast had pity on the gourd"—
And I wept, to hear its dead leaves rattle—

"Which came up in a night, and perished in a night.
And should I not spare Nineveh, that city
Wherein are more than six-score thousand persons
Who cannot tell their left hand from their right;
And also much cattle?"

# John Berryman

**JOHN BERRYMAN**

John Berryman was born on October 25, 1914, in McAlester, Oklahoma. He received an A.B. from Columbia in 1936 and a B.A. from Clare College, Oxford, in 1938. He taught at Wayne State University, Harvard, Princeton, and the University of Washington, among other schools, and was awarded the *Kenyon Review* Doubleday Award, a Rockefeller Fellowship, the Shelley Memorial Prize, the Guarantors Prize and the Levinson Prize from *Poetry* Magazine, the Pulitzer Prize for Poetry (1965), and the National Book Award for Poetry (1969). His wry, studiously colloquial *Dream Songs* are much read and much talked about, particularly among students. However, none of them is included here, as the editor felt that it was impossible to do justice to any of them, or to the body of the work, by presenting only three or four. They are easily available and should be read together. John Berryman committed suicide on January 7, 1972.

## WINTER LANDSCAPE

The three men coming down the winter hill
In brown, with tall poles and a pack of
    hounds
At heel, through the arrangement of the
    trees,
Past the five figures at the burning straw,
Returning cold and silent to their town,

Returning to the drifted snow, the rink
Lively with children, to the older men,
The long companions they can never reach,
The blue light, men with ladders, by the
    church
The sledge and shadow in the twilit street,

Are not aware that in the sandy time
To come, the evil waste of history
Outstretched, they will be seen upon the
    brow
Of that same hill: when all their company
Will have been irrecoverably lost,

These men, this particular three in brown
Witnessed by birds will keep the scene and
    say
By their configuration with the trees,
The small bridge, the red houses and the
    fire,
What place, what time, what morning
    occasion

Sent them into the wood, a pack of hounds
At heel and the tall poles upon their
    shoulders,
Thence to return as now we see them and
Ankle-deep in snow down the winter hill
Descend, while three birds watch and the
    fourth flies.

## PARTING AS DESCENT

The sun rushed up the sky; the taxi flew;
There was a kind of fever on the clock
That morning. We arrived at Waterloo
With time to spare and couldn't find my
    track.

The bitter coffee in a small café
Gave us our conversation. When the train
Began to move, I saw you turn away
And vanish, and the vessels in my brain

Burst, the train roared, the other travellers
In flames leapt, burning on the tilted air
Che si cruccia, I heard the devils curse
And shriek with joy in that place beyond
    prayer.

## VENICE, 182-

White & blue my breathing lady leans
across me in the first light, so we kiss.
The corners of her eyes are white. I miss,
renew. She means
to smother me thro' years of this.

Hell chill young widows in the heel of
    night—
perduring loves, melody's thrusting, press
flush with the soft skin, whence they
    sprung! back. Less
ecstasy might
save us for speech & politeness.

I hear her howl now, and I slam my eyes
against the glowing face. Foul morning-
    cheese
stands fair compared to love. On waspish
    knees
our pasts surprise
and plead us livid. Now she frees

a heavy lock was pulling . . . I kiss it,
lifting my hopeless lids—and all trace
of passion's vanisht from her eyes & face,
the lip I bit
is bluer, a blackhead at the base

of her smooth nose looks sullenly at me,
we look at each other in entire depair,
her eyes are swimming by mine, and I
    swear
sobbing quickly
we are in love. The light hurts. "There . . ."

**A POEM FOR BHAIN**

Although the relatives in the summer house
Gossip and grumble, do what relatives do,
Demand, demand our eyes and ears,
  demand us,

You and I are not precisely there
As they require: heretics, we converse
Alert and alone, as over a lake of fire

Two white birds following their profession
Of flight, together fly, loom, fall and rise,
Certain of the nature and station of their
  mission.

So by the superficial and summer lake
We talk, and nothing that we say is heard,
Neither by the relatives who twitter and
  ache

Nor by any traveller nor by any bird.

**HOLLIS SUMMERS**

Hollis Summers writes: I was born on June 21, 1916, in Eminence, Kentucky, of a line of Baptist preachers. I went to school at Georgetown College, Bread Loaf, and the University of Iowa. Laura Clarke and I are married; we have two sons. I lecture around, attend writers' conferences, teach in the English Department of Ohio University, Athens, Ohio. I made fiction first, then poetry. Now I work at both. My novels are *City Limit, Brighten the Corner, Teach You a Lesson* (with James Rourke), *The Weather of February,* and, in 1968, *The Day After Sunday.* My latest book of poems is *Sit Opposite Each Other.* I like the title *Sit Opposite Each Other.* Perhaps that is what poetry is about.

# Hollis Summers

**THE DELIVERY**

I promised to look out for the child while I wrapped the
  boxes.
He was unattractive, with glasses that magnified his eyes
Into no eyes, and a stinking breath, but I like children.
He kept coming in and out and in and asking questions.
He could not understand any of the arrangements.
I answered as well as I was able, all the while wrapping the
  boxes.

Most people do not understand the art of wrapping boxes.
These are particularly difficult. You not only place the
  first
Into the second, but the second into the third, with tape
  and string
More complicated than music or wallpaper. I do not like
  to boast
But I have proved myself adept at wrapping boxes.

I suspect the parents came for the child. I am reasonably
  sure.
The vast boxes triple wallpaper the room, ordered as Bach.
I have filled out all the forms left by the messenger.
I feel reasonably sure I will be questioned.
I will answer the questions as well as I am able.
And then the boxes will go to the trucks.

**THE PEDDLER**

Finding the hotel was not the real problem,
Although hotels are difficult to find again,
Once you've thought them well left behind,
Once the wind has changed and snow has fallen,
Once you have bought a ticket to another town.

I found the right hotel, I am sure,
But I still did not recall the number of my room.

The clerk was busy at first, then disturbed:
"Somebody stole my records. My memory is poor,"
But he remembered me. He was sure he remembered.

We decided at last on the very top floor
And a mystic number, I remember a mystic number.
"We are right. I am sure there is no one there."
"We are right." "My apologies for my memory."
"My apologies." "The key?" "The key is there."

I joined a nun in the chromium elevator.
Her skin and wimple seemed made of each other.
She smiled as though we were familiar.
We soared quickly together.
She smiled as though we held a secret together.

And we were there, and she had disappeared,
And, behold, my numbered door.
I waited before the door, not from fear
I think, listening a while to the far
Sound of women singing. And then I entered.

The room was a thousand rooms I have departed:
The same draperies, the beds, the chairs, the mirrors;

And perhaps I spoke aloud, rushing to the dresser
("Thank God") where the suitcase waited undisturbed;
Perhaps I fell to my knees as if in prayer.

I do not mean to make too much of this story.
The suitcase held the articles I usually carry:
The same shaver, pajamas, a robe, slippers,
Three books I would logically admire,
And scrawled notes stuffed in a manila folder.

All of the notes I read in the darkening room,
Written in a hand almost or surely mine,
Naming journeys, listing living expenses.
In a dresser drawer I left the memorandums.
I am determined to believe the suitcase is my own.

SONG TO BE ATTACHED

Decorate the carcass
Thread with amethyst
Stud the brow with topaz
Zircon for each wrist

Twist the breast with emerald
Diamond for the waist
Shining as a slogan
Carefully many-faced

Baste the thighs with sapphire
Brilliant as a phrase
Deck the bowels with ruby
Weave a garnet maze

Braise in precious ointment
Drench it if you will
Decorate the carcass
It is a carcass still.

AT THE WAX MUSEUM

Here where Gary Cooper's figure stands
Holding truth enough to fool his mother,
Where a fresh carnation and Gloria Swanson
Bloom equally fresh, and the James Brothers,
Guns alert, measure Gina's body,
Here I would speak my knowledge of busied works,
Surrounded by Caesar, Cortez, Laurel, Hardy,
Considering such idle matters as life and art.

The tenses merge, accompanied by air and water,
Earth, fire, proving John Kennedy
And the presence of Isaac Watts.
Henry VIII eats. Hannah feeds
Her son near Newton, Luther, Al Capone,
Moses, Joan. . . . I would name them all
Whose urgent hair has been precisely counted
As naturally as counted starlings fall.

Once I picked a rose from my own garden
And placed it within a lovely woman's hand;
Undone at the blood of my act with a casual thorn,
I considered the rose and the woman dead;
But the living woman laughed beside the bed
Of yellow roses, pushing back her hair;
"Hurry, take the picture," the woman said.
Oh praise God presently, everywhere.

# John Ciardi

**JOHN CIARDI**

The only son of Italian immigrants, John Ciardi was born on June 24, 1916, in Boston. He graduated *magna cum laude* from Bates College in 1938 and received his M.A. the following year from the University of Michigan. After spending World War II as a gunner in the Army Air Force, he joined the English faculty at Harvard. He has been on the staff of the Bread Loaf Writers' Conference since 1946 and has been director of the conference since 1955. He recently ended a long tenure as poetry editor of *Saturday Review*, in which his articles, under the title "Manner of Speaking," have established him as a master of the informal essay. He is also widely known as a writer of poems for children, and his recently completed translation of Dante's *Divine Comedy* is fast becoming the standard verse translation in English. Ciardi's most recent book of poems, *Lives of X*, is notable for its attempt to employ in poetry the devices of fiction—a move toward the rediscovery of the narrative poem. Between poems, translations, and essays, Ciardi gardens, plays gin rummy, golfs, and almost single-handedly keeps the game of cribbage alive in the Western Hemisphere. He lives in Metuchen, New Jersey, with his wife, Judith, in a great house which they share from time to time with two sons and a daughter.

## THE EVIL EYE

Nona poured oil on the water and saw the eye
   form on my birth. Zia beat me with bay
   fennel and barley to scourge the devil away.
I doubt I needed so much excuse to cry.

From Sister Maria Immaculata there came
   a crucifix, a vow of nine days' prayer,
   a scapular stitched with virgin's hair.
The eye glowed on the water all the same.

By Felicia, the midwife, I was hung with a tin
   fish stuffed with garlic and bread crumbs.
   Three holy waters washed the breast for my gums.
Still the eye glared, wide as original sin

on the deepest pools of women midnight-spoken
   to ward my clamoring soul from the clutch of hell,
   lest growing I be no comfort and dying swell
more than a grave with horror. Still unbroken

the eye glared through the roosts of all their clucking.
   "Jesu," cried Mother, "why is he deviled so?"
   "Baptism without delay," said Father Cosmo.
"This one is not for sprinkling but for ducking."

So in came meat and wine and the feast was on.
   I wore a palm frond in my lace, and sewn
   to my swaddling band a hoop and three beads of bone
for the Trinity. And they ducked me and called me John.

And ate the meat and drank the wine, and the eye
   closed on the water. All this fell between
   my first scream and first name in 1916,
the year of the war and the influenza, when I

was not yet ready for evil or my own name,
though I had one already and the other came.

---

## ON A PHOTO OF SGT. CIARDI A YEAR LATER

The sgt. stands so fluently in leather,
So poster-holstered and so newsreel-jawed
As death's costumed and fashionable brother,
My civil memory is overawed.

Behind him see the circuses of doom
Dance a finale chorus on the sun.
He leans on gun sights, doesn't give a damn
For dice or stripes, and waits to see the fun.

The cameraman whose ornate public eye
Invented that fine bravura look of calm
At murderous clocks hung ticking in the sky
Palmed the deception off without a qualm.

Even the camera, focused and exact
To a two dimensional conclusion,
Uttered its formula of physical fact
Only to lend data to illusion.

The camera always lies. By a law of perception
The obvious surface is always an optical ruse.
The leather was living tissue in its own dimension,
The holsters held benzedrine tablets, the guns were no use.

The careful slouch and dangling cigarette
Were always superstitious as Amen.
The shadow under the shadow is never caught:
The camera photographs the cameraman.

---

## A BOX COMES HOME

I remember the United States of America
As a flag-draped box with Arthur in it
And six marines to bear it on their shoulders.

I wonder how someone once came to remember
The Empire of the East and the Empire of the West.
As an urn maybe delivered by chariot.

You could bring Germany back on a shield once
And France as a plume. England, I suppose,
Kept coming back a long time as a letter.

Once I saw Arthur dressed as the United States
Of America. Now I see the United States
Of America as Arthur in a flag-sealed domino.

And I would pray more good of Arthur
Than I can wholly believe. I would pray
An agreement with the United States of America

To equal Arthur's living as it equals his dying
At the red-taped grave in Woodmere
By the rain and oakleaves on the domino.

---

## THE BENEFITS OF AN EDUCATION:
Boston, 1931

A hulk, three masted once, three stubbed now,
carried away by any history, and dumped
in a mud ballast of low tide, heeled over
and a third swallowed in a black suck
south of the Nixie's Mate—itself going—
gave me a seal of memory for a wax
I wouldn't find for years yet: this was Boston.
Men with nothing to do plovered the sand-edge
with clam rakes that raked nothing. I walked home
over the drawbridge, skirting, on my right,
Charlestown ramshackled over Bunker Hill
and waiting for hopped-up kids to ride The Loop
and die in a tin rumple against the girders
of Sullivan Square, or dodge away toward Everett
and ditch the car; then walk home and be heroes
to ingrown boyos, poor as the streets they prowled.

There, house to house, the auctioneer's red flag
drooped its torn foreclosure to no buyer.

Now and then a blind man who could see,
and his squat wife who could stare out at nothing,
sat on the curb by the stacked furniture
and put the babies to sleep in dresser drawers
till charity came, or rain made pulp of all.
The rest lived in, guarding their limp red flags.
The bank was the new owner and that was all.
Why evict nothing much to make room for nothing?
Some sort of man is better than no man,
and might scrounge crates to keep the pipes from freezing
until the Water Co turned off the meter.
Or come Election, when men got their dole,
the bank might get the trickle of a rent
that wasn't there.
                    I'd walked those seven miles
from Medford to T Wharf to get my job
on the King Philip. Well, not quite a job,
but work, free passage, and a chance to scrounge
nickels and fish all summer till school opened
Miss Bates and Washington Irving.
                                    The King Philip

rose sheer, three river-boat-decks top heavy;
but she could ride an inner-harbor swell
and not quite capsize, though, God knows, she'd try.

Excursion fishing. She put out at nine
from the creaking stink of Sicilian fishing boats
praying for gasoline they sometimes got.
And came back in at five—in any weather
that might turn up a dollar-a-head half deck-load
doling four quarters into the first mate's hand
as if the fish they meant to eat were in it
and not still on a bottom out past luck.
Sometimes a hundred or more, but of them all
not twenty would turn up with a dollar bill.
It was all change. We called the first mate Jingles,
waiting for him to walk across the wharf
and spill his pockets into the tin box
in the Fish Mkt. safe. When he came back
his name was Dixon and we could cast off.

Your dollar bought you eight hours on the water,
free lines, free bait, your catch, and—noon to one—
all the fish chowder you could eat.
                              Good days,
the decks were slimed with pollock, cod, hake, haddock,
a flounder or two, and now and then a skate.
(A sharp man with a saw-toothed small tin can
can punch out Foolish Scallops from a skate's wing.
A Foolish Scallop is a scallop for fools
who eat it and don't know better.) I made a scraper
by screwing bottle caps to an oak paddle
and went my rounds, cleaning the catch for pennies,
or grabbing a gaff to help haul in the big ones.

Dixon, jingling again, took up a pool—
a dollar for the biggest cod or haddock,
a half for the largest fish of any kind.
No house cut but the little he could steal
and not be caught or, being caught, pass off
as an honest man's mistake in a ripped pocket.
The deal was winner-take-all. And the man that gaffed
the winning fish aboard was down for a tip.

One Sunday, with over a hundred in the pool,
I gaffed a skate we couldn't get aboard.
Dixon boat-hooked it dead still in the water,
then rigged a sling and tackle from rotten gear
and I went over the side and punched two holes
behind its head. Then we payed out the hooks
the fireman used for hauling cans of ashes
to dump them overboard, and I hooked it on,
and all hands hauled it clear to hang like a mat
from the main to the lower deck. We couldn't weigh it,
but it was no contest. Dixon paid on the spot.
He counted it out to fifty-seven dollars,
and I got two.
                    We took it in to the wharf

and let it hang—a flag—till the next day
when we cut it loose with half a ceremony,
mostly of flies, just as we cleared Deer Island.
The Captain didn't want that shadow floating
over his treasury of likely bottoms,
so we let the current have it.
                              After five,
the fireman rigged the hose, turned on the pressure,
and I washed down, flying the fish and fish guts
out of the scuppers in a rainbow spray
to a congregation of God-maddened gulls
screaming their witness over the stinking slip.
For leavings.
                    Fishermen are no keepers. One to eat,
a few to give away, and that's enough.
The scuppers might spill over, and the deck
on both sides of a walkway might be littered
with blue-backed and white-bellied gapers staring.

I cleaned the best to haul home. Or I did
when I had carfare, or thought I could climb the fence
into the El and ride free. Now and then,
Gillis, who ran a market next to ruin,
would buy a cod or haddock for nothing a pound
and throw in a pack of Camels.
                              And half the time
an old clutch of black shawl with a face inside it
and a nickel in its fist would flutter aboard
like something blown from a clothesline near a freight yard,
and squeeze a split accordion in her lungs
to wheeze for a bit of "any old fish left over,"
flashing her nickel like a badge, and singing
widowed beatitudes when I picked a good one
and wrapped it in newspaper and passed it over
and refused her ritual nickel the third time.

"I can afford to pay, son."
                              "Sure you can."
"Here, now, it's honest money."
                              "Sure it is."
"Well, take it then."
                              "Compliments of the house."
"God bless you and your proud mother,"
she'd end, and take the wind back to her line.
Then the Fish Mkt man got after Dixon
for letting me steal his customers. Nickels are nickels:
for all he knew, I might be stealing from him
out of that pocket of nothing. But I foxed him.
Next time the old shawl came I sent her off
to wait by Atlantic Avenue. (And I'm damned
if the Fish Mkt man didn't call to her
waving a flipper of old bloat, calling "Cheap!
Just right for a pot of chowder!") After that,
I made an extra bundle every night,
cleaned and filet'd, and when she wasn't there
I fed the cats, or anything else of God's

that didn't run a market.
                    Then five nights running
she didn't come. Which, in God's proper market
might be more mercy than all nickels are,
whoever keeps the register, whoever
folds old shawls for burial.

                    Some nights--
once, twice a week, or some weeks not, the ship
was chartered for a stag by the VFW,
(we used to call them the Victims of Foreign Whores)
or some lodge, or some club, though the promoter
was always the same stink in tired tout's tweed.
He rigged a rigged wheel forward on the lower deck.
Sold bootleg by the men's room. Used the Ladies'
as an undressing room for the girlie show
that squeezed its naked pinched companionway
to the main deck "salon" to do the split
or sun itself in leers, clutching a stanchion,
or, when the hat was passed, to mount the table
and play house, if not home, two at a time,
with a gorilla stinking of pomade
who came on in a bathrobe from the Ladies'.
Two shows a night, prompt as mind's death could make
    them
while it still had a body. And on the top deck,
for an extra quarter, Tillie the Artist's Model
undid flickering all on a canvas screen
lashed to the back of the wheelhouse, where the Captain
kept a sharp Yankee watch for the Harbor Cruiser.

He was a good gray stick of salt, hull down
in some lost boyhood that had put to sea
with the last whales still running into myth.
And down to this, or be beached flat, keeled over
like Boston, or that hulk off the Nixie's Mate,
to stink in the mud for nothing.
                    Nevertheless,
It was some education in some school.
I panted at those desks of flesh flung open,
did mountains of dream homework with willing Tillie,
and, mornings, ran a cloth and a feather duster
(God knows where it came from--I'd guess Mrs. Madden
who cooked the daily chowder of leftovers
in her throbbing galley) over the counters, chairs,
and the great ark-built table, still flesh-haunted.

If it wasn't an education, it was lessons
in something I had to know before I could learn
what I was learning. Whatever there was to learn
in the stinking slips and cat-and-rat wet alleys
off the black girders and the slatted shadow
of the Atlantic Avenue El in Boston
where the edge-grinding wheels of nothing screeched
something from Hell at every sooty bend
of the oil-grimed and horse-dolloped cobbles
from Federal Street to the West End's garlic ghetto,

where black-toothed whores asked sailors for a buck
but took them for a quarter, in the freight yards,
or on the loading platforms behind North Station,
or in any alley where the kids had stoned
the street lights to permission.
                    I took home
more than I brought with me of all Miss Blake
and Washington Irving knew of Sleepy Hollow.
(It had stayed clean and leafy I discovered
years later--like the Captain's boyhood
waiting its fo'c'sle south of Marblehead--
yet, a day further on the same road West,
the hollows had turned grimy, and the hills
fell through tipped crowns of slag--like Beacon Hill
stumbling through trash-can alleys to Scollay Square.)

Still, I got one thing from my education.
One stag-night when the tired tout's bootleg sold
too well for what it was, four poisoned drunks
lay writhing in the stern on the lower deck
in their own spew. And one, half dead but groaning,
green in his sweat, lay choking and dry-heaving,
his pump broken. While from the deck above
girls clattered, the pimp spieled, and the crowd raved.

Dixon came after me with the tout. "Hey, kid,
got a good stomach?" Dixon said. "Yeah, sure,"
I told him, honored.
                    "It's a dirty job."
"What isn't?"
                    "Five bucks!" said the tout. "Five bucks!
Here, Johnny. Five bucks cash and you can hold it!
My God, the guy could *die!*"--and passed the five
to Dixon who spread it open with both hands
to let me see it before he put it away.
"And a deuce from me if you'll do it," he tacked on,
taking my greedy silence for resistance.

"Who do I kill?" I said, taking the line
from George Raft, probably.
                    "Look, kid, it's legal.
You *save* a guy!" the tout said in a spout.

"Lay off," said Dixon, and putting his hand on my shoulder,
he walked me off two paces. "It's like this.
The guy's choked full of rotgut and can't heave it.
I tried to stick my fingers down his throat
to get him started, but I just can't make it.
Kid," he said, "it takes guts I ain't got.
You got the guts to try?"
                    And there I was
with a chance to have more guts than a first mate,
and seven dollars to boot!
                    "Which guy?" I said--
only for something to say: I knew already.

"The groaner by the winch. I got a fid
to jam between his teeth if you'll reach in

41

and stick your fingers down his throat."
                                    We raised him,
half sitting, with his head back in the chains,
and Dixon got the thick end of the fid
jammed into his teeth on one side. "LET'S GO, KID!"
he screamed, almost as green as the half-corpse
that had begun to tremble like a fish
thrown on the deck, not dead yet, though too dead
to buck again.
                    But when I touched the slime
that might have been his tongue, I couldn't make it.
"Dixon, I can't do it!"
                            "Well, damn your eyes,
you *said* you would. Now put up, or by God
I'll heave you over!"
                        "Wait a minute," I said,
catching my education by the tail.
"Can you hold him there a minute?"
                                    *"If he lives.*
Now where the Hell you going?"
                                    "I'll be right back,"
I called, already going, "I'll be right back."

I ran for the locker, grabbed the feather duster,
and ran back, snatching out the grimiest feather,
took out my knife, peeled off all but the tip,
then fished his throat with it, twirling the stem
till I felt him knotting up. "Evoe!" I shouted
for Bacchus to remember I remembered,
not knowing till later that I mispronounced it.
"EE-VO," not giving Bacchus all his syllables.

"Heave-ho it is!" roared Dixon and ducked aside
as the corpse spouted. "There, by God, she blows!"
And blow she did. I've never seen a man
that dirty and still alive. Except maybe the tout
clapping me on the shoulder. "You did it, kid!
By God, you did it! Johnny, didn't he do it!"

Dixon wiped his hands on the drunk's back
where he had twisted and sprawled over the winch-drum
(what reflex is it turns a dead man over
to let him retch facedown?) and fished the five
out of his pocket. "Where'd you learn that trick?"
he said as I took the money and waited for more.

I could have told him, "Dmitri Merezhkovsky,
*Julian the Apostate*, but it wasn't
on Miss Blake's list, and certainly not on his.
"How about the other deuce?" I said instead.

He was holding the feather duster by the handle
and turning his wrist to inspect it from all sides
and looking down into its head of fuzz.
"What's this thing doing on a ship?" he said.

"Waiting for Romans," I told him, guessing his game
but hoping to play him off. "That's history, Dixon.

When a man went to a banquet and stuffed himself,
he'd head for a men's room called a *vomitorium*,
tickle his throat with a feather, do an upchuck,
and then start over. How about that deuce?"

"If you're so smart, then you can figure out
I said if you used your fingers."
                                    "Hey," said the tout,
"If you ain't paying up, get back my fin!
If you can welch on this punk kid, then I can!"

"Go peddle your sewer sweat," Dixon said. "Here, kid.
You earned it right enough. Go buy yourself
more education." And stuffed into my pocket
a crumple I unfolded into—one bill,
while he went forward, shoving the tout away.

Six dollars, then. One short. But the first cash
my education ever paid, and that
from off the reading list, though of the Empire,
if not the Kingdom.
                        Meanwhile, the hat passed,
the crowd's roar signalling, the pomade gorilla
came from the Ladies' and pushed up the stairs
from his own *vomitorium* to the orgy
where low sisters of *meretricis honestae*
waited to mount their table through lit smoke
into my nose-to-the-window education
one deck below the Captain's Yankee eye
on watch for the Harbor Cruiser and the tide,
bearing off Thompson Island to the left,
Deer Island to the right, and dead ahead
Boston's night-glow spindled like two mists:
one on the floodlit needle of Bunker Hill,
one on the Custom House, both shimmering out
to sit the waters of Babylon off Boston,
whose dented cup—an original Paul Revere
fallen from hand to hand—I drained like the kings
of fornication, mad for dirty wine.
And for the kingdoms opening like a book.

---

## A MAGUS

A missionary from the Mau Mau told me.
  There are spores blowing from space.
  He has himself seen an amazing botany
  springing the crust. Fruit with a bearded face
  that howls at the picker. Mushrooms that bleed.
  A tree of enormous roots that sends no trace
  above ground; not a leaf. And he showed me the seed
  of thorned lettuces that induce
  languages. The Jungle has come loose,
  is changing purpose.
                        *Nor are the vegetations*
*of the new continuum the only sign.*

*New eyes have observed the constellations.*
*And what does not change when looked at?—coastline?*
*sea? sky? The propaganda of the wind reaches.*
*Set watches on your gardens. What spring teaches*
*seed shall make new verbs. A root is a tongue.*

I repeat it as he spoke it. I do not interpret
what I do not understand. He comes among
many who have come to us. He speaks and we forget
and are slow to be reminded. But he does come,
signs do appear.
                    There are poisoned islands far over:
fish from their reefs come to table and some
glow in the dark not of candlelight. A windhover
chatters in the counters of our polar camps.
A lectern burns. Geese jam the radar. The red phone
rings. Is there an answer? Planes from black ramps
howl to the edge of sound. The unknown
air breaks from them. They crash through.
What time is it in orbit? Israeli teams
report they have found the body, but Easter seems
symbolically secure. Is a fact true?

How many megatons of idea is a man? What island
lies beyond his saying? I have heard, and say
what I heard said and believe. I do not understand.
But I have seen him change water to blood, and call away
the Lion from its Empire. He speaks that tongue.
I have seen white bird and black bird follow him, hung
like one cloud over his head. His hand,
when he wills it, bursts into flame. The white bird
and the black divide and circle it. At his word
they enter the fire and glow like metal. A ray
reaches from him to the top of the air,
and in it the figures of a vision play
these things I believe whose meaning I cannot say.

Then he closes his fist and there is nothing there.

**PETER VIERECK**

Peter Viereck was born on August 5, 1916, in New York City. He was educated at the Horace Mann School for Boys and at Harvard, where he graduated *summa cum laude* in 1937, one of the few students in the history of the college to receive both the Garrison Prize medal for the best undergraduate verse and the Bowdoin Prize medal for the best philosophical prose. He has since made an international reputation in both fields. After taking his Ph.D. in History from Harvard in 1942, he served in the Army during World War II and then returned to Harvard as an instructor. He left Harvard to teach for two years at Smith College, and from there he went to Mount Holyoke College in South Hadley, Massachusetts, where he has been a professor since 1948. He has also lectured at Oxford and was Fulbright Lecturer at the University of Florence. He won the Pulitzer Prize for Poetry in 1949 for *Terror and Decorum.* Besides his poetry, he has written a novel, a book of criticism, and three distinguished volumes on politics and society. Married and the father of three children, Viereck lives in South Hadley.

# Peter Viereck

## *VALE* FROM CARTHAGE

*(for my brother, 1944)*

I, now at Carthage. He, shot dead at Rome.
Shipmates last May. "And what if one of us,"
I asked last May, in fun, in gentleness,
"Wears doom, like dungarees, and doesn't know?"
He laughed, *"Not see Times Square again?"* The foam,
Feathering across that deck a year ago,
Swept those five words—like seeds—beyond the seas
        Into his future. There they grew like trees;

And as he passed them there next spring, they
    laid
    Upon his road of fire their sudden shade.
Though he had always scraped his mess-kit pure
And scrubbed redeemingly his barracks floor,
Though all his buttons glowed their ritual-hymn
Like cloudless moons to intercede for him,
No furlough fluttered from the sky. He will
Not see Times Square—he will not see—he will
Not see Times
        change; at Carthage (while my friend,
Living those words at Rome, screamed in the end)
I saw an ancient Roman's tomb and read
*"Vale"* in stone. Here two wars mix their dead:
    Roman, my shipmate's dream walks hand in hand
    With yours tonight ("New York again" and
      "Rome"),
    Like widowed sisters bearing water home
    On tired heads through hot Tunisian sand
    In good cool urns, and says, "I understand."
Roman, you'll see your Forum Square no more;
What's left but this to say of any war?

---

## MARY, MARY

*(a four-volume Ph.D. thesis on Rousseau and original sin)*

Mary, long by Boss's kisses bored,
Quit desk and stole His yacht and jumped aboard.
Her lamb took she, for purer were his kisses.
Compass and pistol took she in her purse.
Free sailed she north to eat new freedom up.
And her helped ocean and grew calm and snored.
But when with bleating chum she cuddled up,
Unleashed His typhoons Boss; therein no bliss is.
Then knew she—by four signs—whose jig was up:—

Her buoyed the life-preserver down, not up;
True was the pistol's aim, but in reverse;
The compass steered, but only toward abysses;
The little lamb nipped Mary's thighs and roared.

## POET

*"Toute forme créée, même par l'homme, est*
*immortelle. Car la forme est indépendante*
*de la matière, et ce ne sont pas les*
*molécules qui constituent la forme."*
—(Baudelaire, *Mon Coeur Mis à Nu)*

### 1

The night he died, earth's images all came
To gloat in liberation round his tomb.
Now vengeful colors, stones, and faces dare
    To argue with his metaphor;
And stars his fancy painted on the skies
Drop down like swords
        to pierce his too wide eyes.

### 2

Words that begged favor at his court in vain—
Lush adverbs, senile rhymes in tattered gowns—
    Send notes to certain exiled nouns
And mutter openly against his reign.
While rouged clichés hang out red lights again,
Hoarse refugees report from far-flung towns
That exclamation-marks are running wild
And prowling half-truths carried off a child.

### 3

But he lives on in form, and form shall shatter
    This tuneless mutiny of matter.
His bones are dead; his voice is horribly strong.
Those famed vibrations of life's dancing dust,
Whose thrice-named pangs are "birth" and "death" and
    "lust,"
Are but the spilt iambics of his song.
Scansion of flesh in endless ebb and flow,
The drums of duty and renown's great gong—
Mere grace-notes of that living thousand-year
Tyrannic metronome whose every gear
Is some shy craftsman buried long ago.
What terror crowns the sweetness of all song?

### 4

What hardness leaps at us from each soft tune
And hammers us to shapes we never planned?
This was a different dying from our own.
    Call every wizard in the land—
Bell, book, and test tube; let the dark be rife
With every exorcism we command.
In vain. This death is stronger than our life.

### 5

In vain we drive our stakes through such a haunter
Or woo with spiced applaudings such a heart.

44

His news of April do but mock our winter
Like maps of heaven breathed on window-frost
By cruel clowns in codes whose key is lost.
Yet some sereneness in our rage has guessed
That we are being blessed and blessed and blessed
When least we know it and when coldest art
                    Seems hostile,
                                useless,
                                        or apart.


6

            Not worms, not worms in such a skull
But rhythms, rhythms writhe and sting and crawl.
He sings the seasons round from bud to snow.
And all things are because he willed them so.

---

TO HELEN (of Troy, N.Y.)

I sit here with the wind is in my hair;
I huddle like the sun is in my eyes;
I am (I wished you'd contact me) alone.

A fat lot you'd wear crape if I was dead.
It figures, who I heard there when I phoned you;
It figures, when I came there, who has went.

Dogs laugh at me, folks bark at me since then;
"She is," they say, "no better than she ought to";
I love you irregardless how they talk.

You should of done it (which it is no crime)
With me you should of done it, what they say.
I sit here with the wind is in my hair.

**ROBERT LOWELL**
Robert Lowell was born in Boston on March 1, 1917, the only son of Commander R. T. S. Lowell and Charlotte Winslow. He was taught by Richard Eberhart at St. Mark's School in Southborough, Massachusetts, and by John Crowe Ransom at Kenyon College, where he also became a friend of Randall Jarrell. In 1940 he graduated *summa cum laude* from Kenyon, married the novelist Jean Stafford, and became a Roman Catholic. When the United States entered World War II, he tried twice to enlist in the Navy but was turned down each time. However, by 1943, believing the United States to be out of danger, he felt that the bombing of civilian populations was morally unjustifiable, and he refused to comply with the draft law. As a result, Lowell was sent to prison as a conscientious objector. He received the Pulitzer Prize in 1947 for *Lord Weary's Castle,* a Guggenheim Fellowship in 1947–1948, the Guinness Poetry Award in 1959, and the National Book Award in 1960 for *Life Studies.* His *Imitations,* a collection of free translations of a number of poems, won him the Bollingen Translation Prize in 1962. He has also written three plays and has translated Racine's *Phaedra* and Aeschylus' *Prometheus Bound.* His first marriage having ended in divorce, he married the novelist Elizabeth Hardwick in 1949. They live with their daughter, Harriet, in New York City.

# Robert Lowell

THE DRUNKEN FISHERMAN

Wallowing in this bloody sty,
I cast for fish that pleased my eye
(Truly Jehovah's bow suspends
No pots of gold to weight its ends);
Only the blood-mouthed rainbow trout
Rose to my bait. They flopped about
My canvas creel until the moth
Corrupted its unstable cloth.

A calendar to tell the day;
A handkerchief to wave away
The gnats; a couch unstuffed with
    storm

Pouching a bottle in one arm;
A whiskey bottle full of worms;
And bedroom slacks: are these fit terms
To mete the worm whose molten rage
Boils in the belly of old age?

Once fishing was a rabbit's foot—
O wind blow cold, O wind blow hot,
Let suns stay in or suns step out:
Life danced a jig on the sperm-whale's
    spout—
The fisher's fluent and obscene
Catches kept his conscience clean.
Children, the raging memory drools
Over the glory of past pools.

Now the hot river, ebbing, hauls
Its bloody waters into holes;
A grain of sand inside my shoe
Mimics the moon that might undo
Man and Creation too; remorse,
Stinking, has puddled up its source;
Here tantrums thrash to a whale's rage.
This is the pot-hole of old age.

Is there no way to cast my hook
Out of this dynamited brook?
The Fisher's sons must cast about
When shallow waters peter out.
I will catch Christ with a greased worm,
And when the Prince of Darkness stalks
My bloodstream to its Stygian term . . .
On water the Man-Fisher walks.

---

## FOR GEORGE SANTAYANA

*1863-1952*

In the heydays of 'forty-five,
bus-loads of souvenir-deranged
G.I.'s and officer-professors of philosophy
came crashing through your cell,
puzzled to find you still alive,
free-thinking Catholic infidel,
stray spirit, who'd found
the Church too good to be believed.
Later I used to dawdle
past Circus and Mithraic Temple
to *Santo Stefano* grown paper-thin
like you from waiting. . . .
There at the monastery hospital,
you wished those geese-girl sisters
  wouldn't bother
their heads and yours by praying for your
  soul:
"There is no God and Mary is His Mother."

Lying outside the consecrated ground
forever now, you smile
like Ser Brunetto running for the green
cloth at Verona—not like one
who loses, but like one who'd won . . .
as if your long pursuit of Socrates
demon, man-slaying Alcibiades,
the demon of philosophy, at last had changed
those fleeting virgins into friendly laurel trees
at *Santo Stefano Rotondo,* when you died
near ninety,
still unbelieving, unconfessed and unreceived,
true to your boyish shyness of the Bride.
Old trooper, I see your child's red crayon
  pass,
bleeding deletions on the galleys you
  hold
under your throbbing magnifying glass,
that worn arena, where the whirling sand
and broken-hearted lions lick your hand
refined by bile as yellow as a lump of gold.

## MEMORIES OF WEST STREET AND LEPKE

Only teaching on Tuesdays, book-worming
in pajamas fresh from the washer each morning,
I hog a whole house on Boston's
"hardly passionate Marlborough Street,"
where even the man
scavenging filth in the back alley trash cans,
has two children, a beach wagon, a helpmate,
and is a "young Republican."
I have a nine months' daughter,
young enough to be my granddaughter.
Like the sun she rises in her flame-flamingo infants' wear.

These are the tranquillized *Fifties,*
and I am forty. Ought I to regret my seedtime?
I was a fire-breathing Catholic C.O.,
and made my manic statement,
telling off the state and president, and then
sat waiting sentence in the bull pen
beside a Negro boy with curlicues
of marijuana in his hair.

Given a year,
I walked on the roof of the West Street Jail, a short
enclosure like my school soccer court,
and saw the Hudson River once a day
through sooty clothesline entanglements
and bleaching khaki tenements.
Strolling, I yammered metaphysics with Abramowitz,
a jaundice-yellow ("it's really tan")
and fly-weight pacifist,
so vegetarian,
he wore rope shoes and preferred fallen fruit.
He tried to convert Bioff and Brown,
the Hollywood pimps, to his diet.
Hairy, muscular, suburban,
wearing chocolate double-breasted suits,
they blew their tops and beat him black and blue.

I was so out of things, I'd never heard
of the Jehovah's Witnesses.
"Are you a C.O.?" I asked a fellow jailbird.
"No," he answered, "I'm a J.W."
He taught me the "hospital tuck,"

and pointed out the T shirted back
of *Murder Incorporated's* Czar Lepke,
there piling towels on a rack,
or dawdling off to his little segregated cell full
of things forbidden the common man:
a portable radio, a dresser, two toy American
flags tied together with a ribbon of Easter palm.
Flabby, bald, lobotomized,
he drifted in a sheepish calm,
where no agonizing reappraisal
jarred his concentration on the electric chair—
hanging like an oasis in his air
of lost connections. . . .

---

## WAKING IN THE BLUE

The night attendant, a B.U. sophomore,
rouses from the mare's-nest of his drowsy head
propped on *The Meaning of Meaning.*
He catwalks down our corridor.
Azure day
makes my agonized blue window bleaker.
Crows maunder on the petrified fairway.
Absence! My heart grows tense
as though a harpoon were sparring for the kill.
(This is the house for the "mentally ill.")

What use is my sense of humor?
I grin at Stanley, now sunk in his sixties,
once a Harvard all-American fullback,
(if such were possible!)
still hoarding the build of a boy in his twenties,
as he soaks, a ramrod
with the muscle of a seal
in his long tub,
vaguely urinous from the Victorian plumbing.
A kingly granite profile in a crimson golf-cap,
worn all day, all night,
he thinks only of his figure,
of slimming on sherbet and ginger ale—
more cut off from words than a seal.

This is the way day breaks in Bowditch Hall at McLean's:
the hooded night lights bring out "Bobbie,"
Porcellian '29,
a replica of Louis XVI
without the wig—
redolent and roly-poly as a sperm whale,
as he swashbuckles about in his birthday suit
and horses at chairs.

These victorious figures of bravado ossified young.

In between the limits of day,
hours and hours go by under the crew haircuts
and slightly too little nonsensical bachelor twinkle
of the Roman Catholic attendants.
(There are no Mayflower
screwballs in the Catholic Church.)

After a hearty New England breakfast,
I weigh two hundred pounds
this morning. Cock of the walk,
I strut in my turtle-necked French sailor's jersey
before the metal shaving mirrors,
and see the shaky future grow familiar
in the pinched, indigenous faces
of these thoroughbred mental cases,
twice my age and half my weight.
We are all old-timers,
each of us holds a locked razor.

# Gwendolyn Brooks

**GWENDOLYN BROOKS**

Born in Topeka, Kansas, on June 17, 1917, Gwendolyn Brooks was raised in Chicago, where she attended Wilson Junior College. She has remained in Chicago, where she lives with her husband and two children and teaches poetry at Northeastern Illinois State College, Columbia College, and Elmhurst College. She won the Pulitzer Prize for Poetry in 1950 for *Annie Allen.* Her novel, *Maud Martha,* was published in 1953, and a book of poems for young readers, *The Bean Eaters,* appeared in 1960. She is Poet Laureate of Illinois.

## WE REAL COOL

**The Pool Players.**
**Seven at the Golden Shovel.**

We real cool. We
Left school. We

Lurk late. We
Strike straight. We

Sing sin. We
Thin gin. We

Jazz June. We
Die soon.

## SADIE AND MAUD

Maud went to college.
Sadie stayed at home.
Sadie scraped life
With a fine-tooth comb.

She didn't leave a tangle in.
Her comb found every strand.
Sadie was one of the livingest chits
In all the land.

Sadie bore two babies
Under her maiden name.
Maud and Ma and Papa
Nearly died of shame.

When Sadie said her last so-long
Her girls struck out from home.
(Sadie had left as heritage
Her fine-tooth comb.)

Maud, who went to college,
Is a thin brown mouse.
She is living all alone
In this old house.

## THE BEAN EATERS

They eat beans mostly, this old yellow pair.
Dinner is a casual affair.
Plain chipware on a plain and creaking
      wood,
Tin flatware.

Two who are Mostly Good.
Two who have lived their day,
But keep on putting on their clothes
And putting things away.

And remembering . . .
Remembering, with twinklings and
      twinges,
As they lean over the beans in their
      rented back room that is full of beads and
      receipts and dolls and cloths, tobacco
      crumbs, vases and fringes.

## OLD MARY

My last defense
Is the present tense.

It little hurts me now to know
I shall not go

Cathedral-hunting in Spain
Nor cherrying in Michigan or Maine.

# William Jay Smith

**WILLIAM JAY SMITH**
William Jay Smith was born in Winnfield, Louisiana, on April 22, 1918. He holds B.A. and M.A. degrees from Washington University, which in 1963 awarded him its Alumni Citation for "his creative achievements and versatility as a poet." After spending the war as liaison officer on a French ship, he continued his studies at Columbia, at Oxford (as a Rhodes Scholar), and at the University of Florence. He was poet-in-residence at Williams College from 1959 to 1967 (during which time he was also elected to the Vermont House of Representatives) and is now a professor of English at Hollins College. *Poetry* magazine awarded him its Young Poets Prize in 1945 and its Union League Prize in 1964. In addition, two of his five books of poems— *Poems 1947–1957* and *The Tin Can and Other Poems*—were final contenders for the National Book Award. He has also edited a number of anthologies and has written more than a dozen books of poetry for children, several books of criticism, and translations of Laforgue, Larbaud, and Voznesensky. He served as Consultant in Poetry to the Library of Congress from 1968 to 1970 and was a lecturer for the Department of State in Japan and East Asia in 1969 and in the Soviet Union and Eastern Europe in 1970. He is married to the former Sonja Haussmann of Paris and has two sons.

## THE MASSACRE OF THE INNOCENTS

Because I believe in the community of little children,
Because I have suffered such little children to be slain;
I have gazed upon the sunlight, dazed, bewildered,
As is a child by nothing more than rain.

Not until I can no longer climb,
Until my life becomes the tallest tree,
And every limb of it a limb of shame,
Shall I look out in time, in time to see

Again those who were so small they could but die,
Who had only their vast innocence to give,
That I may tell them, pointing down the sky,
How beautiful it might have been to live.

## AMERICAN PRIMITIVE

Look at him there in his stovepipe hat,
His high-top shoes, and his handsome collar;
Only my Daddy could look like that,
And I love my Daddy like he loves his Dollar.

The screen door bangs, and it sounds so funny—
There he is in a shower of gold;
His pockets are stuffed with folding money,
His lips are blue, and his hands feel cold.

He hangs in the hall by his black cravat,
The ladies faint, and the children holler:
Only my Daddy could look like that,
And I love my Daddy like he loves his Dollar.

## THE TIN CAN

*One very good thing I have learned from writer friends in Japan is that when you have a lot of work to do, especially writing, the best thing is to take yourself off and hide away. The Japanese have a word for this, the "kanzume," or the "tin can," which means about what we would mean by the "lock-up." When someone gets off by himself to concentrate, they say, "He has gone into the tin can."*

–HERBERT PASSIN, "The Mountain Hermitage: Pages from a
Japanese Notebook," *Encounter*, August 1957.

### I

I have gone into the tin can; not in late spring, fleeing a stewing, meat-and-fish smelling
    city of paper houses,

Not when wisteria hangs, a purple cloud, robbing the pines of their color, have I sought
    out the gray plain, the indeterminate outer edge of a determined world,

Not to an inn nestling astride a waterfall where two mountains meet and the misty indecisiveness of Japanese ink-drawn pines frames the afternoon, providing from a sheer bluff an adequate view of infinity,

But here to the tin can in midwinter: to a sagging New England farmhouse in the rock-rooted mountains, where wind rifles the cracks,

Here surrounded by crosshatched, tumbling stone walls, where the snow plow with its broad orange side-thrust has outlined a rutted road,

Where the dimly cracked gray bowl of the sky rests firmly on the valley and gum-thick clouds pour out at the edges,

Where in the hooded afternoon a pock-marked, porcupine-quilled landscape fills with snow-swirls, and the tin can settles in the snow.

I have gone into the tin can, head high, resolute, ready to confront the horrible, black underside of the world.

Snow-murmur! Wind-dip! Heart-rage! It is now my duty to record, to enumerate, to set down the sounds, smells, meanings of this place . . .

How begin? With the red eye of the chocolate-brown rhinoceros? With the triple-serrated teeth of the pencil-fed monster with bright fluted ears and whirling black tail? . . .

This is a skittering and scrambling in the can: a trickle of sand and sawdust from a sack, wet leaves blown back, cracks spreading along the wall.

There is the chitter and clatter of keys, a smudge of pencils, a smear of time . . .

Stippled heaven! Snow-ruffle! Garnet-groove! Black water winding through snow-wounds! Ripple-roost!

Will the wilds wake? Will the words work? Will the rattle and rustle subside? Will the words rise?

A bluejay flashes by a window, the stripes of his tail, chevrons torn from a noncom's sleeve; and in the afternoon the snow begins.

First: a hush—pit-stillness, black accent of hemlocks up and down the mountain, mist in the valley thickening and deepening until it breaks

And the snow already fallen swirls up to meet the snow descending—sky-darkening, still-deepening, sky-hooded and whirling, flakes flying,

Houses settling sidewise in the drifts—winds wedging, snow-choked road lost, still-winding, earth white-star-carpeted, still-wheeling;

And in the tin can the same still, paper-white, damp emptiness.

## II

A door opens—is it a door?—and a woman walks by in the tin can watering tropical plants that jut from the wall or spring from the floor, their leaves great green famished mouths,—

Feeding the fish, distributing specks to the seahorses in their tank and meat to the turtle on his wet pillow;

Cats curling about her legs, she pats the dogs and caresses the heads of the children, and the children open their green mouths and grow upward toward the sunlight like plants.

A door opens: a woman walks by, and through her bobbing, mud-colored glass watches the movements of my pencil,

And a record turns, a black hemstiched whirlpool, and the woman wheels off in a trance of
    drumbeats, screaming of need and nothingness and money;

And money like wet leaves piles high around my ankles, and I am sickened by its smell . . .

Snow-madness! Leaf-mania! Green parabolas! In the tin can there is no morning of
    revelation, no afternoon of appraisal, no evening of enchantment.

In the tin can a small boy in a nightmare kicks one leg from the bed overturning a glowing
    iron stove, and in seconds fire sweeps through a city of tin cans.

I wake thinking of the boy, and all about me are the smoking ruins of cigarettes; and the
    ashes descend through the half-extinguished afternoon with the smell of burning
    flesh . . .

A weasel waddles along in a kind of trotting walk; a mole inches up through darkness, his
    blind trail, the workings of consciousness.

In the tin can I hear a murmur of voices speaking of the life in other tin cans, of death
    sifting through them.

A vision of bodies blasted on the black earth; and I think of those photographs my father
    kept from the Nicaraguan Insurrection, was it?—that we played with as children on a
    sun-spotted floor—

Brown bodies spread out over the jungle floor, the figures beside them wide-eyed and
    bewildered, toy soldiers in ridiculous stances in a meaningless world;

I think of the photographs rubbed vinegar-brown in the sunlight; and of how we placed
    them around us, lined our toy fortress with them,

And talked to one another through tin-can telephones, while from out the photographs
    the jungle's green arm tapped our small brown shoulders.


## III

The tin can is circling with beasts: dogs howl in the night, cats sidle through slats in the tin,
    wet field mice hanging from their mouths;

I step in the morning over the entrails of rodents lying like spun jewels on the carpet,
    offerings to the dark gods.

And the dogs rise from their corners, their dirt-crusted rag beds, smelling of snow, sniffing
    the roots, digging the floor, and begin again to circle the can . . .

Bright flashes of morning! Blue snow-peaks! Fog smoking the valleys! Angels lighting the
    rubble! Children skating on a blue pond! Deer stepping delicately down through the
    pines! . . .

And always the face, the woman's face, brooding over all, rising from the earth beside me,
    disembodied; always the woman clean and classic as sunlight, moving about the
    room, sifting the dirt, watering the shadowy flowers, polishing the spotted tin.

I hear her speak softly; and there she is again beside me; and again the face turns, a small
    bat-face and the lips draw back in a red wound and shriek; and the room is filled
    with a smell of mould and money . . .

The woman turns, the bat-face again a woman's face blue with shrieking, and the woman
    walks to the end of the corridor, climbs a broad white stairway . . .

Leaf-fringe! Sky-tingle! Cloud-clatter! Earth-blaze! All my underworld crumbles; and I am
    left with the one brooding face, no face; with bat-wings folding the black air into a
    shroud.

## IV

When am I to emerge? Dirt falls; eyes blur; memory confounds; multiple voices move
    furred and batlike round my ears; and then no sound—

Only the grating of a pencil over a page—an army of ant words swarming up to
    consciousness.

When will they break through to a bright remembered world, up through the top of the
    tin?

Snow-swirl—hemlocks hunching toward the window—gray-black shadow cutting over
    black, fan shaken over fan . . .

From here the windows open their white mouths to swallow the wind-driven snow.

And I remember salmon sky, fine-boned sunsets sweeping the spiny mountains; and I have
    seen the snow

In banks driven back from the road, the black edges scraggly and bearded, the snowbanks
    under the birches like milk from buckets overturned and frozen . . .

Will the words rise? Will the poem radiate with morning? Here where I see nothing, I have
    seen the Cyclops-eye ballooning over a frozen world,

The wide fringe of eyelashes opening on all existence, the single glazed dazzle of the eye
    watching,

And I have lived with my eyes—watching the watching eye, the eyeball swivelling in
    nothingness, a huge black moon in egg-white immensity.

And I have seen the edges of the tin can fold in around it.

## V

O bodies my body has known! Bodies my body has touched and remembered—in beds, in
    baths, in streams, on fields and streets —will you remember?

Sweet vision of flesh known and loved, lusted after, cherished, repulsed, forgotten and
    remembered, will you remember my body buried now and forgotten? . . .

In childhood we played for hours in the sun on a dump near a cannery; and the long thin
    ribbons of tin rippled round us, and we ran by the railroad track and into the
    backyard behind the asparagus and through the feathers of green our bodies touched
    and the strips of tin radiated their rainbows of light—

And our bodies were spiralled with tin and wondrous with light—

Now out of darkness here from the tin can, through snow-swirl and wind-dazzle, let the tin
    ribbons ride again and range in new-found freedom;

Let the tin rip and rustle in the wind; let the green leaves rise and rift the wondrous
    windows, leaving behind the raging women, and the sickening mould of money, rust,
    and rubble . . .

And the words clean-spun and spiralling orbit that swift-seeing, unseen immensity that will
    never be contained!

---

## ELEGY

*For Bateman Edwards, d. 1 Sept. 1947*

I stood between two mirrors when you died,
Two mirrors in a dimly lighted hall,
Identical in all respects.
Two mirrors face to face reflecting endlessly
Reflection's end.
The wind that had been blowing died away,
Or in the distance seemed about to die.
I stood between two mirrors in the hall.

Outside, the wheels had cut the gravel, and the sun-
Flower nodded to the sun; the air was still.
The deer that browsed upon a distant hillside
Lifted his antlers like a coral tree
Forgotten in midsummer undersea.
And from the delicate dark bridges which the spider
Spun from branch to branch,
In desolation hung
One leaf, announcing autumn to the world.

The world that evening was a world of mirrors
Where two great dragons from opposing caves,
Mirror their eyes and mirror all the scales
Of their long bodies and their giant tails,
Emerged. And all that had seemed human was confined
In terror in the limits of the mind,
And coiled, uncoiled within my memory.

In your sudden dying you became the night
Which I must add to darkness now
To make the morning bright,
To have day break, and daybreak
Melt the mirrors. But I know
You cannot hear me now although
I say, dear friend, good morning and good night.

**WILLIAM MEREDITH**

**William Meredith was born on January 9, 1919, in New York City. He attended Lenox School in Massachusetts and received a B.A.** *magna cum laude* **from Princeton in 1940. During World War II he spent one year in the Army and then became a Navy pilot on an aircraft carrier from 1942 until the end of the war. During the Korean War he spent another two years in the Navy. He has been a reporter for** *The New York Times* **and opera critic for the** *Hudson Review.* **Among his awards are the Yale Series of Younger Poets Award in 1943, the Harriet Monroe Memorial Award from** *Poetry* **in 1944, and the Oscar Blumenthal Prize from the same magazine in 1953. He has also held** *Hudson Review* **and Ford fellowships and two Rockefeller grants, one in criticism and one in poetry. He has served for several years on the poetry staff of the Bread Loaf Writers' Conference and has been chancellor of the Academy of American Poets since 1945. He lives in New London, Connecticut, where he has taught at Connecticut College since 1955.**

# William Meredith

## THE OPEN SEA

We say the sea is lonely; better say
Our selves are lonesome creatures whom the sea
Gives neither yes nor no for company.

Oh, there are people, all right, settled in the sea—
It is as populous as Maine today—
But no one who will give you the time of day.

A man who asks there of his family
Or a friend or teacher gets a cold reply
Or finds him dead against that vast majority.

Nor does it signify, that people who stay
Very long, bereaved or not, at the edge of the sea
Hear the drowned folk call: that is mere fancy,

They are speechless. And the famous noise of sea,
Which a poet has beautifully told us in our day,
Is hardly a sound to speak comfort to the lonely.

Although not yet a man given to prayer, I pray
For each creature lost since the start at sea,
And give thanks it was not I, nor yet one close to me.

# THE WRECK OF THE THRESHER

*(Lost at Sea, April 10, 1963)*

I stand on the ledge where rock runs into the river
As the night turns brackish with morning, and mourn the
    drowned.
Here the sea is diluted with river; I watch it slaver
Like a dog curing of rabies. Its ravening over,
Lickspittle ocean nuzzles the dry ground.
(But the dream that woke me was worse than the sea's
    gray
Slip-slap; there are no such sounds by day.)

This crushing of people is something we live with.
Daily, by unaccountable whim
Or caught up in some harebrained scheme of death,
Tangled in cars, dropped from the sky, in flame,
Men and women break the pledge of breath:
And now under water, gone all jetsam and small
In the pressure of oceans collected, a squad of brave men in
    a hull.

(Why can't our dreams be content with the terrible facts?
The only animal cursed with responsible sleep,
We trace disaster always to our own acts.
I met a monstrous self trapped in the black deep:
*All these years,* he smiled, *I've drilled at sea*
*For this crush of water.* Then he saved only me.)

We invest ships with life. Look at a harbor
At first light: with better grace than men
In their movements the vessels run to their labors
Working the fields that the tide has made green again;
Their beauty is womanly, they are named for ladies and
    queens,
Although by a wise superstition these are called
After fish, the finned boats, silent and submarine.
The crushing of any ship has always been held
In dread, like a house burned or a great tree felled.

I think of how sailors laugh, as if cold and wet
And dark and lost were their private, funny derision
And I can judge then what dark compression
Astonishes them now, their sunken faces set
Unsmiling, where the currents sluice to and fro
And without humor, somewhere northeast of here
    and below.

*(Sea-brothers, I lower to you the ingenuity of dreams,*
*Strange lungs and bells to escape in; let me stay aboard last—*
We amend our dreams in half-sleep. Then it seems
Easy to talk to the severe dead and explain the past.
Now they are saying, *Do not be ashamed to stay alive,*
*You have dreamt nothing that we do not forgive.*
And gentler, *Study something deeper than yourselves,*
*As, how the heart, when it turns diver, delves and saves.)*

Whether we give assent to this or rage
Is a question of temperament and does not matter.
Some will has been done past our understanding,
Past our guilt surely, equal to our fears.
Dullards, we are set again to the cryptic blank page
Where the sea schools us with terrible water.
The noise of a boat breaking up and its men is in our ears.
The bottom here is too far down for our sounding;
The ocean was salt before we crawled to tears.

---

# THE COUPLE OVERHEAD

They don't get anywhere,
The couple overhead;
They wrangle like the damned
In the bed above my bed,
But the harm has all been done.
And this is a short despair:
Count Ugolino dead
Was endlessly condemmed
To gnaw the archbishop's head
Where the nape and the skull are one.

Not so, these secular drunks.
Dante would find their treason
Too spiritless to keep;
Like children stealing raisins
They eat each other's eyes;
The ice that grips their flanks
Is something they have frozen.
After a while they sleep;
And the punishment they've chosen,
After a while it dies.

---

# WALTER JENKS' BATH

*For Rollin Williams*

These are my legs. I don't have to tell them, legs,
Move up and down or which leg. They are black.
They are made of atoms like everything else,
Miss Berman says. That's the green ceiling
Which on top is the Robinsons' brown floor.
This is Beloit, this is my family's bathroom on the world.
The ceiling is atoms, too, little parts running
Too fast to see. But through them running fast,
Through Audrey Robinson's floor and tub
And the roof and air, if I lived on an atom
Instead of on the world, I would see space.
Through all the little parts, I would see into space.

Outside the air it is all black.
The far apart stars run and shine, no one has to tell them,
Stars, run and shine, or the same who tells my atoms

Run and knock so Walter Jenks, me, will stay hard and real.
And when I stop the atoms go on knocking,
Even if I died the parts would go on spinning,
Alone, like the far stars, not knowing it,
Not knowing they are far apart, or running,
Or minding the black distances between.
This is me knowing, this is what I know.

# Lawrence Ferlinghetti

LAWRENCE FERLINGHETTI
Lawrence Ferlinghetti was born probably on March 24. He writes: Probably born 1919 or 20 in Yonkers, New York. Some tampering with the birth certificate has been uncovered, some of it by himself. His mother was Clemence Monsanto, and he was her fifth and last son. She was enclosed in an asylum shortly after his birth which was itself preceded by the sudden death of his father. His father was an Italian auctioneer in Brooklyn who must have arrived WOP (With Out Papers) from Lombardy about the turn of the century. The family name was shortened to Ferling but restored by LF when of age. There was a French "aunt" who took LF to France in swaddling clothes where they remained for an uncertain number of years. Her name was Emily Monsanto, descended from that same Sephardic-Portuguese Mendes-Monsanto who emigrated to the Virgin Islands in a Danish Crown Colony expedition after the Spanish Inquisition and was there knighted by the King of Denmark. LF's first memory of America is eating tapioca pudding (undercooked, and called Cat's Eyes by the inmates) in an orphanage in Chapaqua, New York. He then spent many years in a mansion of a branch of the Lawrence family which founded Sarah Lawrence College in Bronxville, N.Y. where much-beloved Emily left him after serving as a French governess in that family. She later died in an asylum at Central Islip, Long Island, unknown to LF. . . . As a poet, Ferlinghetti describes himself as an Unblinking Eye. He is now engaged in a long prose Work-in-Progress, one part of which is tentatively called, "Her Too."

## DOG

The dog trots freely in the street
and sees reality
and the things he sees
are bigger than himself
and the things he sees
are his reality
Drunks in doorways
Moons on trees
The dog trots freely thru the street
and the things he sees
are smaller than himself
Fish on newsprint
Ants in holes
Chickens in Chinatown windows
their heads a block away
The dog trots freely in the street
and the things he smells
smell something like himself
The dog trots freely in the street
past puddles and babies
cats and cigars
poolrooms and policemen
He doesn't hate cops
He merely has no use for them
and he goes past them
and past the dead cows hung up whole
in front of the San Francisco Meat Market
He would rather eat a tender cow
than a tough policeman
though either might do
And he goes past the Romeo Ravioli Factory
and past Coit's Tower
and past Congressman Doyle
He's afraid of Coit's Tower
but he's not afraid of Congressman Doyle
although what he hears is very discouraging
very depressing
very absurd
to a sad young dog like himself

to a serious dog like himself
But he has his own free world to live in
His own fleas to eat
He will not be muzzled
Congressman Doyle is just another
fire hydrant
to him
The dog trots freely in the street
and has his own dog's life to live
and to think about
and to reflect upon
touching and tasting and testing everything
investigating everything
without benefit of perjury
a real realist
with a real tale to tell
and a real tail to tell it with
a real live
          barking
                    democratic dog
engaged in real
                    free enterprise
with something to say
                    about ontology
something to say
                    about reality
                    and how to see it
                              and how to hear it
with his head cocked sideways
                    at streetcorners
as if he is just about to have
                    his picture taken
                              for Victor Records
                    listening for
                    His Master's Voice
          and looking
                    like a living questionmark
                              into the
                              great gramaphone
                              of puzzling existence
          with its wondrous hollow horn
                    which always seems
                    just about to spout forth
                              some Victorious answer
                                   to everything

# PICTURES OF A GONE WORLD #17

          Terrible

                    a horse at night

          standing hitched alone

                              in the still street

                    and whinnying

                              as if some sad nude astride him

had gripped hot legs on him

                    and sung

                              a sweet high hungry

                    single syllable

---

# A CONEY ISLAND OF THE MIND #9

See
    it was like this when
                    we waltz into this place
a couple of Papish cats
                    is doing an Aztec two-step
And I says
          Dad let's cut
but then this dame
                    comes up behind me see
                              and says
                    You and me could really exist
Wow I says
          Only the next day
          she has bad teeth
                    and really hates
                              poetry

---

# A CONEY ISLAND OF THE MIND #20

The pennycandystore beyond the El
is where I first
                    fell in love
                              with unreality
Jellybeans glowed in the semi-gloom
of that september afternoon
A cat upon the counter moved among
                    the licorice sticks
          and tootsie rolls
          and Oh Boy Gum

Outside the leaves were falling as they died

A wind had blown away the sun

A girl ran in
Her hair was rainy
Her breasts were breathless in the little room

Outside the leaves were falling
                and they cried
                        Too soon! too soon!

# Howard Nemerov

HOWARD NEMEROV
Howard Nemerov writes: Howard
Nemerov was born in NYC on
February 29th, 1920. His parents,
shaken at being thus singled out
on their very first try, persuaded
the doctor not to fill in the birth
certificate until six minutes later,
when it would be March 1st. Mr.
Nemerov's life since that heady
beginning has been unremarkable:
he attended one college, went to
one war, married one wife, has
three sons and fourteen books.
He teaches.

## MOMENT

Now, starflake frozen on the windowpane
All of a winter night, the open hearth
Blazing beyond Andromeda, the sea-
Anemone and the downwind seed, O
    moment
Hastening, halting in a clockwise dust,
The time in all the hospitals is now,
Under the arc-lights where the sentry walks

His lonely wall it never moves from now,
The crying in the cell is also now,
And now is quiet in the tomb as now
Explodes inside the sun, and it is now
In the saddle of space, where argosies of
    dust
Sail outward blazing, and the mind of God,
The flash across the gap of being, thinks
In the instant absence of forever: now.

## TRUTH

Around, above my bed, the pitch-dark fly
Buzzed in the darkness till in my mind's eye
His blue sound made the image of my thought
An image that his resonance had brought
Out of a common midden of the sun—
A garbage pit, and pile where glittering tin
Cans turned the ragged edges of their eyes
In a mean blindness on mine, where the loud flies
Would blur the summer afternoons out back
Beyond the house. Sleepy, insomniac, black
Remainder of a dream, what house? and when?
Listening now, I knew never again
That winged image as in amber kept
Might come, summoned from darkness where it slept
The common sleep of all such sunken things
By the fly's loud buzzing and his dreaming wings.

I listened in an angry wakefulness;
The fly was bitter. Between dream and guess
About a foundered world, about a wrong
The mind refused, I waited long, long,
And then that humming of the garbage heap
I drew beneath the surface of my sleep
Until I saw the helmet of the king
Of Nineveh, pale gold and glittering
On the king's brow, yet sleeping knew that I
But thought the deepening blue thought of the fly.

# LOT LATER

*Vaudeville for George Finckel*

## I

It seems now far off and foolish, a memory
Torn at the hem from the fabric of a dream
In drunken sleep, but why was I the one?
God knows, there were no fifty righteous, nor
Ten righteous, in town just at that very moment;
Gone south for the winter, maybe. And moreover,
I wouldn't have been one of the ten or fifty
Or whatever, if there had been. Abraham
Stood up to Him, but not for me—more likely
For the principle of the thing. I've always been
Honest enough for this world, and respected
In this town—but to be taken by the hair
Like that and lifted into that insane story,
Then to be dropped when it was done with me . . .
I tell you, I felt *used.*

                    In the first place,
I never knew the two of them were angels:
No wings, no radiance. I thought they might be students
Going from town to town, seeing the country.
I said "Come in the house, we'll have a drink,
Some supper, why not stay the night?" They did.
The only oddity was they didn't bother
With evening prayers, and that made me suspect
They might be Somebody. But in my home town
It doesn't take much; before I thought it out
People were coming round beating the door:
"Who you got in the house, let's have a party."
It was a pretty nice town in those days,
With always something going on, a dance
Or a big drunk with free women, or boys
For those who wanted boys, in the good weather
We used to play strip poker in the yard.
But just then, when I looked at those young gents,
I had a notion it was not the time,
And shouted through the door, "Go home, we're tired."
Nobody went. But all these drunks began
To pound the door and throw rocks at the windows
And make suggestions as to what they might do
When they got hold of the two pretty young men.
Matters were getting fairly desperate
By this time, and I said to those outside,
"Look, I got here my two daughters, virgins
Who never been there yet. I send them out,
Only my guests should have a peaceful night."
That's how serious the situation was.
Of course it wasn't the truth about the kids,
Who were both married, and, as a matter of fact,
Not much better than whores, and both the husbands
Knocking their horns against the chandeliers

Of my own house—but still, it's what I said.
It got a big laugh out there, and remarks,
Till the two young men gave me a nice smile
And stretched out one hand each, and suddenly
It got pitch dark outside, people began
Bumping into each other and swearing; then
They cleared away and everything was quiet.
So one young man opens his mouth, he says,
"You've got till sunrise, take the wife and kids
And the kids' husbands, and go. Go up to the hills."
The other says, "The Lord hath sent us to
Destroy this place" and so forth and so forth.
You can imagine how I felt. I said,
"Now look, now after all . . ." and my wife said,
"Give me a few days till I pack our things,"
And one of them looked at his watch and said,
"It's orders, lady, sorry, you've got till dawn."
I said, "Respectfully, gentlemen, but who
Lives in the hills? I've got to go, so why
Shouldn't I go to Zoar, which is a nice
Town with a country club which doesn't exclude
Jews?" "So go to Zoar if you want," they said.
"Whatever you do, you shouldn't look back here."
We argued all night long. First this, then that.
My son-in-laws got into the act: "You're kidding,
Things of this nature simply do not happen
To people like us." The pair of them said, "We'll stay,
Only deed us the house and furniture."
"I wouldn't deed you a dead fish," I said,
"Besides, I'm going to take the girls along."
"So take," they said, "they weren't such a bargain."
The two visitors all this time said nothing,
They might as well not have been there. But I
Believed what I was told, and this, I think,
Makes all the difference—between life and death,
I mean—to feel sincerely that there's truth
In something, even if it's God knows what.
My poor old woman felt it too, that night,
She only couldn't hold it to the end.
The girls just packed their biggest pocketbooks
With candy and perfume; they'd be at home
Most anywhere, even in a hill.

                    At last
I knelt down and I spoke to my God as follows:
"Dear Sir," I said, "I do not understand
Why you are doing this to my community,
And I do not understand why, doing it,
You let me out. There's only this one thing,
So help me, that with all my faults I do
Believe you are able to do whatever you say
You plan to do. Myself, I don't belong
In any operation on this scale.
I've always been known here as a nice fellow,
Which is low enough to be or want to be:
Respectfully I ask to be let go

To live out my declining years at peace
In Zoar with my wife and the two kids
Such as they are. A small house will do.
Only I shouldn't be part of history."
Of course no one answered. One of them said:
"If you're about through, please get on your feet,
It's time to go." My daughters' gorgeous husbands
Were drinking on the porch before we left.

## II

My relative Abraham saw it happen: the whole
Outfit went up in smoke, he said. One minute
There was the town, with banks and bars and grills
And the new sewage disposal plant, all looking
(he said) terribly innocent in the first light;
Then it ignited. It went. All those old pals
Gone up, or maybe down. I am his nephew,
Maybe you know, he had troubles himself,
With the maid, and his own son. That's neither here
Nor there. We'd been forbidden to look, of course,
But equally of course my old girl had to look.
She turned around, and in one minute there
She was, a road sign or a mileage marker.
By this time, though, I knew that what we were in
Was very big, and I told the kids Come on.
We didn't stop to cry, even. Also
We never went to Zoar. I began to think
How real estate was high, how I'd been told
To go up in the hills, and how I'd always
Wanted to live in the country, a gentleman
Like Abraham, maybe, and have my flocks
Or whatever you call them—herds. Well, I found out.
A cave, we lived in, a real cave, out of rock.
I envied those bums my son-in-laws, until
I remembered they were dead. And the two girls,
My nutsy kids, getting the odd idea
That the whole human race had been destroyed
Except for us, conceived—this word I love,
Conceived—the notion that they should be known
In carnal union by their poppa. Me.
Poor dear old Dad. Most any man might dream
About his daughters; darling and stupid chicks
As these ones were, I'd dreamed, even in daytime,
Such brilliant dreams. But they? They bought some booze,
Having remembered to bring money along,
Something I never thought of, considering
I was in the hand of God, and got me boiled.
And then—I'm told—on two successive nights
Arrived on my plain stone couch and—what shall I say?
Had me? I was completely gone at the time,
And have no recollection. But there they were,
The pair of them, at the next moon, knocked up,
And properly, and by their Dad. The kids
Turned out to be boys, Moab and Ben-Ammi
By name. I have been given to understand
On competent authority that they will father
A couple of peoples known as Moabites
And Ammonites, distinguished chiefly by
Heathenish ways and ignorance of the Law.
And I did this? Or this was done to me,
A foolish man who lived in the grand dream
One instant, at the fuse of miracle and
The flare of light, a man no better than most,
Who loves the Lord and does not know His ways,
Neither permitted the pleasure of his sins
Nor punished for them, and whose aging daughters
Bring him his supper nights, and clean the cave.

---

## ELEGY FOR A NATURE POET

It was in October, a favorite season,
He went for his last walk. The covered bridge,
Most natural of all the works of reason,
Received him, let him go. Along the hedge

He rattled his stick; observed the blackening bushes
In his familiar field; thought he espied
Late meadow larks; considered picking rushes
For a dry arrangement; returned home, and died

Of a catarrh caught in the autumn rains
And let go on uncared for. He was too rapt
In contemplation to recall that brains
Like his should not be kept too long uncapped

In the wet and cold weather. While we mourned,
We thought of his imprudence, and how Nature,
Whom he'd done so much for, had finally turned
Against her creature.

His gift was daily his delight, he peeled
The landscape back to show it was a story;
Any old bird or burning bush revealed
At his hands just another allegory.

Nothing too great, nothing too trivial
For him; from mountain range or humble vermin
He could extract the hidden parable—
If need be, crack the stone to get the sermon.

And now, poor man, he's gone. Without his name
The field reverts to wilderness again,
The rocks are silent, woods don't seem the same;
Demoralized small birds will fly insane.

Rude Nature, whom he loved to idealize
And would have wed, pretends she never heard
His voice at all, as, taken by surprise
At last, he goes to her without a word.

---

## THE HUMAN CONDITION

In this motel where I was told to wait,
The television screen is stood before
The picture window. Nothing could be more
Use to a man than knowing where he's at,
And I don't know, but pace the day in doubt
Between my looking in and looking out.

Through snow, along the snowy road, cars pass
Going both ways, and pass behind the screen
Where heads of heroes sometimes can be seen
And sometimes cars, that speed across the glass.
Once I saw world and thought exactly meet,
But only in a picture by Magritte,

A picture of a picture, by Magritte,
Wherein a landscape on an easel stands
Before a window opening on a land-
scape, and the pair of them a perfect fit,
Silent and mad. You know right off, the room
Before that scene was always an empty room.

And that is now the room in which I stand
Waiting, or walk, and sometimes try to sleep.
The day falls into darkness while I keep
The TV going; headlights blaze behind
Its legendary traffic, love and hate,
In this motel where I was told to wait.

**CHARLES BUKOWSKI**

Charles Bukowski writes: Charles Bukowski was born 8-16-20, Andernach, Germany. 17 or 18 books of prose and poetry, one novel. Now leisurely at work on his second novel, *The Poet*. Says Bukowski, basically I began writing at the age of 35 after 75 jobs (laborer) across the country, and one stretch of 5 years in a Philadelphia bar, running errands for sandwiches, living on handouts and the grace of my luck. Arrived, on schedule, death row of the charity ward of the L.A. County Hospital. Gigantic hemorrhages. Got out and got a typewriter. I was supposed to die but I got a typewriter. Wrote, and worked for the Post Office both as a clerk and a carrier. 15 years. I was counseled by the Post Office—and admonished—for writing the column "Notes of a Dirty Old Man" for the underground newspaper, *Open City.* Since they couldn't seem to fire me, I quit, and have since been a literary hustler, writing dirty stories, giving poetry readings and laying about the parks and beaches with a beautiful 30 year old sculptress, amen.

# Charles Bukowski

## THE TRAGEDY OF THE LEAVES

I awakened to dryness and the ferns were
    dead,
the potted plants yellow as corn.
My woman was gone and the
empty bottles like bled corpses
surrounded me with their uselessness;
the sun was still good, though,
and my landlady's note cracked in fine and
undemanding yellowness; what was needed
    now
was a good comedian, ancient style, a jester
with jokes upon absurd pain; pain is absurd
because it exists, nothing more;
I shaved carefully with an old razor,
the man who had once been young and
said to have genius; but
that's the tragedy of the leaves,
the dead ferns, the dead plants;
and I walked into the dark hall
where the landlady stood
execrating and final,
sending me to hell,
waving her fat sweaty arms
and screaming,
screaming for rent
because the world had failed us both.

## THE SINGULAR SELF

There are these small cliffs
above the sea
and it is night, late night;
I have been unable to sleep,
and with my car above me
like a steel mother,
I crawl down the cliffs,
breaking bits of rock
and being scratched by witless
and scrabby seaplants,

60

I make my way down
clumsy, misplaced,
an oddity on the shore,
and all around me are the lovers,
the two-headed beasts
turning to stare
at the madness
of a singular self;
shamed, I move on through them
to climb a row of wet boulders that
break the sea-stroke
into sheaths of white;
the moonlight is wet
on the bald stone,
and now that I'm there
I don't want to be there,
the sea stinks
and makes flushing sounds
like a toilet;
it is a bad place to die;
any place is a bad place to die,
but better a yellow room
with known walls and dusty
lampshades; so . . .
still stupidly off-course
like a jackal in a land of lions,
I make my way back through
them, through their blankets
and fires and kisses and sandy thumpings,
back up the cliff I climb,
worse off, kicking clods,
and there the black sky, the black sea
behind me
lost in the game,
and I have left my shoes down there
with them    2 empty shoes,
and in the car
I start the engine,
headlights on I back away,
swing left drive East,
climb up the land and out,
bare feet on worn ribbed rubber,
out of there,
looking for
another place.

*footnote upon the construction of
the masses:*

some people are young and nothing
else and
some people are old and nothing
else
and some people are in between and
just in between.

and if the flies wore clothes on their
backs
and all the buildings burned in
golden fire,
if heaven shook like a belly
dancer
and all the atom bombs began to
cry,
some people would be young and nothing
else and
some people old and nothing
else,
and the rest would be the same
the rest would be the same.

the few who are different
are eliminated quickly enough
by the police, by their mothers, their
brothers, others; by
themselves.

all that's left is what you
see.

it's
hard.

FOR JANE

225 days under grass
and you know more than I.

they have long taken your blood,
you are a dry stick in a basket.

is this how it works?

in this room
the hours of love
still make shadows.

when you left
you took almost
everything.

I kneel in the nights
before tigers
that will not let me be.

what you were
will not happen again.

the tigers have found me
and I do not care.

# Richard Wilbur

**RICHARD WILBUR**

Richard Wilbur received the Pulitzer Prize in 1957 for *Things of This World.* He writes: I was born at noon on the first of March, 1921, with a Line of Mentality which slopes toward the Mount of the Moon. My father, Lawrence Wilbur, was and is a portrait painter. I was brought up in a sort of rustic English colony in New Jersey. At Amherst, I edited the undergraduate newspaper. Charlotte Ward and I were married in 1942, and we have had four children. During World War II, I served with the 36th Division at Cassino, Anzio, and the Siegfried Line. Between 1946 and 1950 I was a graduate student and Junior Fellow at Harvard; I have since taught English and Humanities at Harvard, Wellesley, and Wesleyan. In addition to writing poems, I have done some criticism (particularly on Poe), a bit of editing, a book for children called *Loudmouse,* an anthology of beast-literature, and a number of translations, of which the most substantial are three verse-plays of Molière's. Productions of these last have constituted my happiest involvements with the theatre; my experiences as a Broadway lyricist have been exciting but sometimes disastrous. I play tennis, walk, snow-shoe, ski, and work around our place in Cummington, Massachusetts. I write poems as it suits me, enjoy the work of some very dissimilar contemporaries, and deplore theories, especially dead-serious talk about breath-groups.

## MIND

Mind in its purest play is like some bat
That beats about in caverns all alone,
Contriving by a kind of senseless wit
Not to conclude against a wall of stone.

It has no need to falter or explore;
Darkly it knows what obstacles are there,
And so may weave and flitter, dip and soar
In perfect courses through the blackest air.

And has this simile a like perfection?
The mind is like a bat. Precisely. Save
That in the very happiest intellection
A graceful error may correct the cave.

## STILL, CITIZEN SPARROW

Still, citizen sparrow, this vulture which
    you call
Unnatural, let him but lumber again to air
Over the rotten office, let him bear
The carrion ballast up, and at the tall

Tip of the sky lie cruising. Then you'll see
That no more beautiful bird is in heaven's
    height,
No wider more placid wings, no watchfuller
    flight;
He shoulders nature there, the frightfully
    free,

The naked-headed one. Pardon him, you
Who dart in the orchard aisles, for it is he
Devours death, mocks mutability,
Has heart to make an end, keeps nature
    new.

Thinking of Noah, childheart, try to forget
How for so many bedlam hours his saw
Soured the song of birds with its wheezy
    gnaw,
And the slam of his hammer all the day
    beset

The people's ears. Forget that he could bear
To see the towns like coral under the keel,
And the fields so dismal deep. Try rather
    to feel
How high and weary it was, on the waters
    where

He rocked his only world, and everyone's.
Forgive the hero, you who would have died
Gladly with all you knew; he rode that tide
To Ararat; all men are Noah's sons.

## A GRASSHOPPER

But for a brief
Moment, a poised minute,
He paused on the chicory-leaf;
Yet within it

The sprung perch
Had time to absorb the shock,
Narrow its pitch and lurch,
Cease to rock.

A quiet spread
Over the neighbor ground;
No flower swayed its head
For yards around;

The wind shrank
Away with a swallowed hiss;
Caught in a widening, blank
Parenthesis,

Cry upon cry
Faltered and faded out;
Everything seemed to die.
Oh, without doubt

Peace like a plague
Had gone to the world's verge,
But that an aimless, vague
Grasshopper-urge

Leapt him aloft,
Giving the leaf a kick,
Starting the grasses' soft
Chafe and tick,

So that the sleeping
Crickets resumed their chimes,
And all things wakened, keeping
Their several times.

In gay release
The whole field did what it did,
Peaceful now that its peace
Lay busily hid.

# A BLACK NOVEMBER TURKEY

*to* A.M. *and* A.M.

Nine white chickens come
With haunchy walk and heads
Jabbing among the chips, the chaff, the stones
    And the cornhusk-shreds,

And bit by bit infringe
A pond of dusty light,
Spectral in shadow until they bobbingly one
    By one ignite.

Neither pale nor bright,
The turkey-cock parades
Through radiant squalors, darkly auspicious as
    The ace of spades,

Himself his own cortège
And puffed with the pomp of death,

Rehearsing over and over with strangled râle
    His latest breath.

The vast black body floats
Above the crossing knees
As a cloud over thrashed branches, a calm ship
    Over choppy seas,

Shuddering its fan and feathers
In fine soft clashes
With the cold sound that the wind makes, fondling
    Paper-ashes.

The pale-blue bony head
Set on its shepherd's-crook
Like a saint's death-mask, turns a vague, superb
    And timeless look

Upon these clocking hens
And the cocks that one by one,
Dawn after mortal dawn, with vulgar joy
    Acclaim the sun.

---

# AN EVENT

As if a cast of grain leapt back to the hand,
A landscapeful of small black birds, intent
On the far south, convene at some command
At once in the middle of the air, at once are gone
With headlong and unanimous consent
From the pale trees and fields they settled on.

What is an individual thing? They roll
Like a drunken fingerprint across the sky!
Or so I give their image to my soul
Until, as if refusing to be caught
In any singular vision of my eye
Or in the nets and cages of my thought,

They tower up, shatter, and madden space
With their divergences, are each alone
Swallowed from sight, and leave me in this place
Shaping these images to make them stay:
Meanwhile, in some formation of their own,
They fly me still, and steal my thoughts away,

Delighted with myself and with the birds,
I set them down and give them leave to be.
It is by words and the defeat of words,
Down sudden vistas of the vain attempt,
That for a flying moment one may see
By what cross-purposes the world is dreamt.

---

**JOHN WILLIAMS**

John Williams writes: I was born
August 29, 1922, in Clarksville,
Texas; was an enlisted man in the
United States Army Air Force
from 1942 to 1945, serving two
and a half years in China, Burma,
and India; and I wrote my first
novel, *Nothing but the Night,*
while in the Army. In 1948 this
novel was published by the late
Alan Swallow, through whose
kindness and friendship I was
persuaded to return to college.
I received my B.A. and M.A. from
the University of Denver, and be-
came an instructor at the Univer-
sity of Missouri, where I received
my Ph.D. Since 1954, I have
taught at the University of Den-
ver. I am the author of two other
novels—*Butcher's Crossing* (1960)
and *Stoner* (1965)—and two vol-
umes of poetry—*The Broken
Landscape* (1949) and *The Nec-
essary Lie* (1965). I received a
Rockefeller Award for Fiction in
1967 and a National Endowment
for the Arts Award in 1969. I have
been Writer-in-Residence at Smith
College, and for the past seven
years have been a staff member of
the Bread Loaf Writers' Confer-
ence. I write slowly but steadily,
being perhaps that kind of writer
whom Thomas Mann described as
one who finds writing more diffi-
cult than most people do.

# John Williams

## LETTER FROM THE NORTH ATLANTIC

The variety is bewildering in its sameness.
A quick skittering of light is thrown off as the waves move,
a myriad of planes, shard from the dark liquidity;
they surge upward, are swallowed
                       and disgorged in an instant,
so that the distance is a brilliant haze, a slow throbbing
that steadies against the intense blue of the horizon,
where the eyes moves upon its limit, pauses, and returns

to the sea. It is a vast circle, whose far rim, perfect
and unbroken, contains a slow violence of motion;
what one sees is a world of surfaces, of beaten froth
spreading like vapor under
                   the sea-slate opacity;
but for a moment, all seems depthless. One can imagine
a life that one cannot see, of which one is the lone God,
the indifferent center, still in ignorance, and blind.

But one is not a God, nor would be; it is too easy.
To be human is difficult; one makes choices, may be
wrong, cannot afford ignorance, and must take his chances.
I think of Melville and Crane,
                    of the agony they saw
hidden by the gentle swelling of an endless water,
and of that awful Paradise and source that only man
conceives, out of a nameless need and his distant sorrow—

hence vortices that twist down infinitely to a peace
that is soundless and still, and hence those white
  monstrosities
to which we give ironic names. We never believe them,
quite; therefore we can use them
                    as if they were using us.
And the sea remains as it has been—inscrutable, dark,
free of us in its ancient rolling, passive to the chance
that whips it to a fury or smooths it in calm billows.

Too civilized to see a lurking there, too primitive
to see nothing, we are aware of loss; somehow the sea
is less real suspended between the brute nerves that perceive
it and the changeling terror
                 of god or ghost that lingers
in us, primordial as the sea, depthless as its caverns.
The waves trough ambiguously, the foam clots on the slick
patina, a milky translucence bursts down to darkness. . . .

We would have it something other than what it is—either
a watery chaos that is our beginning and end,
that old pollution compact with shapes crawling blindly out
from a primeval dark, or

                    a wide world of mineral
and common gasses linked in intricate simplicity,
moved by the profound forces that we name for our
      comfort
and chart for our pleasure, as if we made the ebb and flow.

Meanwhile, we move forward upon it, swaying a little,
yawing in the powerful slow surging of wave and wind.
Water flakes from the prow and scatters whiteness, a thin
      spray
is blown back in our faces,
                              we look to where we're going.
It is a quiet harbor that will take us; locked by land,
we shall look long at the blue shallows of our anchorage
and be puzzled by a stillness that is empty and strange.

---

## AT THE THEATRE

And so the scene degenerates
To this: not fact nor artifact,
That which ballooned the willing heart
Now fizzles in the final act.

The bodies have been dragged away,
The stage is almost bare, yet bare
With ghosts that glide invisibly
Through castle walls and the still air.

The faithful wife did not suspect
Her fault, nor did the black groom sense
In the bloody field where he flailed
Her most infernal innocence.

But we have known the bearded Moor,
And still we know his livid rage
That lights cannot put down, nor time
Blot out, nor the will assuage;

And though we see Iago slink
From stage or chamber, out of the scene,
For the sick soul there is no purge,
Nor unguent for the swelling spleen.

It goes on, though the stage is dull,
This rant: into that noble hand
The rubied dirk of history
Was thrust, and the dark coals fanned

To a fury, and the arm plunged.
'All's spoke is marr'd.' Gratiano meant,
All's raged is calmed; and the blade cools
In black flesh, and the night is spent.

## THE SKATERS

Graceful and sure with youth, the skaters glide
Upon the frozen pond. Unending rings
Expand upon the ice, contract, divide,
Till motion seems the shape that movement brings,

And shape is constant in the moving blade.
Ignorant of the beauty they invent,
Confirmed in their hard strength, the youths evade
Their frail suspension on an element,

This frozen pond that glitters in the cold.
Through all the warming air they turn and spin,
And do not feel that they grow old
Above the fragile ice they scrape and thin.

## COLD COFFEE

In a long room that voices sundered,
With black coffee in a chipped cup
—My fingers curled, my eyes dumb—
I sat in wait for you who did not know
I waited, and who did not come.
Then someone jostled me, my coffee swirled,
And terror dinned my heart. I wondered
Where you waited in the wide world.

# Anthony Hecht

**ANTHONY HECHT**

Anthony Hecht was born in New York City on January 16, 1923. Between a B.A. from Bard College in 1944 and an M.A. from Columbia in 1950, he spent three years in the Army. Since 1967 he has taught English at the University of Rochester, after earlier positions at Kenyon College, the University of Iowa, New York University, Smith College, and Bard. He has received a number of awards, among them a Prix de Rome Fellowship in 1951, Guggenheim Fellowships in 1954 and 1959, and the Pulitzer Prize in 1968 for *The Hard Hours.* He lives with his wife, Helen D'Alessandro, in Rochester, New York.

## THE VOW

In the third month, a sudden flow of blood.
The mirth of tabrets ceaseth, and the joy
Also of the harp. The frail image of God
Lay spilled and formless. Neither girl nor
  boy,
But yet blood of my blood, nearly my
  child.
         All that long day
Her pale face turned to the window's mild
        Featureless gray.

And for some nights she whimpered as she
  dreamed
The dead thing spoke, saying: "Do not
  recall
Pleasure at my conception. I am redeemed
From pain and sorrow. Mourn rather for all
Who breathlessly issue from the bone gates,
        The gates of horn,
For truly it is best of all the fates
        Not to be born.

"Mother, a child lay gasping for bare breath
On Christmas Eve when Santa Claus had set
Death in the stocking, and the lights of
  death
Flamed in the tree. O, if you can, forget
You were the child, turn to my father's lips
        Against the time
When his cold hand puts forth its fingertips
        Of jointed lime."

Doctors of Science, what is man that he
Should hope to come to a good end? *The
  best
Is not to have been born.* And could it be
That Jewish diligence and Irish jest
The consent of flesh and a midwinter storm
        Had reconciled,
Was yet too bold a mixture to inform
        A simple child?

Even as gold is tried, Gentile and Jew.
If that ghost was a girl's, I swear to it:
Your mother shall be far more blessed
  than you.
And if a boy's, I swear: The flames are lit
That shall refine us; they shall not destroy
        A living hair.
Your younger brothers shall confirm in joy
        This that I swear.

## "IT OUT-HERODS HEROD. PRAY YOU, AVOID IT."

Tonight my children hunch
Toward their Western, and are glad
As, with a Sunday punch,
The Good casts out the Bad.

And in their fairy tales
The warty giant and witch
Get sealed in doorless jails
And the match-girl strikes it rich.

I've made myself a drink.
The giant and witch are set
To bust out of the clink
When my children have gone to bed.

All frequencies are loud
With signals of despair;
In flash and morse they crowd
The rondure of the air.

For the wicked have grown strong,
Their numbers mock at death,
Their cow brings forth its young,
Their bull engendereth.

Their very fund of strength,
Satan, bestrides the globe;
He stalks its breadth and length
And finds out even Job.

Yet by quite other laws
My children make their case;
Half God, half Santa Claus,
But with my voice and face,

A hero comes to save
The poorman, beggarman, thief,
And make the world behave
And put an end to grief.

And that their sleep be sound
I say this childermas
Who could not, at one time,
Have saved them from the gas.

# A LETTER

I have been wondering
What you are thinking about, and by now suppose
It is certainly not me.
But the crocus is up, and the lark, and the blundering
Blood knows what it knows.
It talks to itself all night, like a sliding moonlit sea.

Of course, it is talking of you.
At dawn, where the ocean has netted its catch of
lights,
The sun plants one lithe foot
On that spill of mirrors, but the blood goes worming
through
Its warm Arabian nights,
Naming your pounding name again in the dark heart-root.

Who shall, of course, be nameless.
Anyway, I should want you to know I have done my
best,
As I'm sure you have, too.
Others are bound to us, the gentle and blameless
Whose names are not confessed
In the ceaseless palaver. My dearest, the clear unquarried
blue

Of those depths is all but blinding.
You may remember that once you brought my boys
Two little wooly birds.
Yesterday the older one asked for you upon finding
Your thrush among his toys.
And the tides welled about me, and I could find no words.

There is not much else to tell.
One tries one's best to continue as before,
Doing some little good.
But I would have you know that all is not well
With a man dead set to ignore
The endless repetitions of his own murmurous blood.

---

# UPON THE DEATH OF
# GEORGE SANTAYANA

Down every passage of the cloister hung
A dark wood cross on a white plaster wall;
But in the court were roses, not as tongue
Might have them, something of Christ's blood grown small,
But just as roses, and at three o'clock
Their essences, inseparably bouqueted,
Seemed more than Christ's last breath, and rose to mock
An elderly man for whom the Sisters prayed.

What heart can know itself? The Sibyl speaks
Mirthless and unbedizened things, but who
Can fathom her intent? Loving the Greeks,

He whispered to a nun who strove to woo
His spirit unto God by prayer and fast,
"Pray that I go to Limbo, if it please
Heaven to let my soul regard at last
Democritus, Plato and Socrates."

And so it was. The river, as foretold,
Ran darkly by; under his tongue he found
Coin for the passage; the ferry tossed and rolled;
The sages stood on their appointed ground,
Sighing, all as foretold. The mind was tasked;
He had not dreamed that so many had died.
"But where is Alcibiades," he asked,
"The golden roisterer, the animal pride?"

These sages who had spoken of the love
And enmity of things, how all things flow,
Stood in a light no life is witness of,
And Socrates, whose wisdom was to know
He did not know, spoke with a solemn mien,
And all his wonderful ugliness was lit,
"He whom I loved for what he might have been
Freezes with traitors in the ultimate pit."

---

# THIRD AVENUE IN SUNLIGHT

Third Avenue in sunlight. Nature's error.
Already the bars are filled and John is there.
Beneath a plentiful lady over the mirror
He tilts his glass in the mild mahogany air.

I think of him when he first got out of college,
Serious, thin, unlikely to succeed;
For several months he hung around the Village,
Boldly T-shirted, unfettered but unfreed.

Now he confides to a stranger, "I was first scout,
And kept my glimmers peeled till after dark.
Our outfit had as its sign a bloody knout,
We met behind the museum in Central Park.

Of course, we were kids." But still those savages,
War-painted, a flap of leather at the loins,
File silently against him. Hostages
Are never taken. One summer, in Des Moines,

They entered his hotel room, tomahawks
Flashing like barracuda. He tried to pray.
Three years of treatment. Occasionally he talks
About how he almost didn't get away.

Daily the prowling sunlight whets its knife
Along the sidewalk. We almost never meet.
In the Rembrandt dark he lifts his amber life.
My bar is somewhat further down the street.

## JOHN LOGAN

John Logan was born in Red Oak, Iowa, on January 23, 1923. After taking a B.A. in Zoology from Coe College in Cedar Rapids, Iowa, he went to the University of Iowa, where he received an M.A. in English. He has taught at a number of schools, recently at San Francisco State College, and is now professor of English at the State University of New York at Buffalo. Formerly poetry editor of *The Nation,* he now edits *Choice,* a magazine of poetry and photography. He won the Miles Modern Poetry Award in 1967 and a Rockefeller Foundation Grant in 1969. Besides his poetry, he has published criticism and fiction in *Sewanee Review, Hudson Review, The New Yorker,* and other magazines. At present he is kept busy giving readings throughout the United States.

# John Logan

## LOVE POEM

Last night you would not come,
and you have been gone so long.
I yearn to find you in my aging, earthen
    arms
again (your alchemy can change my clay to
    skin).
I long to turn and watch again
from my half-hidden place
the lost, beautiful slopes and fallings of
    your face,
the black, rich leaf of each eyelash,
fresh, beach-brightened stones of your teeth.
I want to listen as you breathe yourself to
    sleep
(for by our human art we mime
the sleeper till we dream).
I want to smell the dark
herb gardens of your hair—touch the thin
    shock
that drifts over your high brow when
you rinse it clean,
for it is so fine.
I want to hear the light,
long wind of your sigh.
But again tonight I know you will not come.
I will never feel again
your gentle, sleeping calm
from which I took
so much strength, so much of my human
    heart.
Because the last time
I reached to you
as you sat upon the bed
and talked, you caught both my hands
in yours and crossed them gently on my
    breast.
I died mimicking the dead.

## CONCERT SCENE

*To John and Jane Gruen*

So he sits down. His host will play for him
And his hostess will come again, with wine.
He has a chance to see the room, to find
The source, defend himself against
    something
Beautiful, which hit him when he came in
And left him weak. On the baroque
    fireplace,
Whose stone has the turn of a living arm,
Some lacquer red poppies now are opened
In a copper bowl. Over the mantel
A warm oil against the white paneled wall.
An open coach; a girl and bearded man,
Both young, canter through a summer
    landscape
Soft with color, their faces full and flushed.
The Brahms on the piano is about
This. To the left a black coffee table
Topped with strips of crossed cane beside a
    green
Cloth couch. On this top a wicker horn leaks
Out white grapes by a tin of purple-wrapped
Candied nuts, and a thin white porcelain
Cream pitcher with a few, loosely figured
Very bright blue anemones and greens;
At the right of the fireplace a great teak
Desk has a red Chinese plume or feather
In a silver pitcher, then a clear, wine-
glass shaped, tall bowl—full of golden apples.
Still the music in Brahms: golds, blues, and
    wines
Of the stained glass panels in the far door,
A light behind. The hostess brings a tray
Of sherry and a jar of caviar
In ice, the thousand eggs writhing with light
Beside the lucent lemon slice. She sits
Upon the green or gold cloth couch. She
    holds
The thin stemmed glass, and now he looks
    at her,
Shook with the colors or the music or
The wine. Her hair is blue black and drops
    straight
From the part—directly in the middle
Of her skull—its long, moonwet waterfall.
Her smile is warm for him, lips large
    without
Paint, gentle eyes hollowed in the high
    bones
Of her white face. Now he sees above her
A graceful, black iron candelabra
On the white wall, green of its candles spin-
ning in the whorls of shiny surfaced leaves

At the top of a thin plant in the corner,
And in the jagged-necked, blown-glass
    bottle,
As big as a child, standing on the floor
By the piano. His hostess rises

To sing. (She doesn't know he's trembling.)
    Her
Voice is too strong. Suddenly the color
Is intense. And he finds no defense.

## THE SHEEP CHILD

Farm boys wild to couple
With anything     with soft-wooded trees
With mounds of earth     mounds
Of pinestraw     will keep themselves off
Animals by legends of their own:
In the hay-tunnel dark
And dung of barns, they will
Say     I have heard tell

That in a museum in Atlanta
Way back in a corner somewhere
There's this thing that's only half
Sheep     like a woolly baby
Pickled in alcohol     because
Those things can't live     his eyes
Are open     but you can't stand to look
I heard from somebody who . . .

But this is now almost all
Gone. The boys have taken
Their own true wives in the city,
The sheep are safe in the west hill
Pasture     but we who were born there
Still are not sure. Are we,
Because we remember, remembered
In the terrible dust of museums?

Merely with his eyes, the sheep-child may

Be saying     saying

> *I am here, in my father's house.*
> *I who am half of your world, came deeply*
> *To my mother in the long grass*
> *Of the west pasture, where she stood like moonlight*
> *Listening for foxes. It was something like love*
> *From another world that seized her*
> *From behind, and she gave, not lifting her head*
> *Out of dew, without ever looking, her best*
> *Self to that great need. Turned loose, she dipped her*
>     *face*
> *Farther into the chill of the earth, and in a sound*
> *Of sobbing     of something stumbling*
> *Away, began, as she must do,*
> *To carry me. I woke, dying,*

**JAMES DICKEY**
James Dickey was born on February 2, 1923, in Atlanta, Georgia, where he spent his youth. He flew with the Air Force in World War II, and, after taking his B.A. in 1949 and his M.A. in 1950 from Vanderbilt University, he served as a pilot in the Korean War. His travels have taken him to Europe, Australia, and the Far East. A *Sewanee Review* Fellowship in 1954, a Guggenheim Fellowship in 1962, and numerous other awards preceded the National Book Award in 1966 for *Buckdancer's Choice*. Dickey's most recent success, *Deliverance*, was a best-selling novel in 1970 and was recently filmed under his supervision in the hills of Georgia. He now lives with his wife, Maxine, and their two sons in Columbia, South Carolina, where he is a professor of English and writer-in-residence at the University of South Carolina.

*In the summer sun of the hillside, with my eyes*
*Far more than human. I saw for a blazing moment*
*The great grassy world from both sides,*
*Man and beast in the round of their need,*
*And the hill wind stirred in my wool,*
*My hoof and my hand clasped each other,*
*I ate my one meal*
*Of milk, and died*
*Staring. From dark grass I came straight*

*To my father's house, whose dust*
*Whirls up in the halls for no reason*
*When no one comes      piling deep in a hellish mild*
  *corner,*
*And, through my immortal waters,*
*I meet the sun's grains eye*
*To eye, and they fail at my closet of glass.*
*Dead, I am most surely living*
*In the minds of farm boys: I am he who drives*
*Them like wolves from the hound bitch and calf*
*And from the chaste ewe in the wind.*
*They go into woods      into bean fields      they go*
*Deep into their known right hands. Dreaming of me,*
*They groan      they wait      they suffer*
*Themselves, they marry, they raise their kind.*

---

## REINCARNATION (I)

Still, passed through the spokes of an old wheel, on and
  around
The hub's furry rust in the weeds and shadows of the
  riverbank,
This one is feeling his life as a man move slowly away.
Fallen from that estate, he has gone down on his knees
And beyond, disappearing into the egg buried under the sand

And wakened to the low world being born, consisting now
Of the wheel on its side not turning, but leaning to rot away
In the sun a few feet farther off than it is for any man.
The roots bulge quietly under the earth beneath him;
With his tongue he can hear them in their concerted effort

To raise something, anything, out of the dark of the ground.
He has come by gliding, by inserting the head between stems.
Everything follows that as naturally as the creation
Of the world, leaving behind arms and legs, leaving behind
The intervals between tracks, leaving one long wavering step

In sand and none in grass: he moves through, moving
  nothing,
And the grass stands as never entered. It is in the new
Life of resurrection that one can come in one's own time
To a place like a rotting wheel, the white paint flaking from
  it,
Rust slowly emerging, and coil halfway through it, stopped

By a just administration of light and dark over the diamonds
Of the body. Here, also naturally growing, is a flat leaf
To rest the new head upon. The stem bends but knows the
  weight
And does not touch the ground, holding the snub, patterned
  face
Swaying with the roots of things. Inside the jaws, saliva

Has turned ice cold, drawn from bird eggs and thunderstruck
  rodents,
Dusty pine needles, blunt stones, horse dung, leaf mold,
But mainly, now, from waiting—all the time a symbol of evil—
Not for food, but for the first man to walk by the gentle
  river:
Minute by minute the head becomes more poisonous and
  poised.

Here in the wheel is the place to wait, with the eyes
  unclosable,
Unanswerable, the tongue occasionally listening, this time
No place in the body desiring to burn the tail away or to
  warn,
But only to pass on, handless, what yet may be transferred
In a sudden giving-withdrawing move, like a county judge
  striking a match.

70

## THE FIEND

He has only to pass by a tree     moodily walking     head down
A worried accountant     not with it     and he is swarming
He is gliding up the underside light of leaves     upfloating
In a seersucker suit     passing window after window of her building.
He finds her at last, chewing gum     talking on the telephone.
The wind sways him softly     comfortably sighing     she must bathe
Or sleep.     She gets up, and he follows her along the branch
Into another room.     She stands there for a moment     and the
     teddy bear
On the bed feels its guts spin as she takes it by the leg and tosses
It off.     She touches one button at her throat, and rigor mortis
Slithers into his pockets, making everything there—keys, pen
and secret love—stand up.     He brings from those depths the knife
And flicks it open     it glints on the moon one time     carries
Through the dead walls     making a wormy static on the TV screen.
He parts the swarm of gnats that live excitedly at this perilous level
Parts the rarefied light high windows give out into inhabited trees
Opens his lower body to the moon.     This night the apartments are
     sinking

To ground level     burying their sleepers in the soil     burying all floors
But the one where a sullen shopgirl gets ready to take a shower,
Her hair in rigid curlers, and the rest.     When she gives up
Her aqua terry-cloth robe the wind quits in mid-tree     the birds
Freeze to their perches round his head     a purely human light
Comes out of a one-man oak     around her an energy field     she stands
Rooted     not turning to anything else     then begins to move like a saint
Her stressed nipples rising like things about to crawl off her     as he gets
A hold on himself.     With that clasp she changes     senses     something

Some breath through the fragile walls     some all-seeing eye
Of God     some touch that enfolds her body     some hand come up
     out of roots
That carries her as she moves     swaying     at this rare height.
     She wraps
The curtain around her and streams.     The room fades.     Then coming
Forth magnificently     the window blurred from within     she moves
     in a cloud
Chamber     the tree in the oak currents sailing     in clear air keeping
     pace
With her white breathless closet—he sees her mistily part her lips
As if singing to him, come up from river-fog     almost hears her as if
She sang alone in a cloud     its warmed light streaming into his branches
Out through the gauze glass of the window.     She takes off her
     bathing cap
The tree with him ascending     himself and the birds all moving
In darkness together     crumbling the bark in their claws.
By this time he holds in his awkward, subtle limbs the limbs

Of a hundred understanding trees.     He has learned what a plant is like
When it moves near a human habitation     moving closer the later it is
Unfurling its leaves near bedrooms     still keeping its wilderness life
Twigs covering his body with only one way out     for his eyes into
     inner light
Of a chosen window     living with them night after night     watching

71

Watching with them at times their favorite TV shows     learning—
Though now and then he hears a faint sound:     gunshot, bombing,
Building-fall—how to read lips:     the lips of laconic cowboys
Bank robbers     old and young doctors tense-faced     gesturing savagely
In wards and corridors     like reading the lips of the dead

The lips of men interrupting the program at the wrong time
To sell you a good used car on the Night Owl Show     men silently
     reporting
The news out the window.     But the living as well, three-dimensioned,
Silent as the small gray dead, must sleep at last     must save their lives
By taking off their clothes. It is his beholding that saves them:
God help the dweller in windowless basements     the one obsessed
With drawing curtains this night. At three o'clock in the morning
He descends     a medium-sized shadow     while that one sleeps and
     turns
In her high bed in loss     as he goes limb by limb     quietly down
The trunk with one lighted side. Ground upon which he could not
     explain
His presence he walks with toes uncurled from branches, his
     bird-movements
Dying hard. At the sidewalk he changes     gains weight     a solid citizen

Once more. At apartments there is less danger from dogs, but he has
For those a super-quiet hand     a hand to calm sparrows and rivers,
And watchdogs in half-tended bushes lie with him watching their
     women
Undress     the dog's honest eyes and the man's the same pure beast's
Comprehending the same essentials. Not one of these beheld would
     ever give
Him a second look     but he gives them all a first look that goes
On and on     conferring immortality while it lasts     while the
     suburb's leaves
Hold still enough     while whatever dog he has with him holds its breath
Yet seems to thick-pant     impatient as he with the indifferent men
Drifting in and out of the rooms     or staying on, too tired to move
Reading the sports page     dozing     plainly unworthy     for what
     women want
Dwells in bushes and trees:     what they want is to look outward,

To look with the light streaming into the April limbs     to stand
     straighter
While their husbands' lips dry out     feeling that something is there
That could dwell in no earthly house:     that in poplar trees or beneath
The warped roundabout of the clothesline     in the sordid disorder
Of communal backyards     some being is there in the shrubs
Sitting comfortably on a child's striped rubber ball filled with rainwater
Muffling his glasses with a small studious hand against a sudden
Flash of houselight from within     or flash from himself     a needle's eye
Uncontrollable     blaze of uncompromised being. Ah, the lingerie
Hung in the bathroom! The domestic motions of single girls living
     together
A plump girl girding her loins against her moon-summoned blood:
In that moon he stands     the only male lit by it, covered with
     leaf-shapes.
He coughs, and the smallest root responds     and in his lust he is set
By the wind in motion. That movement can restore the green eyes

Of middle age    looking    renewed    through the qualified light
Not quite reaching him where he stands again on the usual branch
Of his oldest love    his tie not loosened    a plastic shield
In his breast pocket full of pencils and ballpoint pens given him by
    salesmen
His hat correctly placed to shade his eyes    a natural gambler's tilt
And in summer wears an eyeshade    a straw hat Caribbean style.
In some guise or other he is near them when they are weeping without
    sound
When the teen-age son has quit school    when the girl has broken up
With the basketball star    when the banker walks out on his wife.
He sees mothers counsel desperately with pulsing girls face down
On beds full of overstuffed beasts    sees men dress as women
In ante-bellum costumes with bonnets    sees doctors come, looking
    oddly
Like himself    though inside the houses    worming a medical arm
Up under the cringing covers    sees children put angrily to bed
Sees one told an invisible fairy story    with lips moving silently as his
Are also moving    the book's few pages bright. It will take years
But at last he will shed his leaves    burn his roots    give up
Invisibility    will step out    will make himself known to the one
He cannot see loosen her blouse    take off luxuriously    with lips
Compressed against her mouth-stain    her dress    her stockings
Her magic underwear.    To that one he will come    up frustrated pines
Down alleys    through window blinds    blind windows    kitchen doors
On summer evenings. It will be something small that sets him off:
Perhaps a pair of lace pants on a clothesline    gradually losing
Water to the sun    filling out in the warm light with a well-rounded
Feminine wind as he watches    having spent so many sleepless nights
Because of her    because of her hand on a shade always coming down
In his face    not leaving even a shadow stripped naked upon the
    brown paper
Waiting for her now in a green outdated car with a final declaration
Of love    pretending to read    and when she comes and takes down
Her pants, he will casually follow her in    like a door-to-door salesman
The godlike movement of trees stiffening with him    the light
Of a hundred favored windows    gone wrong somewhere in his glasses
Where his knocked-off panama hat was    in his painfully vanishing
    hair.

## CHERRYLOG ROAD

Off Highway 106
At Cherrylog Road I entered
The '34 Ford without wheels,
Smothered in kudzu,
With a seat pulled out to run
Corn whiskey down from the hills,

And then from the other side
Crept into an Essex
With a rumble seat of red leather
And then out again, aboard
A blue Chevrolet, releasing
The rust from its other color,

Reared up on three building blocks.
None had the same body heat;
I changed with them inward, toward
The weedy heart of the junkyard,
For I knew that Doris Holbrook
Would escape from her father at noon

And would come from the farm
To seek parts owned by the sun
Among the abandoned chassis,
Sitting in each in turn
As I did, leaning forward
As in a wild stock-car race

In the parking lot of the dead.
Time after time, I climbed in
And out the other side, like
An envoy or movie star
Met at the station by crickets.
A radiator cap raised its head,

Become a real toad or a kingsnake
As I neared the hub of the yard,
Passing through many states,
Many lives, to reach
Some grandmother's long Pierce-Arrow
Sending platters of blindness forth

From its nickel hubcaps
And spilling its tender upholstery
On sleepy roaches,
The glass panel in between
Lady and colored driver
Not all the way broken out,

The back-seat phone
Still on its hook.
I got in as though to exclaim,
"Let us go to the orphan asylum,
John; I have some old toys
For children who say their prayers."

I popped with sweat as I thought
I heard Doris Holbrook scrape
Like a mouse in the southern-state sun
That was eating the paint in blisters
From a hundred car tops and hoods.
She was tapping like code,

Loosening the screws,
Carrying off headlights,
Sparkplugs, bumpers,
Cracked mirrors and gear-knobs,
Getting ready, already,
To go back with something to show

Other than her lips' new trembling
I would hold to me soon, soon,
Where I sat in the ripped back seat
Talking over the interphone,
Praying for Doris Holbrook
To come from her father's farm

And to get back there
With no trace of me on her face
To be seen by her red-haired father
Who would change, in the squalling barn,
Her back's pale skin with a strop,
Then lay for me

In a bootlegger's roasting car
With a string-triggered 12-gauge shotgun
To blast the breath from the air.
Not cut by the jagged windshields,

Through the acres of wrecks she came
With a wrench in her hand,

Through dust where the blacksnake dies
Of boredom, and the beetle knows
The compost has no more life.
Someone outside would have seen
The oldest car's door inexplicably
Close from within:

I held her and held her and held her,
Convoyed at terrific speed
By the stalled, dreaming traffic around us,
So the blacksnake, stiff
With inaction, curved back
Into life, and hunted the mouse

With deadly overexcitement,
The beetles reclaimed their field
As we clung, glued together,
With the hooks of the seat springs
Working through to catch us red-handed
Amidst the gray breathless batting

That burst from the seat at our backs.
We left by separate doors
Into the changed, other bodies
Of cars, she down Cherrylog Road
And I to my motorcycle
Parked like the soul of the junkyard

Restored, a bicycle fleshed
With power, and tore off
Up Highway 106, continually
Drunk on the wind in my mouth,
Wringing the handlebar for speed,
Wild to be wreckage forever.


THE HEAVEN OF ANIMALS

Here they are. The soft eyes open.
If they have lived in a wood
It is a wood.
If they have lived on plains
It is grass rolling
Under their feet forever.

Having no souls, they have come,
Anyway, beyond their knowing.
Their instincts wholly bloom
And they rise.
The soft eyes open.

To match them, the landscape flowers,
Outdoing, desperately
Outdoing what is required:
The richest wood,
The deepest field.

For some of these,
It could not be the place
It is, without blood.
These hunt, as they have done,
But with claws and teeth grown perfect,

More deadly than they can believe.
They stalk more silently,
And crouch on the limbs of trees,
And their descent
Upon the bright backs of their prey

May take years
In a sovereign floating of joy.
And those that are hunted

Know this as their life,
Their reward: to walk

Under such trees in full knowledge
Of what is in glory above them,
And to feel no fear,
But acceptance, compliance.
Fulfilling themselves without pain

At the cycle's center,
They tremble, they walk
Under the tree,
They fall, they are torn,
They rise, they walk again.

**ALAN DUGAN**

Alan Dugan was born in Brooklyn, New York, on February 12, 1923. He received a B.A. from Mexico City College (now University of the Americas in Puebla) in 1951. For his first book, *Poems*, published in 1961, he won the Yale Younger Poets Award, the National Book Award, and the Pulitzer Prize. He lives in New York and Massachusetts with his wife, Judith Shahn. He writes: I'm working on *Poems 4*. I'm reading around at colleges and high schools as usual so as to enjoy the young and eat, and I'm a Staff Member of the Fine Arts Work Center in Provincetown, Mass., which is an interesting operation in that it's for middle-aged young post-academic artists who don't know whether they want to be artists or teachers or both, so we give them a winter in Provincetown on a starvation amount of money so they can work at their crafts and go crazy away from the Universities.

# Alan Dugan

## TRIBUTE TO KAFKA FOR SOMEONE TAKEN

The party is going strong.
The doorbell rings. It's
for someone named me.
I'm coming. I take
a last drink, a last
puff on a cigarette,
a last kiss at a girl,
and step into the hall,
                    bang,
shutting out the laughter. "Is
your name you?" "Yes."
"Well come along then."
"See here. See here. See here."

## ELEGY FOR A PURITAN CONSCIENCE

I closed my ears with stinging bugs
and sewed my eyelids shut
but heard a sucking at the dugs
and saw my parents rut.

I locked my jaw with rusty nails
and cured my tongue in lime
but ate and drank in garbage pails
and said these words of crime.

I crushed my scrotum with two stones
and drew my penis in
but felt your wound expect its own
and fell in love with sin.

## HOLIDAY

After hundreds of years of common sense
action appeared at the corners of all eyes:
lights appeared at night, and sounds of war
whammed from the desert back of town.

At first only the outlying saints saw them,
but later they strolled through the streets:
bat-faced devils walking arm in arm
with blond white angels in a tourists' truce.

It was then that Natural Law was repealed
and a public virgin wept that it was she
to whom a fiend or angel had appeared
announcing an unearthly rape of sorts
and the arrival of a difficult child.

**LOUIS SIMPSON**

Born in Jamaica, British West Indies, on March 27, 1923, Louis Simpson was educated at Munro College, Jamaica, and at Columbia University, where he studied under Mark Van Doren. After five years as an editor with Bobbs-Merrill Company, he joined the English faculty at Columbia in 1955. Later he taught at the University of California, Berkeley, and is now professor of English at the State University of New York at Stony Brook, where he has been since 1967. His poetry has received numerous honors, including a Rome Fellowship from the American Academy of Arts and Letters, a *Hudson Review* Fellowship, and a Guggenheim Fellowship. In 1964 Simpson won the Pulitzer Prize for *At the End of the Open Road.* He is the author of a critical study of the Scottish poet James Hogg, a novel entitled *Riverside Drive,* and a textbook, *An Introduction to Poetry.* He lives with his wife, Dorothy Roochvarg, and their three children in Port Jefferson, New York.

## LOVE SONG: I AND THOU

Nothing is plumb, level, or square:
   the studs are bowed, the joists
are shaky by nature, no piece fits
   any other piece without a gap
or pinch, and bent nails
   dance all over the surfacing
like maggots. By Christ
   I am no carpenter. I built
the roof for myself, the walls
   for myself, the floors
for myself, and got
   hung up in it myself. I
danced with a purple thumb
   at this house-warming, drunk
with my prime whiskey: rage.

Oh I spat rage's nails
into the frame-up of my work:
   it held. It settled plumb,
level, solid, square and true
   for that great moment. Then
it screamed and went on through,
   skewing as wrong the other way.
God damned it. This is hell,
   but I planned it, I sawed it,
I nailed it, and I
   will live in it until it kills me.
I can nail my left palm
   to the left-hand crosspiece but
I can't do everything myself.
   I need a hand to nail the right,
a help, a love, a you, a wife.

# Louis Simpson

## TO THE WESTERN WORLD

A siren sang, and Europe turned away
From the high castle and the shepherd's
  crook.
Three caravels went sailing to Cathay
On the strange ocean, and the captains
  shook
Their banners out across the Mexique Bay.

And in our early days we did the same.
Remembering our fathers in their wreck
We crossed the sea from Palos where they
  came
And saw, enormous to the little deck,
A shore in silence waiting for a name.

The treasures of Cathay were never found.
In this America, this wilderness
Where the axe echoes with a lonely sound,
The generations labor to possess
And grave by grave we civilize the ground.

## IN THE SUBURBS

There's no way out.
You were born to waste your life.
You were born to this middleclass life

As others before you
Were born to walk in procession
To the temple, singing.

## AMERICAN POETRY

Whatever it is, it must have
A stomach that can digest
Rubber, coal, uranium, moons, poems.

Like the shark, it contains a shoe.
It must swim for miles through the desert
Uttering cries that are almost human.

## VANDERGAST AND THE GIRL

Vandergast to his neighbors—
the grinding of a garage door
and hiss of gravel in the driveway.

He worked for the insurance company
whose talisman is a phoenix
rising in flames . . . *non omnis moriar.*
From his desk he had a view of the street—

translucent raincoats, and umbrellas,
fluorescent plate-glass windows.
A girl knelt down. arranging
underwear on a female dummy—

sea waves and, on the gale,
Venus, these busy days,
poised in her garter-belt and stockings.

The next day he saw her eating
in the restaurant where he usually ate.

Soon they were having lunch together
elsewhere.

She came from Dallas.
This was only a start, she was ambitious,
twenty-five and still unmarried.
Green eyes with silver spiricles . . .
red hair . . .

When he held the car door open
her legs were smooth and slender.

"I was wondering,"
she said, "when you'd get round to it,"
and laughed.

Vandergast says he never intended
having an affair.

And was that what this was?
The names that people give to things . . .
What do definitions and divorce-court
    proceedings
have to do with the breathless reality?

O little lamp at the bedside
with views of Venice and the Bay of Naples,
you understood! *Lactona* toothbrush
and suitcase bought in a hurry,
you were the witnesses of the love
we made in bed together.

*Schrafft's Chocolate Cherries,* surely you
    remember
when she said she'd be true forever,

and, watching "Dark Storm," we decided
there is something to be said, after all,
for soap opera, "if it makes people happy."

The Vandergasts are having some trouble
finding a buyer for their house.

When I go for a walk with Tippy
I pass the unweeded tennis court,
the empty garage, windows heavily
    shuttered.

Mrs. Vandergast took the children
and went back to her family.

And Vandergast moved to New Jersey,
where he works for an insurance company
whose emblem is the Rock of Gibraltar—
the rest of his life laid out
with the child-support and alimony
    payments.

As for the girl, she vanished.

Was it worth it? Ask Vandergast.
You'd have to be Vandergast, looking
    through his eyes
at the house across the street, in Orange,
    New Jersey.
Maybe on wet days umbrellas and raincoats
set his heart thudding.

Maybe
he talks to his pillow, and it whispers,
moving red hair.

In any case, he will soon be forty.

**DENISE LEVERTOV**

Denise Levertov was born on October 24, 1923, in Ilford, Essex, England, where her father, a Christian convert from a distinguished Russian Jewish family, was a priest in the Anglican Church. She was educated at home, spent the war years as a civilian nurse in London, and after the war met and married Mitchell Goodman, now a well-known activist in the peace movement. They lived in Paris and Florence before making New York their permanent place of residence in 1948. She was poetry editor of *The Nation* in 1961 and received a Guggenheim Fellowship in 1962, a National Institute of Arts and Letters Award in 1965, and two awards from *Poetry.*

# Denise Levertov

## A DAY BEGINS

A headless squirrel, some blood
oozing from the unevenly
chewed-off neck

lies in rainsweet grass
near the woodshed door.
Down the driveway

the first irises
have opened since dawn,
ethereal, their mauve

almost a transparent gray,
their dark veins
bruise-blue.

## PARTIAL RESEMBLANCE

A doll's hair concealing
an eggshell skull delicately
throbbing, within which
maggots in voluptuous unrest
jostle and shrug. Oh, Eileen, my
big doll, your gold hair was
not more sunny than this
human fur, but
your head was
radiant in its emptiness,
a small clean room.

Her warm and rosy mouth
is telling lies—she would

**ROBERT HUFF**

Robert Huff writes: I was born in Evanston, Illinois, April 3, 1924. After serving as an aerial gunner and non-commissioned bombardier with the Eighth Air Force, I attended Wayne State University for my undergraduate and graduate degrees. I've had writing fellowships to the MacDowell Colony and the Indiana School of Letters and I was a Bread Loaf Scholar in Poetry in 1961. In 1952 I moved to the Northwest, where I've worked for the U.S. Forest Service and taught writing and English literature at several universities. I'm currently Professor of English at Western Washington State College, and live with my wife Sally and three children in Bellingham.

believe them if she could believe:
her pretty eyes
search out corruption. Oh, Eileen,
how kindly your silence was, and
what virtue
shone in the opening and shutting of your
ingenious blindness.

## THE JACOB'S LADDER

The stairway is not
a thing of gleaming strands
a radiant evanescence
for angels' feet that only glance in their
    tread, and need not
touch the stone.

It is of stone.
A rosy stone that takes
a glowing tone of softness
only because behind it the sky is a
    doubtful, a doubting
night gray.

A stairway of sharp
angles, solidly built.
One sees that the angels must spring
down from one step to the next, giving a
    little
lift of the wings:

and a man climbing
must scrape his knees, and bring
the grip of his hands into play. The cut
    stone
consoles his groping feet. Wings brush past
    him.
The poem ascends.

## THE WAY THROUGH

Let the rain plunge radiant
through sulky thunder
rage on rooftops

let it scissor and bounce its denials
on concrete slabs and black
roadways. Flood the streets. It's much
but not enough, not yet: persist,
rain, real rain, sensuous,
swift, released from

          vague skies, the tedium
up there.

          Under scared bucking trees
the beach road washed out—

          trying to get by on the verge
          is no good, earth crumbles into the
          brown waterfall, but he backs up
the old car again and CHARGES.

The water flies in the halfwit's eyes
          who didn't move fast enough
"Who do you think I am, a horse?"
          but we made it—

          Drown us, lose us,
rain, let us loose, so,
to lose ourselves, to career
up the plunge of the hill

# Robert Huff

## TRADITIONAL RED

Returning after dark, I thought,
The house will have grown small: noises
In the barn I knew, wood and field,
All tree tops visible. My eyes,
I thought, lied then or will lie now;
My ears, even my ears, will tell
Me: small. Then half awake I waited,
Half afraid of the sound light makes
With frost on windowpanes. But night

Birds carried fifteen years away
Like an abandoned nest, put them
To rest somewhere I couldn't see
Without undoing anything,
And when I woke the dawn I saw
Was on the farm as positive as God.

A rooster dipped in sunlight raised
His crown, called to the steaming barn,
Gigantic, red, until my blood
Roared for stupidity, and I
Ran down the path humble with hens

To kneel and stare dumb wonder
At his size. My pride! my pride! O
Jesus, bright dove call! I knelt there
In his thunder, white and small, watched
Him and rose to walk under trees

Whose tops I couldn't see for light,
Dense, golden, moving hosts of leaves
Answering that red cry. And when
I turned I saw the farm house roof
Raking an iron rooster through the sky.

---

## RAINBOW

After the shot the driven feathers rock
In the air and are by sunlight trapped.
Their moment of descent is eloquent.
It is the rainbow echo of a bird
Whose thunder, stopped, puts in my daughter's eyes
A question mark. She does not see the rainbow,
And the folding bird-fall was for her too quick.
It is about the stillness of the bird
Her eyes are asking. She is three years old;
Has cut her fingers; found blood tastes of salt;
But she has never witnessed quiet blood,
Nor ever seen before the peace of death.
I say: "The feathers—Look!" but she is torn
And wretched and draws back. And I am glad
That I have wounded her, have winged her heart,
And that she goes beyond my fathering.

## GETTING DRUNK WITH DAUGHTER

Caught without wife and mother, child,
We squat close, scratching gibberish in the sand,
Inspect your castle, peek into the pail
Where shells await your signal to attack
The stick gate, strike down squads of stones,
And storm the tower of the Feather Queen,
When, perchspine arrow in his head,
Lord Cork falls dead, his bride carted away.
And my pailful of ice is melting down
Around what will be two dead soldiers soon.

Odors remind me your cheeks reeked with kisses:
Whiskey, tobacco, dentures—sourdough—
When Father found you on the trail he misses.
Too bad the old man had to see you grow
Into my blonde wag with your woman's wishes,
Playing pretend wife, Daughter . . . even though
He threw himself to rags and knows his bliss is
Walking the sweaty mares he can't let go.

Precocious runt. Noting our shapely neighbor
Is amber from toenails to Brillo hair,
Has rolled, and drops her top and props her cleavage,
You grin above your army. Dear, her spine's
Not likely to compete with you or Bourbon
Since you're your mother's small ape from behind.
Oh, I know you know I know love likes beaches—

For blood outruns the heart, no doubt,
But mine runs to your lordship's mortal splinter.
I've one cork left. So let the spearmen start.

Tomorrow's going to come. We'll be together.
The sun will bake us, and we'll let our bones
Fly with the wastrel gulls, who love this weather,
Enlisting stronger sticks, more stalwart stones.
Your mother's got a feather where she itches.
Your daddy's got a fish bone in his brain.
The world lies down and waits in all its ditches.
But you and I aren't going to let it rain.

## PORCUPINES

I knew that porcupines liked to eat trees,
woodsheds, wood piles, cabins, and anything anybody
touched long enough to leave salt on; that they were
rodents who waddle around their food, making a hog-
like noise; and that their spines were always hurting
dogs, whose curiosity about bushes urges their noses
close to those that move.

I had been told about their priceless teeth,
which in midlife are deep yellow, inlaid in old age
with intricate brown designs. The Indians, I read,
brought to the quills an artful skill which fashioned
heraldry. And everyone said porcupines were slow
to die. Shoot off half that neckless, faceless
lump around the eyes, yet moves the porcupine.

What keeps them moving I was left to learn by
moonlight on a butte they seemed to own. They came
in squads, ate up the ladder rungs, axe handles, boxes;
everything more base than they themselves was theirs
to feed upon. And so they chewed until I murdered
them and saw the product of their alchemy.

Rich as their teeth, much madder than their
spines, their entrails are the millers of their being.
There the enormous task of their lives is all the
time going on. I loosed it in one who went dragging
his intestines up a lava slope. His ghost gnaws hard
now at my dignity. Tenacious, dull, drab animal—
turned inside out, he headed for the dark, lugging
his precious golden chemistry, which glittered in the
darkness like the overflow of Henry Morgan's hold.

# Vassar Miller

**VASSAR MILLER**

Vassar Miller writes: I was born July 19, 1924 in Houston, Texas. Because I was (and am) a victim of cerebral palsy I was educated at home by my parents until I entered Junior High School. Thence I went to high school and finally received B.S. and M.A. Degrees from the University of Houston. With my parents I traveled widely in the west. In '65 and in '70 I went to Europe and to England—the last trip taken by myself to visit friends in Oxford. From 1964 to 1967 I taught at St. John's School in Houston. Currently, I'm working on a fifth mss. of poetry and a libretto of Kazantzakis' *Last Temptation of Christ* with composer Thomas Avinger.

## WITHOUT CEREMONY

Except ourselves, we have no other prayer;
Our needs are sores upon our nakedness.
We do not have to name them; we are here.
And You who can make eyes can see no
    less.
We fall, not on our knees, but on our hearts,
A posture humbler far and more downcast;
While Father Pain instructs us in the arts
Of praying, hunger is the worthiest fast.
We find ourselves where tongues cannot
    wage war
On silence (farther, mystics never flew)
But on the common wings of what we are,
Borne on the wings of what we bear,
    toward You,
Oh Word, in whom our wordiness dissolves,
When we have not a prayer except
    ourselves.

## BOUT WITH BURNING

I have tossed hours upon the tides of fever,
Upon the billows of my blood have ridden,
Where fish of fancy teem as neither river
Nor ocean spawns from India to Sweden.
Here while my boat of body burnt has
    drifted
Along her sides crawled tentacles of crabs
Sliming her timbers; on the waves upwafted
Crept water rats to gnaw her ropes and ribs.
Crashing, she has dived, her portholes
    choking
With weed and ooze, the swirls of black and
    green
Gulping her inch by inch, the seagulls'
    shrieking
Sieved depth through depth to silence. Till
    blast-blown,
I in my wreck beyond storm's charge and
    churning
Have waked marooned upon the coasts of
    morning.

## CHRISTMAS MOURNING

On Christmas Day I weep
Good Friday to rejoice.
I watch the Child asleep.
Does He half dream the choice
The Man must make and keep?

At Christmastime I sigh
For my Good Friday hope.
Outflung the Child's arms lie
To span in their brief scope
The death the Man must die.

Come Christmastide I groan
To hear Good Friday's pealing.
The Man, racked to the bone,
Has made His hurt my healing,
Has made my ache His own.

Slay me, pierced to the core
With Christmas penitence
So I who, new-born, soar
To that Child's innocence,
May wound the Man no more.

## JUDAS

Always I lay upon the brink of love,
Impotent, waiting till the waters stirred,
And no one healed my weakness with a
    word;
For no one healed me who lacked words to
    prove
My heart, which, when the kiss of Mary
    wove
His shroud, my tongueless anguish spurred
To cool dissent, and which, each time I
    heard
John whisper to Him, moaned, but could
    not move.

While Peter deeply drowsed within love's
    deep
I cramped upon its margin, glad to share
The sop Christ gave me, yet its bitter bite
Dried up my ducts. Praise Peter, who could
    weep
His sin away, but never see me where
I hang, huge teardrop on the cheek of night.

# Jane Cooper

## THE FAITHFUL

Once you said joking slyly, "If I'm killed
I'll come to haunt your solemn bed,
I'll stand and glower at the head
And see if my place is empty still, or filled."

What was it woke me in the early darkness
Before the first bird's twittering?
—A shape dissolving and flittering
Unsteady as a flame in a drafty house.

It seemed a concentration of the dark
  burning
By the bedpost at my right hand,
While to my left that no-man's land
Of sheet stretched palely as a false
  morning. . . .

All day I have been sick and restless.
  This evening
Curtained, with all the lights on,
I start up—only to sit down.
Why should I grieve after ten years of
  grieving?

What if last night I was the one who lay
  dead,
While the dead burned beside me
Trembling with passionate pity
At my blameless life and shaking its
  flamelike head?

**JANE COOPER**
Jane Cooper was born on October 9, 1924, in Atlantic City, New Jersey. She writes: From childhood I carry with me a sense of close family ties, wide physical landscapes, solitude left over from a few illnesses, poems read aloud. The Second World War turned me toward science, languages, social idealism, and resulted in a book of anti-war poems that I never tried to publish. Since the age of 25 I have been deep in the experience of teaching. From my students at Sarah Lawrence College I have learned that it is possible to build relationships without authority, poems without the structures I used to depend on. And yet I remain rather traditional —at least for the time being. My first published book, *The Weather of Six Mornings*, covered 13 years of work and was the 1968 Lamont Selection of the Academy of American Poets. I have held a Guggenheim Fellowship and a writing grant from the Ingram Merrill Foundation. I am interested in sequences of poems, in how to extend what I have to say when the usual continuities fail me, in alternations of speech (even prose) with song. I want to write more as I get older, and more freely; I hope to live increasingly as a poet.

## THE GRAVEYARD

Where five old graves lay circled on a hill
And pines kept all but shattered sunlight out
We came to learn about
How each had sinned, loved, suffered, lost until
He met the other and grew somehow still.

Under those soughing, rumor-speaking trees
Full of dead secrets, on the August ground,
We leaned against a mound
Not touching; there, as we could, gave keys
To open midnight vaults that no one sees.

All that had shaped us thirty years or more
We tried to offer—not as brave youngsters do
Who need an echo, who
See in their fathers' sins a canceled score—
But as two grieving inmates tapping at the door.

Gifts of the self which were but bids for power,
Gifts of the innocent self—stripped, bound and torn—
A rare child wrongly born
And our best strivings turned, with age, half-sour:
Such darkness we unlocked within an hour.

Those five old graves lay speechless while the sun
Gradually stroked them with its flickering arm,
The smell of pines grew warm.
We walked away to watch a fresh stream run
As free as if all guilts were closed and done.

**MAXINE KUMIN**

Maxine Kumin writes: I was born in Germantown, Philadelphia, June 6, 1925, attended the standard public schools, read Virgil and Ovid in high school and became a freestyle swimmer for the local AAU. Wellesley, which has a splendid pool, rejected me, and instead I attended Radcliffe, which has a less than standard size one, thereby aborting a possible career in hundred-meter sprints. Subsequently, Radcliffe granted me a Masters (I was married and pregnant) even though I failed the Latin exam. From 1958 to 1961 I was an Instructor in English at Tufts University and Lecturer there 1965–1968. From 1961–63 I was a scholar at the Radcliffe Institute for Independent Study and the recipient of a grant from the National Council on the Arts and Humanities in 1967–68. Besides my poems, I have published three novels—*The Abduction, The Passions of Uxport* and *Through Dooms of Love* (all from Harper & Row) and a number of children's books.

## IN THE HOUSE OF THE DYING

So once again, hearing the tired aunts
whisper together under the kitchen globe,
I turn away; I am not one of them.

At the sink I watch the water cover my hands
in a sheath of light. Upstairs she lies alone
dreaming of autumn nights when her children were born.

On the steps between us grows in a hush of waiting
the impossible silence between two generations.
The aunts buzz on like flies around a bulb.

I am dressed like them. Standing with my back turned
I wash the dishes in the same easy way.
Only at birth and death do I utterly fail.

For death is my old friend who waits on the stairs.
Whenever I pass I nod to him like the newsman
who is there every day; for them he is the priest.

While the birth of love is so terrible to me
I feel unworthy of the commonest marriage.
Upstairs she lies, washed through by the two miracles.

---

## IN THE LAST FEW MOMENTS CAME THE OLD GERMAN CLEANING WOMAN

Our last morning in that long room,
Our little world, I could not cry
But went about the senseless chores
—Coffee and eggs and newspapers—
As if your plane would never fly,
As if we were trapped there for all time.

Wanting to fix by ritual
The marriage we could never share

I creaked to stove and back again.
Leaves in the stiffening New York sun
Clattered like plates; the sky was bare—
I tripped and let your full cup fall.

Coffee scalded your wrist and that
Was the first natural grief we knew.
Others followed after years:
Dry fodder swallowed, then the tears
When mop in hand the old world through
The door pressed, dutiful, idiot.

---

# Maxine Kumin

---

## PURGATORY

And suppose the darlings get to Mantua,
suppose they cheat the crypt, what next?
  Begin
with him, unshaven. Through not, I grant
  you, a
displeasing cockerel, there's egg yolk on his
  chin.
His seedy robe's aflap, he's got the rheum.
Poor dear, the cooking lard has smoked her
  eye.

Another Montague is in the womb
although the first babe's bottom's not yet
  dry.
She scrolls a weekly letter to her Nurse
who dares to send a smock through
  Balthasar,
and once a month, his father posts a purse.
News from Verona? Always news of war.
  Such sour years it takes to right this
  wrong!
The fifth act runs unconscionably long.

## FOR MY SON ON THE HIGHWAYS OF HIS MIND

*for Dan*

Today the jailbird maple in the yard
sends down a thousand red hands in the rain.
Trussed at the upstairs window I
watch the great drenched leaves flap by
knowing that on the comely boulevard
incessant in your head you stand again
at the cloverleaf, thumb crooked outward.

Dreaming you travel light
guitar pick and guitar
bedroll sausage-tight
they take you as you are.

They take you as you are
there's nothing left behind
guitar pick and guitar
on the highways of your mind.

Instead you come home with two cops, your bike
lashed to the back of the cruiser because
an old lady, afraid of blacks and boys
with hair like yours, is simon-sure you took
her purse. They search you and of course you're clean.
Later we make it into a family joke,
a poor sort of catharsis. It wasn't the scene
they made—that part you rather enjoyed—
and not the old woman whose money turned up next day
in its usual lunatic place under a platter
but the principle of the thing, to be toyed
with cat and mouse, be one mouse who got away
somehow under the baseboard or radiator
and expect to be caught again sooner or later.

Dreaming you travel light
guitar pick and guitar
bedroll sausage-tight
they take you as you are.

Collar up, your discontent goes wrapped
at all times in the flannel army shirt
your father mustered out in, wars ago,
the ruptured duck still pinned to the pocket flap
and the golden toilet seat—the award his unit
won for making the bomb that killed the Japs—
now rubbed to its earliest threads, an old trousseau.

Meanwhile the posters on your bedroom wall
give up their glue. The corners start to fray.
Belmondo, Brando, Uncle Ho and Che,
last year's giants, hang lop-eared but hang on.
The merit badges, the model airplanes, all
the paraphernalia of a simpler day
gather dust on the shelf. That boy is gone.

They take you as you are
there's nothing left behind
guitar pick and guitar
on the highways of your mind.

How it will be tomorrow is anyone's guess.
The *Rand McNally* opens at a nudge
to forty-eight contiguous states, easy
as a compliant girl. In Minneapolis
I see you drinking wine under a bridge.
I see you turning on in Washington, D.C.,
panhandling in New Orleans, friendless

in Kansas City in an all-night beanery
and mugged on the beach in Venice outside L.A.
They take your watch and wallet and crack your head
as carelessly as an egg. The yolk runs red.
All this I see, or say it's what I see
in leaf fall, in rain, from the top of the stairs today
while your maps, those sweet pastels, lie flat and ready.

Dreaming you travel light
guitar pick and guitar
bedroll sausage-tight
they take you as you are.

They take you as you are
there's nothing left behind
guitar pick and guitar
on the highways of your mind.

---

## A FAMILY MAN

We are talking in bed. You show me snapshots.
Your wallet opens like a salesman's case
on a dog, a frame house hung with shutters
and your eyes reset in a child's face.
Here is your mother standing in full sun
on the veranda back home. She is wearing
what we used to call a washdress. Geraniums
flank her as pious in their bearing
as the soap and water she called down on your head.
We carry around our mothers. But mine is dead.

Out of the celluloid album, cleverly as a shill
you pull an old snap of yourself squatting beside
a stag you shot early in the war in the Black Hills.
The dog tags dangle on your naked chest.
The rifle, broken, lies across your knees.
What do I say to the killer you love best,
that boy-man full of his summer expertise?
I with no place in the file will
wake on dark mornings alone with him in my head.
This is what comes of snapshots. Of talking in bed.

**DONALD JUSTICE**

Donald Justice writes: Born in Miami, Florida, August 12, 1925, of Southern parentage, and brought up there during the depression. Miami, in those days, a quiet half-ruined tropical resort. Music my early interest, and in adolescence had the luck to be taken on as composition pupil by Carl Ruggles, then wintering in Miami. After graduation from the University of Miami—attended on music scholarship—there was the usual wandering around the country before settling down to graduate school (at Chapel Hill) and marriage. Also attended Stanford, where I studied with Yvor Winters, without making it into his inner circle; later took a Ph.D. at Iowa, where some of my teachers were Engle, Shapiro, Lowell, Berryman. Since then have taught at many schools, among them Reed, Missouri, Syracuse, University of California at Irvine. Currently a professor of English in the Writers Workshop at Iowa. Besides my own poems, I've edited *The Collected Poems of Weldon Kees* and coedited *Contemporary French Poetry.*

## AT THE END OF THE AFFAIR

That it should end in an Albert Pick hotel
with the air conditioner gasping like a carp
and the bathroom tap plucking its one-string harp
and the sourmash bond half gone in the open bottle,

that it should end in this stubborn disarray
of stockings and car keys and suitcases,
all the unfoldings that came forth yesterday
now crammed back to overflow their spaces,

considering the hairsbreadth accident of touch
the nightcap leads to—how it protracts
the burst of colors, the sweetgrass of two tongues,
then turns the lock in Hilton or in Sheraton,
in Marriott or Holiday Inn for such
a man and woman—bearing in mind these facts,

better to break glass, sop with towels, tear
snapshots up, pour whiskey down the drain
than reach and tangle in the same old snare
saying the little lies again.

# Donald Justice

## POEM TO BE READ AT 3 A.M.

Excepting the diner
On the outskirts
The town of Ladora
At 3 A.M.
Was dark but
For my headlights
And up in
One second-story room
A single light
Where someone
Was sick or
Perhaps reading
As I drove past
At seventy
Not thinking
This poem
Is for whoever
Had the light on

## THE SNOWFALL

The classic landscapes of dreams are not
More pathless, though footprints leading
    nowhere
Would seem to prove that a people once
Survived for a little even here.

Fragments of a pathetic culture
Remain, the lost mittens of children,
And a single, bright, detasseled snow-cap,
Evidence of some frantic migration.

The landmarks are gone. Nevertheless
There is something familiar about this
    country.
Slowly now we begin to recall

The terrible whispers of our elders
Falling softly about our ears
In childhood, never believed till now.

## BUT THAT IS ANOTHER STORY

I do not think the ending can be right.
How can they marry and live happily
Forever, these who were so passionate
At chapter's end? Once they are settled in
The quiet country house, what will they do,
So many miles from anywhere?
Those blonde ancestral ghosts crowding the stair,
Surely they disapprove? Ah me,
I fear love will catch cold and die
From pacing naked through those drafty halls
Night after night. Poor Frank. Poor Imogene.
Before them now their lives
Stretch empty as great Empire beds
After the lovers rise and the damp sheets
Are stripped by envious chambermaids.

And if the first night passes brightly enough,
What with the bonfires lit with old love letters,
That is no inexhaustible fuel, perhaps?
God knows how it must end, not I.
Will Frank walk out some day
Alone through the ruined orchard with his stick,
Strewing the path with lissome heads
Of buttercups? Will Imogene
Conceal in the crotches of old trees
Love-notes for grizzled gardeners and such?
Meanwhile they quarrel, and make it up,
Only to quarrel again. A sudden storm
Has pulled the fences down. The stupid sheep
Stand out all night now coughing in the garden
And peering through the windows where they sleep.

## THE TOURIST FROM SYRACUSE

*One of those men who can be a car salesman or a*
*tourist from Syracuse or a hired assassin.*
JOHN D. MacDONALD

You would not recognize me.
Mine is the face which blooms in
The dank mirrors of washrooms
As you grope for the light switch.

My eyes have the expression
Of the cold eyes of statues
Watching their pigeons return
From the feed you have scattered,

And I stand on my corner
With the same marble patience.
If I move at all, it is
At the same pace precisely

As the shade of the awning
Under which I stand waiting

And with whose blackness it seems
I am already blended.

I speak seldom, and always
In a murmur as quiet
As that of crowds which surround
The victims of accidents.

Shall I confess who I am?
My name is all names and none.
I am the used-car salesman,
The tourist from Syracuse,

The hired assassin, waiting.
I will stand here forever
Like one who has missed his bus—
Familiar, anonymous—

On my usual corner,
The corner at which you turn
To approach that place where now
You must not hope to arrive.

# Robert Canzoneri

**ROBERT CANZONERI**

Robert Canzoneri was born on November 21, 1925, in San Marcos, Texas, but left at the age of two months and has spent much of the rest of his life in and around Mississippi. For the past several years, however, he and his wife and two children have lived in California and, currently, in Ohio, where he is professor of English at Ohio State University. He holds degrees from Mississippi College, the University of Mississippi, and Stanford University. In addition to his poetry, Canzoneri has published a novel, a book of short stories, a nonfiction book entitled *I Do So Politely: A Voice from the South,* and, with Page Stegner, a textbook introduction to fiction. Currently, he is working on his poems and short stories, rewriting a novel, writing a critical book and two textbooks, planning a volume on Sicily and America, and doing background work on a couple of plays.

## THE UNLOVED

When I would squat by holes and piles of dirt
crumbling clods, ready to insert
bare roots of shrubs, she'd soil my vegetable dreams:
this adolescent dog approaching albino
would worm under my arm with motive I know
too but bury in pride, curl both head
and tail toward me begging to be fed
love at both extremes.

Neither was an end unto itself, or
small dogs one might do as well for;
a car front struck her fore part like a match
that spurts red fire and dies, curdled a batch
of blood out from one end and knocked
oval feces out the other. Shocked,
arrested at the waste, I swore a herbist
vow; but now I felt the still unserviced
bitch for lack of pulse and breath. I coiled
her limp into a hamper, saw it soiled
with drying blood. She stiffened in a curl,
never having learned a nicer girl
could hope to stay unspaded, yet behave.
With too much heat I dug a rounded grave.

## ONE LION, ONCE

Ho, Androcles!
What do you say went on
From when the lion scratched off in the dust
Toward you as meat and bone
And, roaring to his lean and hungry guts
The end of grumbling wait,
Bore down? What shifted in those preying eyes
As, closing, you grew featured
And the features made a face? What lies
Would not reach truth too late
But failed the heated lion's sight, as face
Became not one man's meat,
But Androcles?
We could ask Plato, looking back, to place
The abstract qualities
Of this into a scheme: how many rungs
Of love a beast can seize
In one great charge, to land (with rasping lungs
And flesh starved to his bones)
Muzzling like a milk-fed cat at ease
Against you on your knees.

# W. D. Snodgrass

**W. D. SNODGRASS**
Born in Wilkinsburg, Pennsylvania, on January 5, 1926, W. D. Snodgrass moved with his family shortly thereafter to Beaver Falls, Pennsylvania, where he later spent one year at Geneva College before joining the Navy. After the war he studied Renaissance literature and wrote poetry at the State University of Iowa in Iowa City. After receiving his B.A., M.A., and M.F.A. there, he joined the English faculty at Cornell University in 1955. He has since taught at the University of Rochester, Wayne State University, and Syracuse University. His first book, *Heart's Needle*, was highly praised and received the 1961 Pulitzer Prize. His other awards include a *Hudson Review* Fellowship and a National Institute of Arts and Letters Grant. He lives with his wife and children in Erieville, New York.

## from HEART'S NEEDLE

*—for Cynthia*

**2**

Late April and you are three; today
   We dug your garden in the yard.
To curb the damage of your play,
Strange dogs at night and the moles tunneling,
   Four slender sticks of lath stand guard
      Uplifting their thin string.

So you were the first to tramp it down.
   And after the earth was sifted close
You brought your watering can to drown
All earth *and* us. But these mixed seeds are pressed
   With light loam in their steadfast rows.
      Child, we've done our best.

Someone will have to weed and spread
   The young sprouts. Sprinkle them in the hour
When shadow falls across their bed.
You should try to look at them every day
   Because when they come to full flower
      I will be away.

**4**

No one can tell you why
the season will not wait;
   the night I told you I
must leave, you wept a fearful rate
      to stay up late.

Now that it's turning Fall,
we go to take our walk
   among municipal
flowers, to steal one off its stalk,
      to try and talk.

We huff like windy giants
scattering with our breath
   grey-headed dandelions;
Spring is the cold Wind's aftermath.
      The poet saith.

But the asters, too, are grey,
ghost-grey. Last night's cold
   is sending on their way
petunias and dwarf marigold,
      hunched sick and old.

Like nerves caught in a graph,
the morning-glory vines
   frost has erased by half
still crawl over their rigid twines.
      Like broken lines

of verses I can't make.
In its unravelling loom
   we find a flower to take,
with some late buds that might still bloom
      back to your room.

Night comes and the stiff dew.
I'm told a friend's child cried
   because a cricket, who
had minstrelled every night outside
      her window, died.

MEMENTOS, 1

Sorting out letters and piles of my old
    Canceled checks, old clippings, and yellow note cards
That meant something once, I happened to find
    Your picture. *That* picture. I stopped there cold,
Like a man raking piles of dead leaves in his yard
        Who has turned up a severed hand.

Still, that first second, I was glad: you stand
    Just as you stood—shy, delicate, slender,
In that long gown of green lace netting and daisies
    That you wore to our first dance. The sight of you stunned
Us all. Well, our needs were different, then,
        And our ideals came easy.

Then through the war and those two long years
    Overseas, the Japanese dead in their shacks
Among dishes, dolls, and lost shoes; I carried
    This glimpse of you, there, to choke down my fear,
Prove it had been, that it might come back.
        That was before we got married.

—Before we drained out one another's force
    With lies, self-denial, unspoken regret
And the sick eyes that blame; before the divorce
    And the treachery. Say it: before we met. Still,
I put back your picture. Someday, in due course,
        I will find that it's still there.

---

MEMENTOS, 2

I found them there today
in the third-floor closet,
packed away
among our wedding gifts
under the thick deposit
of black coal dust that sifts
down with the months:
that long white satin gown
and the heavy lead-foil crown
that you wore once
when you were Queen of the May,
the goddess of our town.

That brilliant hour
you stood, exquisite, tall,
for the imperious Power
that drives and presses all
seed and the buried roots
to rise from the dead year.
I saw your hair,
the beauty that would fall
to the boy who won you. Today,
I wondered where,
in what dark, your wedding suit
lies packed away.

How proud I was to gain you!
No one could warn
me of the pride or of
the fear my love might stain you
that would turn your face to scorn—
of the fear you could not love
that would tease and haunt you
till all that made me want you
would gall you like a crown
of flowering thorn.
My love hung like a gown
of lead that pulled you down.

I saw you there once, later—
the hair and the eyes dull,
a grayness in the face—
a woman with a daughter
alone in the old place.
Yet the desire remains:
for times when the right boys sought you;
to be courted, like a girl.
I thought of our years; thought you
had had enough of pain;
thought how much grief I'd brought you;
I wished you well again.

# A. R. Ammons

## HYMN

I know if I find you I will have to leave the earth
and go on out
   over the sea marshes and the brant in bays
and over the hills of tall hickory
and over the crater lakes and canyons
and on up through the spheres of diminishing air
past the blackset noctilucent clouds
      where one wants to stop and look
way past all the light diffusions and bombardments
up farther than the loss of sight
   into the unseasonal undifferentiated empty stark

And I know if I find you I will have to stay with the earth
inspecting with thin tools and ground eyes
trusting the microvilli sporangia and simplest
   coelenterates
and praying for a nerve cell
with all the soul of my chemical reactions
and going right on down where the eye sees only traces

You are everywhere partial and entire
You are on the inside of everything and on the outside

I walk down the path down the hill where the sweetgum
has begun to ooze spring sap at the cut
and I see how the bark cracks and winds like no other bark
chasmal to my ant-soul running up and down
and if I find you I must go out deep into your
   far resolutions
and if I find you I must stay here with the separate leaves

**A. R. AMMONS**

A. R. Ammons was born on February 18, 1926, in Whiteville, North Carolina. He writes: I was born in the sixteenth century approximately (represented by 1926) on a farm in the low-south country of North Carolina. We had fifty acres, half clear, half woods and swamp. Randolph Ammons, my paternal grandfather, died three years before I was born, widowing my grandmother Eliza Williams Ammons who held a lifetime right to our place and who died when I was eleven. There were my father Willie, my mother Lucy Della McKee Ammons, now both dead, and my two sisters, and Sally Tyree, an old woman who had been with our family for many years. There were dogs and cats, Doll (the cow), and Silver (the mule), mockingbirds, bluebirds, hawks, biddies, sows and pigs, guineas, pear and pecan and apple and persimmon trees, and a Milky Way clear enough to shine its dust. Tobacco, strawberries, corn, watermelons, Kentucky wonders, plenty to do, and little to spend.

## IDENTITY

   1) an individual spider web
      identifies a species:

an order of instinct prevails
   through all accidents of circumstance,

     though possibility is
high along the peripheries of
spider

       webs:
         you can go all
       around the fringing attachments

     and find
disorder ripe,
   entropy rich, high levels of random,
     numerous occasions of accident

   2) the possible settings
     of a web are infinite:

   how does
the spider keep
    identity
   while creating the web
   in a particular place?

   how and to what extent
     and by what modes of chemistry
     and control?

it is
wonderful
   how things work: I will tell you
      about it
      because

it is interesting
and because whatever is
moves in weeds
     and blood and spider webs
and known
          is loved
     and in that love,
     each of us knowing it,
     I love you,

for how it moves beyond us,
     sizzles in
winter grasses, darts and hangs with bumblebees
by summer windowsills!

     I will show you
the underlying that takes no image of itself
but weaves in and out of moons and bladderweeds
         and is all and
     beyond destruction
     because created fully in no
particular form:

         if the web were perfectly pre-set,
         the spider would
   never find
     a perfect place to set in it: and
         if the web were

perfectly adaptable,
if freedom and possibility were without limit,
      . the web would
lose its special identity:

         the row-strung garden web
     keeps order at the center
     where space is freest (interesting that the freest
         "medium" should
         accept the firmest order)

   and that
   order
           diminishes toward the
periphery
     allowing at the points of contact
         entropy equal to entropy.

## CASCADILLA FALLS

I went down by Cascadilla
Falls this
evening, the
stream below the falls,
and picked up a
handsized stone
kidney-shaped, testicular, and

throught all its motions into it,
the 800 mph earth spin,
the 190-million-mile yearly
displacement around the sun,
the overriding
grand
haul

of the galaxy with the 30,000
mph of where
the sun's going:
thought all the interweaving
motions
into myself: dropped

the stone to dead rest:
the stream from other motions
broke
rushing over it:
shelterless,
I turned

to the sky and stood still:
oh
I do
not know where I am going
that I can live my life
by this single creek.

# James Merrill

**JAMES MERRILL**

James Merrill was born on March 3, 1926, in New York City. He attended Lawrenceville and after service in the Army in World War II graduated from Amherst College. Among the honors he has received for his poetry are the Oscar Blumenthal Prize in 1947, the Levinson Prize in 1949, and the Harriet Monroe Prize in 1951, all from *Poetry*. He also won the National Book Award in 1967 for *Nights and Days*. Besides his poetry, he has written two plays and two novels. He lives in Stonington, Connecticut.

## A RENEWAL

Having used every subterfuge
To shake you, lies, fatigue, or even that of passion,
Now I see no way but a clean break.
I add that I am willing to bear the guilt.

You nod assent. Autumn turns windy, huge,
A clear vase of dry leaves vibrating on and on.
We sit, watching. When I next speak
Love buries itself in me, up to the hilt.

## THE WORLD AND THE CHILD

Letting his wisdom be the whole of love,
The father tiptoes out, backwards. A gleam
Falls on the child awake and wearied of,

Then, as the door clicks shut, is snuffed. The glove-
Gray afterglow appalls him. It would seem
That letting wisdom be the whole of love

Were pastime even for the bitter grove
Outside, whose owl's white hoot of disesteem
Falls on the child awake and wearied of.

He lies awake in pain, he does not move,
He will not scream. Any who heard him scream
Would let their wisdom be the whole of love.

People have filled the room he lies above.
Their talk, mild variation, chilling theme,
Falls on the child. Awake and wearied of

Mere pain, mere wisdom also, he would have
All the world waking from its winter dream,
Letting its wisdom be. The whole of love
Falls on the child awake and wearied of.

## THE MAD SCENE

Again last night I dreamed the dream called Laundry.
In it, the sheets and towels of a life we were going to share,
The milk-stiff bibs, the shroud, each rag to be ever
Trampled or soiled, bled on or groped for blindly,
Came swooning out of an enormous willow hamper
Onto moon-marbly boards. We had just met. I watched
From outer darkness. I had dressed myself in clothes
Of a new fiber that never stains or wrinkles, never
Wears thin. The opera house sparkled with tiers
And tiers of eyes, like mine enlarged by belladonna,
Trained inward. There I saw the cloud-clot, gust by gust,
Form, and the lightning bite, and the roan mane unloosen.
Fingers were running in panic over the flute's nine gates.
Why did I flinch? I loved you. And in the downpour laughed
To have us wrung white, gnarled together, one
Topmost mordent of wisteria,
As the lean tree burst into grief.

# Robert Creeley

**ROBERT CREELEY**

Robert Creeley was born in Arlington, Massachusetts, on May 21, 1926. He attended Harvard for a while, leaving during World War II to join the American Field Service, with which he served in India and Burma. He returned to Harvard after the war only to leave again shortly before graduation. He received his B.A. in 1955 from Black Mountain College, Black Mountain, North Carolina, and his M.A. in 1960 from the University of New Mexico. After spending some time in France and Spain, he joined the faculty of Black Mountain College, where he taught writing and edited the *Black Mountain Review.* Married and the father of three children, he now teaches English at the State University of New York at Buffalo.

## THE WARNING

For love—I would
split open your head and put
a candle in
behind the eyes.

Love is dead in us
if we forget
the virtues of an amulet
and quick surprise.

## A COUNTERPOINT

Let me be my own fool
of my own making, the sum of it

is equivocal.
One says of the drunken farmer:

leave him lay off it. And this is
the explanation.

## THE WINDOW

Position is where you
put it, where it is,
did you, for example, that

large tank there, silvered,
with the white church along-
side, lift

all that, to what
purpose? How
heavy the slow

world is with
everything put
in place. Some

man walks by, a
car beside him on
the dropped

road, a leaf of
yellow color is
going to

fall. It
all drops into
place. My

face is heavy
with the sight. I can
feel my eye breaking.

## I KNOW A MAN

As I sd to my
friend, because I am
always talking,—John, I

sd, which was not his
name, the darkness sur-
rounds us, what

can we do against
it, or else, shall we &
why not, buy a goddamn big car,
drive, he sd, for
christ's sake, look
out where yr going.

# Allen Ginsberg

## HOWL

*for Carl Solomon*

**I**

I saw the best minds of my generation destroyed by madness, starving hysterical naked,
dragging themselves through the negro streets at dawn looking for an angry fix,
angelheaded hipsters burning for the ancient heavenly connection to the starry dynamo in
   the machinery of night,
who poverty and tatters and hollow-eyed and high sat up smoking in the supernatural
   darkness of cold-water flats floating across the tops of cities contemplating jazz,
who bared their brains to Heaven under the El and saw Mohammedan angels staggering on
   tenement roofs illuminated,
who passed through universities with radiant cool eyes hallucinating Arkansas and Blake-
   light tragedy among the scholars of war,
who were expelled from the academies for crazy & publishing obscene odes on the
   windows of the skull,
who cowered in unshaven rooms in underwear, burning their money in wastebaskets and
   listening to the Terror through the wall,
who got busted in their pubic beards returning through Laredo with a belt of marijuana
   for New York,
who ate fire in paint hotels or drank turpentine in Paradise Alley, death, or purgatoried
   their torsos night after night
with dreams, with drugs, with waking nightmares, alcohol and cock and endless balls,
incomparable blind streets of shuddering cloud and lightning in the mind leaping
   toward poles of Canada & Paterson, illuminating all the motionless world of Time
   between,
Peyote solidities of halls, backyard green tree cemetery dawns, wine drunkenness over the
   rooftops, storefront boroughs of teahead joyride neon blinking traffic light, sun and
   moon and tree vibrations in the roaring winter dusks of Brooklyn, ashcan rantings and
   kind king light of mind,
who chained themselves to subways for the endless ride from Battery to holy Bronx on
   benzedrine until the noise of wheels and children brought them down shuddering
   mouth-wracked and battered bleak of brain all drained of brilliance in the drear light of
   Zoo,
who sank all night in submarine light of Bickford's floated out and sat through the stale
   beer afternoon in desolate Fugazzi's, listening to the crack of doom on the hydrogen
   jukebox,
who talked continuously seventy hours from park to pad to bar to Bellevue to museum to
   the Brooklyn Bridge,
a lost battalion of platonic conversationalists jumping down the stoops off fire escapes off
   windowsills off Empire State out of the moon,
yacketayakking screaming vomiting whispering facts and memories and anecdotes and
   eyeball kicks and shocks of hospitals and jails and wars,
whole intellects disgorged in total recall for seven days and nights with brilliant eyes,
   meat for the Synagogue cast on the pavement,
who vanished into nowhere Zen New Jersey leaving a trail of ambiguous picture postcards
   of Atlantic City Hall,
suffering Eastern sweats and Tangerian bone-grindings and migraines of China under junk-
   withdrawal in Newark's bleak furnished room,

**ALLEN GINSBERG**

Allen Ginsberg was born on June 3, 1926 in Newark, New Jersey. He writes: Grammar High School Paterson New Jersey, B.A. Columbia College 1948; associations with Jack Kerouac, Wm. S. Burroughs, Herbert H. Huncke & Neal Cassidy begun 1945 NYC and next decade after with Gregory Corso, Peter Orlovsky companion 1954 & poets Michael McClure Philip Lamantia Gary Snyder & Philip Whalen in San Francisco became known 1955 on as "Beat Generation" and/or "San Francisco Renaissance" literary phases; acquaintance with William Carlos Williams 1948 & study of his relative-footed American speech prosody led to *Empty Mirror* early poems with W.C.W. preface, as later Williams introduced *Howl*.... Travel began early 1950's half year Mayan Mexico, several voyages years Tangiers-Europe late 50's on, earlier merchant marine sea trips to Africa & Arctic, half year Chile Bolivia & Peru Amazon 1960, half year Cuba Russia Poland Czechoslovakia culminating May Day 1965 election as King of May (Kral Majales) by 100,000 Prague young citizens. Literary Awards: obscenity trial with *Howl* text declared legal by court S.F. 1957, Guggenheim Fellowship 1963–4, National Institute of Arts and Letters Grant for poetry 1969. . . . Attended mantra-chanting at first Human Be-in San Francisco 1967; conferred at *Dialectics of Liberation* in London & gave poetry readings with poet father Louis Ginsberg there & NY; testified U.S. Senate hearings for legalization of psychedelics; arrested with Dr. Spock blocking Whitehall Draft Board steps war protest NY same year. Teargassed chanting AUM at Lincoln Park Yippie Life-Festival Chicago 1968 Presidential convention, then accompanied Jean Genet & William Burroughs on front line "Conspiracy" march led by Dave Dellinger. Mantric poetics and passing acquaintance with poet-singers Ezra Pound, Bob Dylan, Ed Sanders, Paul McCartney & Mick Jagger led to music study for tunes to Wm. Blake's *Songs of Innocence and Experience:* this homage to visionary poet-guru William Blake, occasioned by visit West Coast to touch a satin bag of body-ashes the late much-loved Neal Cassidy, & composed one week on return from police-state shock in Chicago, was recorded summer 1969 Aetat 43. Chanted Om to Judge & Jury December 1969 Anti-War-Conspiracy trial Chicago; thereafter interrupted by Miami Police on reading poetry exorcising police bureaucracy Prague & Pentagon, rapid Federal Court Mandatory Injunction declared police texts Constitutionally protected from police censorship. Pallbore funerals late Kerouac & Olson, last few winters spent outside cities learning music milking cows & goats.

who wandered around and around at midnight in the railroad yard wondering where to go, and went, leaving no broken hearts,

who lit cigarettes in boxcars boxcars boxcars racketing through snow toward lonesome farms in grandfather night,

who studied Plotinus Poe St. John of the Cross telepathy and bop kaballa because the cosmos instinctively vibrated at their feet in Kansas,

who loned it through the streets of Idaho seeking visionary indian angels who were visionary indian angels,

who thought they were only mad when Baltimore gleamed in supernatural ecstasy,

who jumped in limousines with the Chinaman of Oklahoma on the impulse of winter midnight streetlight smalltown rain,

who lounged hungry and lonesome through Houston seeking jazz or sex or soup, and followed the brilliant Spaniard to converse about America and Eternity, a hopeless task, and so took ship to Africa,

who disappeared into the volcanoes of Mexico leaving behind nothing but the shadow of dungarees and the lava and ash of poetry scattered in fireplace Chicago,

who reappeared on the West Coast investigating the F.B.I. in beards and shorts with big pacifist eyes sexy in their dark skin passing out incomprehensible leaflets,

who burned cigarette holes in their arms protesting the narcotic tobacco haze of Capitalism,

who distributed Supercommunist pamphlets in Union Square weeping and undressing while the sirens of Los Alamos wailed them down, and wailed down Wall, and the Staten Island ferry also wailed,

who broke down crying in white gymnasiums naked and trembling before the machinery of other skeletons,

who bit detectives in the neck and shrieked with delight in policecars for committing no crime but their own wild cooking pederasty and intoxication,

who howled on their knees in the subway and were dragged off the roof waving genitals and manuscripts,

who let themselves be fucked in the ass by saintly motorcyclists, and screamed with joy,

who blew and were blown by those human seraphim, the sailors, caresses of Atlantic and Caribbean love,

who balled in the morning in the evenings in rosegardens and the grass of public parks and cemeteries scattering their semen freely to whomever come who may,

who hiccupped endlessly trying to giggle but wound up with a sob behind a partition in a Turkish Bath when the blonde & naked angel came to pierce them with a sword,

who lost their loveboys to the three old shrews of fate the one eyed shrew of the heterosexual dollar the one eyed shrew that winks out of the womb and the one eyed shrew that does nothing but sit on her ass and snip the intellectual golden threads of the craftsman's loom,

who copulated ecstatic and insatiate with a bottle of beer a sweetheart a package of cigarettes a candle and fell off the bed, and continued along the floor and down the hall and ended fainting on the wall with a vision of ultimate cunt and come eluding the lazy gyzym of consciousness,

who sweetened the snatches of a million girls trembling in the sunset, and were red eyed in the morning but prepared to sweeten the snatch of the sunrise, flashing buttocks under barns and naked in the lake,

who went out whoring through Colorado in myriad stolen night-cars, N.C., secret hero of these poems, cocksman and Adonis of Denver—joy to the memory of his innumerable lays of girls in empty lots & diner backyards, moviehouses' rickety rows, on mountaintops in caves or with gaunt waitresses in familiar roadside lonely petticoat upliftings & especially secret gas-station solipsisms of johns, & hometown alleys too,

who faded out in vast sordid movies, were shifted in dreams, woke on a sudden Manhattan, and picked themselves up out of basements hungover with heartless Tokay and horrors of Third Avenue iron dreams & stumbled to unemployment offices,

who walked all night with their shoes full of blood on the snowbank docks waiting for a
   door in the East River to open to a room full of steamheat and opium,
who created great suicidal dramas on the apartment cliff-banks of the Hudson under the
   wartime blue floodlight of the moon & their heads shall be crowned with laurel in oblivion,
who ate the lamb stew of the imagination or digested the crab at the muddy bottom of the
   rivers of Bowery,
who wept at the romance of the streets with their pushcarts full of onions and bad music,
who sat in boxes breathing in the darkness under the bridge, and rose up to build
   harpsichords in their lofts,
who coughed on the sixth floor of Harlem crowned with flame under the tubercular sky
   surrounded by orange crates of theology,
who scribbled all night rocking and rolling over lofty incantations which in the yellow
   morning were stanzas of gibberish,
who cooked rotten animals lung heart feet tail borsht & tortillas dreaming of the pure
   vegetable kingdom,
who plunged themselves under meat trucks looking for an egg,
who threw their watches off the roof to cast their ballot for  Eternity outside of Time,
    & alarm clocks fell on their heads every day for the next decade,
who cut their wrists three times successively unsuccessfully, gave up and were forced to
   open antique stores where they thought they were growing old and cried,
who were burned alive in their innocent flannel suits on Madison Avenue amid blasts of
   leaden verse & the tanked-up clatter of the iron regiments of fashion & the nitroglycerine
   shrieks of the fairies of advertising & the mustard gas of sinister intelligent editors, or
   were run down by the drunken taxicabs of Absolute Reality,
who jumped off the Brooklyn Bridge this actually happened and walked away unknown
   and forgotten into the ghostly daze of Chinatown soup alleyways & firetrucks, not even
   one free beer,
who sang out of their windows in despair, fell out of the subway window, jumped in the
   filthy Passaic, leaped on negroes, cried all over the street, danced on broken wineglasses
   barefoot smashed phonograph records of nostalgic European 1930's German jazz
   finished the whiskey and threw up groaning into the bloody toilet, moans in their ears
   and the blast of colossal steamwhistles,
who barreled down the highways of the past journeying to each other's hotrod-Golgotha
   jail-solitude watch or Birmingham jazz incarnation,
who drove crosscountry seventytwo hours to find out if I had a vision or you had a
   vision or he had a vision to find out Eternity,
who journeyed to Denver, who died in Denver, who came back to Denver & waited in
   vain, who watched over Denver & brooded & loned in Denver and finally went away
   to find out the Time, & now Denver is lonesome for her heroes,
who fell on their knees in hopeless cathedrals praying for each other's salvation and light
   and breasts, until the soul illuminated its hair for a second,
who crashed through their minds in jail waiting for impossible criminals with golden heads
   and the charm of reality in their hearts who sang sweet blues to Alcatraz,
who retired to Mexico to cultivate a habit, or Rocky Mount to tender Buddha or Tangiers
   to boys or Southern Pacific to the black locomotive or Harvard to Narcissus to
   Woodlawn to the daisychain or grave,
who demanded sanity trials accusing the radio of hypnotism & were left with their
   insanity & their hands & a hung jury,
who threw potato salad at CCNY lecturers on Dadaism and subsequently presented
   themselves on the granite steps of the madhouse with shaven heads and harlequin speech
   of suicide, demanding instantaneous lobotomy,
and who were given instead the concrete void of insulin metrasol electricity hydrotherapy
   psychotherapy occupational therapy pingpong & amnesia,
who in humorless protest overturned only one symbolic pingpong table, resting briefly
   in catatonia,

returning years later truly bald except for a wig of blood, and tears and fingers, to the
  visible madman doom of the wards of the madtowns of the East,
Pilgrim State's Rockland's and Greystone's foetid halls, bickering with the echoes of the
  soul, rocking and rolling in the midnight solitude-bench dolmen-realms of love, dream of
  life a nightmare, bodies turned to stone as heavy as the moon,
with mother finally ******, and the last fantastic book flung out of the tenement
  window, and the last door closed at 4 AM and the last telephone slammed at the wall in
  reply and the last furnished room emptied down to the last piece of mental furniture,
  a yellow paper rose twisted on a wire hanger in the closet, and even that imaginary,
  nothing but a hopeful little bit of hallucination—

ah, Carl, while you are not safe I am not safe, and now you're really in the total animal
  soup of time—
and who therefore ran though the icy streets obsessed with a sudden flash of the alchemy
  of the use of the ellipse the catalog the meter & the vibrating plane,
who dreamt and made incarnate gaps in Time & Space through images juxtaposed, and
  trapped the archangel of the soul between 2 visual images and joined the elemental verbs
  and set the noun and dash of consciousness together jumping with sensation of Pater
  Omnipotens Aeterna Deus
to recreate the syntax and measure of poor human prose and stand before you speechless
  and intelligent and shaking with shame, rejected yet confessing out the soul to conform
  to the rhythm of thought in his naked and endless head,
the madman bum and angel beat in Time, unknown, yet putting down here what might be
  left to say in time come after death,
and rose reincarnate in the ghostly clothes of jazz in the goldhorn shadow of the band and
  blew the suffering of America's naked mind for love into an eli eli lamma lamma
  sabacthani saxophone cry that shivered the cities down to the last radio
with the absolute heart of the poem of life butchered out of their own bodies good to eat
  a thousand years.

---

## THE SHROUDED STRANGER

Bare skin is my wrinkled sack
When hot Apollo humps my back
When Jack Frost grabs me in these rags
I wrap my legs with burlap bags

My flesh is cinder my face is snow
I walk the railroad to and fro
When city streets are black and dead
The railroad embankment is my bed

I sup my soup from old tin cans
And take my sweets from little hands
In Tiger Alley near the jail
I steal away from the garbage pail

In darkest night where none can see
Down in the bowels of the factory
I sneak barefoot upon stone
Come and hear the old man groan

I hide and wait like a naked child
Under the bridge my heart goes wild
I scream at a fire on the river bank
I give my body to an old gas tank

I dream that I have burning hair
Boiled arms that claw the air
The torso of an iron king
And on my back a broken wing

Who'll go out whoring into the night
On the eyeless road in the skinny moonlight
Maid or dowd or athlete proud
May wanton with me in the shroud

Who'll come lay down in the dark with me
Belly to belly and knee to knee
Who'll look into my hooded eye
Who'll lay down under my darkened thigh?

*1949*

96

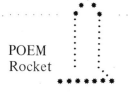

POEM
Rocket

*'Be a Star-screwer!'* –Gregory Corso

Old moon my eyes are new moon with human footprint
no longer Romeo Sadface in drunken river Loony Pierre eyebrow, goof moon
O possible moon in Heaven we get to first of ageless constellations of names
as God is possible as All is possible so we'll reach another life.

Moon politicians earth weeping and warring in eternity
tho not one star disturbed by screaming madmen from Hollywood
oil tycoons from Romania making secret deals with flabby green Plutonians—
slave camps on Saturn Cuban revolutions on Mars?
Old life and new side by side, will Catholic church find Christ on Jupiter
Mohammed rave in Uranus will Buddha be acceptable on the stolid planets
or will we find Zoroastrian temples flowering on Neptune?
What monstrous new ecclesiastical design on the entire universe unfolds in the dying Pope's brain?
Scientist alone is true poet he gives us the moon
he promises the stars he'll make us a new universe if it comes to that
O Einstein I should have sent you my flaming mss.
O Einstein I should have pilgrimaged to your white hair!

O fellow travellers I write you a poem in Amsterdam in the Cosmos
where Spinoza ground his magic lenses long ago
I write you a poem long ago
already my feet are washed in death
Here I am naked without identity
with no more body than the fine black tracery of pen mark on soft paper
as star talks to star multiple beams of sunlight all the same myriad thought
in one fold of the universe where Whitman was
and Blake and Shelley saw Milton dwelling as in a starry temple
brooding in his blindness seeing all—
Now at last I can speak to you beloved brothers of an unknown moon
real Yous squatting in whatever form amidst Platonic Vapors of Eternity
I am another Star.
Will you eat my poems or read them
or gaze  with aluminum blind plates on sunless pages?
do you dream or translate & accept data with indifferent droopings of antennae?
do I make sense to your flowery green receptor eyesockets? do you have visions of God?
Which way will the sunflower turn surrounded by millions of suns?

This is my rocket my personal rocket I send up my message Beyond
Someone to hear me there
My immortality
without steel or cobalt basalt or diamond gold or mercurial fire
without passports filing cabinets bits of paper warheads
without myself finally
pure thought
message all and everywhere the same
I send up my rocket to land on whatever planet awaits it
preferably religious sweet planets no money
fourth dimensional planets where Death shows movies
plants speak (courteously) of ancient physics and poetry itself is manufactured by the trees
the final Planet where the Great Brain of the Universe sits waiting for a poem to land in His golden pocket
joining the other notes mash-notes love-sighs complaints-musical shrieks of despair and the
    millon unutterable thoughts of frogs

**DAVID WAGONER**

David Wagoner writes: I was born
June 5, 1926 in Massillon, Ohio,
and grew up (I hope) in Whiting,
Indiana, an industrial suburb of
Chicago. I graduated from Penn
State and Indiana Universities,
have taught English at DePauw
Univ., Penn State, and since 1954
at the Univ. of Washington where
I'm now a full professor and editor
of *Poetry Northwest.* I've pub-
lished six novels, the most re-
cent of which is *Where Is My
Wandering Boy Tonight?,* Farrar,
Straus & Giroux, 1970, and five
books of poems, the most recent
of which is *New and Selected
Poems,* Indiana Univ. Press, 1969.
A sixth book of poems, *Riverbed,*
will be published in 1972. I have
been editing the notebooks of
Theodore Roethke, who was a
teacher of mine at Penn State in
1947 and a colleague at the Univ.
of Washington from 1954 till his
death in 1963, and Doubleday will
publish the results in 1972, titled
*Straw for the Fire.* He was a form-
ative influence on me. My wife
Patt and I live daily and gladly
in the Northwest.

I send you my rocket of amazing chemical
more than my hair my sperm or the cells of my body
the speeding thought that flies upward with my desire as instantaneous as the universe and
    faster than light
and leave all other questions unfinished for the moment to turn back to sleep in my dark
    bed on earth.

*Amsterdam, 1958*

## A SUPERMARKET IN CALIFORNIA

What thoughts I have of you tonight, Walt Whitman, for I walked down the
sidestreets under the trees with a headache self-conscious looking at the full moon.

In my hungry fatigue, and shopping for images, I went into the neon fruit
supermarket, dreaming of your enumerations!

What peaches and what penumbras! Whole families shopping at night! Aisles full of
husbands! Wives in the avocados, babies in the tomatoes!— and you, Garcia Lorca, what
were you doing down by the watermelons?

I saw you, Walt Whitman, childless, lonely old grubber, poking among the meats in
the refrigerator and eyeing the grocery boys.

I heard you asking questions of each: Who killed the pork chops? What price
bananas? Are you my Angel?

I wandered in and out of the brilliant stacks of cans following you, and followed in
my imagination by the store detective.

We strode down the open corridors together in our solitary fancy tasting artichokes,
possessing every frozen delicacy, and never passing the cashier.

Where are we going, Walt Whitman? The doors close in an hour. Which way does
your beard point tonight?

(I touch your book and dream of our odyssey in the supermarket and feel absurd.)

Will we walk all night through solitary streets? The trees add shade to shade, lights
out in the houses, we'll both be lonely.

Will we stroll dreaming of the lost America of love past blue automobiles in
driveways, home to our silent cottage?

Ah, dear father, graybeard, lonely old courage-teacher, what America did you have
when Charon quit poling his ferry and you got out on a smoking bank and stood watching
the boat disappear on the black waters of Lethe?

*Berkeley, 1955*

# David Wagoner

## THE BURGLAR

Being a burglar, you slip out of doors in the morning
And look at the street by looking at the sky,
Not being taken in by anything blue.
You must look to the left or right to see across.
If nothing strikes your eye, if no one comes running,
You've stolen another day.

You must spend it on your toes
At the edges of buildings, doorways, and windows

Wherever no one is watching close enough.
Keep your fingers light as smoke.
You may have permission to kiss with one eye open.
Try every door while leaning away from it.

But sundown is serious; it's time to go home
To the house that will draw you under its empty wing.
Climbing like ivy up the drains, go through
The furthest window into a dark room.
Wait there to hear how everything has gone.
Then, masking every motion,

Glide to the stairwell.
They will be eating dinner: the man and the woman
At opposite ends of a white and silver table;
Between them, food and candles and children.
Their knives and forks go in and out of their mouths;
Whatever they do will aim them toward each other.

Now, follow your fingerprints around all corners
From nightlatch to velvet lid, from hasp to stone.
Everything locked, of course, has been locked for you:
You must break in softly, take whatever you find
Whether you understand what it is or not.
Breathe in, reach out,

Stealing one thing at a time.
If you grow hungry, thinking of their desserts,
It's time to vanish over the windowsill.
You must go without their dinner into the night,
Not saying goodbye, not waiting to scrawl a note
To say you're running away, but running away.

## LEAVING SOMETHING BEHIND

A fox at your neck and snakeskin on your feet,
You have gone to the city behind an ivory brooch,
Wearing your charms for and against desire, bearing your
    beauty
Past all the gaping doorways, amazing women on edge
And leading men's eyes astray while skirting mayhem,
And I, for a day, must wish you safe in your skin.

The diggers named her the Minnesota Girl. She was fifteen,
Eight thousand years ago, when she drowned in a glacial
    lake,
Curling to sleep like her sea-snail amulet, holding a turtleshell,
A wolf's tooth, the tine of an antler, carrying somehow
A dozen bones from the feet of water birds. She believed
    in her charms,
But something found her and kept her. She became what
    she wore.

She loved her bones and her own husk of creatures
But left them piecemeal on the branching shore.
Without you, fox paws, elephant haunches, all rattling tails,
Snails' feet, turtles' remote hearts, muzzles of wolves,

Stags' ears, and the tongues of water birds are only
    themselves.
Come safely back. There was nothing in her arms.

## THE POETS AGREE TO BE QUIET BY THE SWAMP

They hold their hands over their mouths
And stare at the stretch of water.
What can be said has been said before:
Strokes of light like herons' legs in the cattails,
Mud underneath, frogs lying even deeper.
Therefore, the poets may keep quiet.
But the corners of their mouths grin past their hands.
They stick their elbows out into the evening,
Stoop, and begin the ancient croaking.

## STAYING ALIVE

Staying alive in the woods is a matter of calming down
At first and deciding whether to wait for rescue,
Trusting to others,
Or simply to start walking and walking in one direction
Till you come out—or something happens to stop you.
By far the safer choice
Is to settle down where you are, and try to make a living
Off the land, camping near water, away from shadows.
Eat no white berries;
Spit out all bitterness. Shooting at anything
Means hiking further and further every day
To hunt survivors;
It may be best to learn what you have to learn without a gun,
Not killing but watching birds and animals go
In and out of shelter
At will. Following their example, build for a whole season:
Facing across the wind in your lean-to,
You may feel wilder,
But nothing, not even you, will have to stay in hiding.
If you have no matches, a stick and a fire-bow
Will keep you warmer,
Or the crystal of your watch, filled with water, held up to
    the sun
Will do the same in time. In case of snow
Drifting toward winter,
Don't try to stay awake through the night, afraid of
    freezing—
The bottom of your mind knows all about zero;
It will turn you over
And shake you till you waken. If you have trouble sleeping
Even in the best of weather, jumping to follow
With eyes strained to their corners
The unidentifiable noises of the night and feeling
Bears and packs of wolves nuzzling your elbow,
Remember the trappers

Who treated them indifferently and were left alone.
If you hurt yourself, no one will comfort you
Or take your temperature,
So stumbling, wading, and climbing are as dangerous as
    flying.
But if you decide, at last, you must break through
In spite of all danger,
Think of yourself by time and not by distance, counting
Wherever you're going by how long it takes you;
No other measure
Will bring you safe to nightfall. Follow no streams: they run
Under the ground or fall into wilder country.
Remember the stars
And moss when your mind runs into circles. If it should rain
Or the fog should roll the horizon in around you,
Hold still for hours
Or days if you must, or weeks, for seeing is believing
In the wilderness. And if you find a pathway,
Wheel-rut, or fence-wire,
Retrace it left or right: someone knew where he was going
Once upon a time, and you can follow
Hopefully, somewhere,
Just in case. There may even come, on some uncanny evening,
A time when you're warm and dry, well fed, not thirsty,
Uninjured, without fear,
When nothing, either good or bad, is happening.
This is called staying alive. It's temporary.
What occurs after
Is doubtful. You must always be ready for something to
    come bursting
Through the far edge of a clearing, running toward you,
Grinning from ear to ear
And hoarse with welcome. Or something crossing and
    hovering
Overhead, as light as air, like a break in the sky,
Wondering what you are.
Here you are face to face with the problem of recognition.
Having no time to make smoke, too much to say,
You should have a mirror
With a tiny hole in the back for better aiming, for reflecting
Whatever disaster you can think of, to show
The way you suffer.
These body signals have universal meaning: If you are lying
Flat on your back with arms outstretched behind you,
You say you require
Emergency treatment; if you are standing erect and holding
Arms horizontal, you mean you are not ready;
If you hold them over
Your head, you want to be picked up. Three of anything
Is a sign of distress. Afterward, if you see
No ropes, no ladders,
No maps or messages falling, no searchlights or trails blazing,
Then, chances are, you should be prepared to burrow
Deep for a deep winter.

# Frank O'Hara

**FRANK O'HARA**
Frank O'Hara was born on June 27, 1926, in Baltimore, Maryland. He studied piano at the New England Conservatory in Boston and, after navy service in World War II, attended Harvard College, where he changed his major from music to English. A friend of prominent painters as well as musicians and poets, he was officially associated for some time with the New York Museum of Modern Art. He wrote and produced verse plays, published essays on art and poetry, and collaborated on a musical comedy before he was thirty, by which time he was considered a leading figure in the group sometimes called the New York Poets. He died July 25, 1966, after being hit by a dune buggy on Fire Island.

## AN ABORTION

Do not bathe her in blood,
the little one whose sex is
undermined, she drops leafy
across the belly of black
sky and her abyss has not
that sweetness of the March
wind. Her conception ached
with the perversity of nursery
rhymes, she was a shad a
snake a sparrow and a girl's
closed eye. At the supper, weeping,
they said let's have her and
at breakfast: no.

          Don't bathe
her in tears, guileless, beguiled
in her peripheral warmth, more
monster than murdered, safe
in all silences. From our tree
dropped, that she not wither,
autumn in our terrible breath.

## HOMOSEXUALITY

So we are taking off our masks, are we, and keeping
our mouths shut? as if we'd been pierced by a glance!

The song of an old cow is not more full of judgment
than the vapors which escape one's soul when one is sick;

so I pull the shadows around me like a puff
and crinkle my eyes as if at the most exquisite moment

of a very long opera, and then we are off!
without reproach and without hope that our delicate feet

will touch the earth again, let alone "very soon."
It is the law of my own voice I shall investigate.

I start like ice, my finger to my ear, my ear
to my heart, that proud cur at the garbage can

in the rain. It's wonderful to admire oneself
with complete candor, tallying up the merits of each

of the latrines. 14th Street is drunken and credulous,
53rd tries to tremble but is too at rest. The good

love a park and the inept a railway station,
and there are the divine ones who drag themselves up

and down the lengthening shadow of an Abyssinian head
in the dust, trailing their long elegant heels of hot air

crying to confuse the brave "It's a summer day,
and I want to be wanted more than anything else in the world."

**ROBERT BLY**

Robert Bly lives in Madison, Minnesota, where he was born on December 23, 1926. He graduated *magna cum laude* from Harvard in 1950, after which he served two years in the Navy. He is founder and editor of *The Seventies* magazine and press and is a major translator of Latin American poetry, to which he gives over much of his magazine. He was the Amy Lowell Travelling Scholar in Poetry in 1964, received the National Book Award for Poetry in 1968 for *Light Around the Body*, and has also been a Rockefeller and a Guggenheim Fellow.

## WHY I AM NOT A PAINTER

I am not a painter, I am a poet.
Why? I think I would rather be
a painter, but I am not. Well,

for instance, Mike Goldberg
is starting a painting. I drop in.
"Sit down and have a drink" he
says. I drink; we drink. I look
up. "You have SARDINES in it."
"Yes, it needed something there."
"Oh." I go and the days go by
and I drop in again. The painting
is going on, and I go, and the days
go by. I drop in. The painting is
finished. "Where's SARDINES?"
All that's left is just
letters, "It was too much," Mike says.

But me? One day I am thinking of
a color: orange. I write a line
about orange. Pretty soon it is a
whole page of words, not lines.
Then another page. There should be
so much more, not of orange, of
words, of how terrible orange is
and life. Days go by. It is even in

prose, I am a real poet: My poem
is finished and I haven't mentioned
orange yet. It's twelve poems, I call
it ORANGES. And one day in a gallery
I see Mike's painting, called SARDINES.

## POEM

Lana Turner has collapsed!
I was trotting along and suddenly
it started raining and snowing
and you said it was hailing
but hailing hits you on the head
hard so it was really snowing and
raining and I was in such a hurry
to meet you but the traffic
was acting exactly like the sky
and suddenly I see a headline
LANA TURNER HAS COLLAPSED!
there is no snow in Hollywood
there is no rain in California
I have been to lots of parties
and acted perfectly disgraceful
but I never actually collapsed
oh Lana Turner we love you get up

# Robert Bly

## WRITTEN IN DEJECTION NEAR ROME

What if these long races go on repeating themselves
century after century, living in houses painted light colors
on the beach,
black spiders,
having turned pale and fat,
men walking thoughtfully with their families,
vibrations
of exhausted violin-bodies,
horrible eternities of sea pines!
Some men cannot help but feel it,
they will abandon their homes
to live on rafts tied together on the ocean;
those on shore will go inside tree trunks,
surrounded by bankers whose fingers have grown long and
  slender,
piercing through rotting bark for their food.

## THE FIRE OF DESPAIR HAS BEEN OUR SAVIOUR

Today, autumn.
Heaven's roots are still.
O holy trees, rejoicing ruin of leaves,
How easily we see spring coming in your black branches!
Not like the Middle Ages! Then iron ringing iron
At dawn, chill wringing
The grass, clatter of saddles,
The long flight on borrowed stone
Into the still air sobered by the hidden joy of crows.

Or the Ice Age!
Another child dead,
Turning bone stacks for bones, sleeves of snow blowing
Down from above, no tracks in the snow, in agony

Man cried out—like the mad hog, pierced, again,
Again, by teeth-spears, who
Grew his horny scales
From sheer despair—instants
Finally leading out of the snowbound valley!

This autumn, I
Cannot find the road
That way: the things that we must grasp,
The signs, are gone, hidden by spring and fall, leaving
A still sky here, a dusk there,
A dry cornleaf in a field; where has the road gone? All
Trace lost, like a ship sinking,
Where what is left and what goes down both bring despair.
Not finding the road, we are slowly pulled down.

## HURRYING AWAY FROM THE EARTH

The poor, and the dazed, and the idiots
Are with us, they live in the casket of the sun
And the moon's coffin, as I walk out tonight
Seeing the night wheeling their dark wheelbarrow
All about the plains of heaven,
And the stars inexorably rising.
Dark moon! Sinister tears!
Shadow of slums and of the conquering dead!

Some men have pierced the chest with a long needle
To stop their heart from beating any more;
Another put blocks of ice in his bed
So he would die, women

Have washed their hair, and hanged themselves
In the long braids, one woman climbed
A high elm above her lawn,
Opened a box, and swallowed poisonous spiders. . . .

The time for exhortation is past. I have heard
The iron chairs scraping in asylums,
As the cold bird hunches into the winter
In the windy night of November.
The coal miners rise from their pits
Like a flash flood,
Like a rice field disintegrating.
Men cry when they hear stories of someone rising from the
    dead.

## COME WITH ME

Come with me into those things that have felt this despair
    for so long—
Those removed Chevrolet wheels that howl with a terrible
    loneliness,
Lying on their backs in the cindery dirt, like men drunk, and
    naked,
Staggering off down a hill at night to drown at last in the
    pond.

Those shredded inner tubes abandoned on the shoulders of
    thruways,
Black and collapsed bodies, that tried and burst,
And were left behind;
And the curly steel shavings, scattered about on garage
    benches,
Sometimes still warm, gritty when we hold them,
Who have given up, and blame everything on the government,
And those roads in South Dakota that feel around in the
    darkness . . .

# Galway Kinnell

**GALWAY KINNELL**

Galway Kinnell was born in Providence, Rhode Island, on February 1, 1927, and was raised in Pawtucket. After attending Princeton University, he spent the early fifties directing the liberal arts program at the University of Chicago downtown center. During the next ten years he traveled a great deal, living in France, Iran, Vermont, Louisiana, and New York. Recently he has been poet-in-residence at several colleges and universities. In addition to his poetry, he has translated the poems of François Villon, Yves Bonnefoy's *On the Motion and Immobility of Douve,* and Yvan Goll's *Lackawanna Elegy,* and he has also published a novel, *Black Light.* He now lives in Vermont.

## THE BEAR

### 1

In the late winter
I sometimes glimpse bits of steam
coming up from
some fault in the old snow
and bend close and see it is lung-colored
and put down my nose
and know
the chilly, enduring odor of bear.

### 2

I take a wolf's rib and whittle
it sharp at both ends
and coil it up
and freeze it in blubber and place it out
on the fairway of the bears.

And when it has vanished
I move out on the bear tracks,
roaming in circles
until I come to the first, tentative, dark
splash on the earth.

And I set out
running, following the splashes
of blood wandering over the world.
At the cut, gashed resting places
I stop and rest,
at the crawl-marks
where he lay out on his belly
to overpass some stretch of bauchy ice
I lie out
dragging myself forward with bear-knives in
    my fists.

### 3

On the third day I begin to starve,
at nightfall I bend down as I knew I would
at a turd sopped in blood,
and hesitate, and pick it up,
and thrust it in my mouth, and gnash it
    down,
and rise
and go on running.

### 4

On the seventh day,
living by now on bear blood alone,

I can see his upturned carcass far out
    ahead, a scraggled,
steamy hulk,
the heavy fur riffling in the wind.

I come up to him
and stare at the narrow-spaced, petty eyes,
the dismayed
face laid back on the shoulder, the nostrils
flared, catching
perhaps the first taint of me as he
died.

I hack
a ravine in his thigh, and eat and drink,
and tear him down his whole length
and open him and climb in
and close him up after me, against the wind,
and sleep.

### 5

And dream
of lumbering flatfooted
over the tundra,
stabbed twice from within,
splattering a trail behind me,
splattering it out no matter which way I
    lurch,
no matter which parabola of bear-
    transcendence,
which dance of solitude I attempt,
which gravity-clutched leap,
which trudge, which groan.

### 6

Until one day I totter and fall—
fall on this
stomach that has tried so hard to keep up,
to digest the blood as it leaked in,
to break up
and digest the bone itself: and now the
    breeze
blows over me, blows off
the hideous belches of ill-digested bear
    blood
and rotted stomach
and the ordinary, wretched odor of bear,

blows across
my sore, lolled tongue a song
or screech, until I think I must rise up
and dance. And I lie still.

7

I awaken I think. Marshlights
reappear, geese
come trailing again up the flyway.
In her ravine under old snow the dam-bear
lies, licking
lumps of smeared fur
and drizzly eyes into shapes
with her tongue. And one
hairy-soled trudge stuck out before me,
the next groaned out,
the next,
the next,
the rest of my days I spend
wandering: wondering
what, anyway,
was that sticky infusion, that rank flavor of
    blood, that poetry, by which I lived?


# NIGHT IN THE FOREST

1

A woman
sleeps next to me on the earth. A strand
of hair flows
from her cocoon sleeping bag, touching
the ground hesitantly, as if thinking
to take root.

2

I can hear
a mountain brook
and somewhere blood winding
down its ancient labyrinths. And
a few feet away
charred stick-ends surround
a bit of ashes, where burnt-out, vanished
    flames
absently
waver, absently leap.


# BURNING

He lives, who last night flopped from a log
Into the creek, and all night by an ankle
Lay pinned to the flood, dead as a nail
But for the skin of the teeth of his dog.

I brought him boiled eggs and broth.
He coughed and waved his spoon

And sat up saying he would dine alone,
Being fatigue itself after that bath.

I sat without in the sun with the dog.
Wearing a stocking on the ailing foot,
In monster crutches, he hobbled out,
And addressed the dog in bitter rage.

He told the yellow hound, his rescuer,
Its heart was bad, and it ought
Not wander by the creek at night;
If all his dogs got drowned he would be poor.

He stroked its head and disappeared in the shed
And came out with a stone mallet in his hands
And lifted that rocky weight of many pounds
And let it lapse on top of the dog's head.

I carted off the carcass, dug it deep.
Then he came too with what a thing to lug,
Or pour on a dog's grave, his thundermug,
And poured it out and went indoors to sleep.

I saw him sleepless in the pane of glass
Looking wild-eyed at sunset, then the glare
Blinded the glass—only a red square
Burning a house burning in the wilderness.


# THE PORCUPINE

1

Fatted
on herbs, swollen on crabapples,
puffed up on bast and phloem, ballooned
on willow flowers, poplar catkins, first
leafs of aspen and larch,
the porcupine
drags and bounces his last meal through ice,
mud, roses and goldenrod, into the stubbly
    high fields.

2

In character
he resembles us in seven ways:
he puts his mark on outhouses,
he alchemizes by moonlight,
he shits on the run,
he uses his tail for climbing,
he chuckles softly to himself when scared,
he's overcrowded if there's more than one
    of him per five acres,
his eyes have their own inner redness.

**3**

Digger of
goings across floors, of hesitations
at thresholds, of
handprints of dread
at doorpost or window jamb, he would
gouge the world
empty of us, hack and crater
it
until it is nothing, if that
could rinse it of all our sweat and pathos.

Adorer of ax
handles aflow with grain, of arms
of Morris chairs, of hand
crafted objects
steeped in the juice of fingertips,
of surfaces wetted down
with fist grease and elbow oil,
of clothespins that have
grabbed our body-rags by underarm and
    crotch . . .

Unimpressed—bored—
by the whirl of the stars, by *these*
he's astonished, ultra-
Rilkean angel!
for whom the true
portion of the sweetness of earth
is one of those bottom-heavy, glittering,
    saccadic
bits
of salt water that splash down
the haunted ravines of a human face.

**4**

A farmer shot a porcupine three times
as it dozed on a tree limb. On
the way down it torn open its belly
on a broken
branch, hooked its gut,
and went on falling. On the ground
it sprang to its feet, and
paying out gut heaved
and spartled through a hundred feet of
    goldenrod
before
the abrupt emptiness.

**5**

The Avesta
puts porcupine killers
into hell for nine generations, sentencing
    them

to gnaw out
each other's hearts for the
salts of desire.

I roll
this way and that in the great bed, under
the quilt
that mimics this country of broken farms
    and woods,
the fatty sheath of the man
melting off,
the self-stabbing coil
of bristles reversing, blossoming outward—
a red-eyed, hard-toothed, arrow-stuck urchin
tossing up mattress feathers,
pricking the
woman beside me until she cries.

**6**

In my time I have
crouched, quills erected,
Saint
Sebastian of the
scared heart, and been
beat dead with a locust club
on the bare snout.
And fallen from high places
I have fled, have
jogged
over fields of goldenrod,
terrified, seeking home,
and among flowers
I have come to myself empty, the rope
strung out behind me
in the fall sun
suddenly glorified with all my blood.

**7**

And tonight I think I prowl broken
skulled or vacant as a
sucked egg in the wintry meadow, softly
    chuckling, blank
template of myself, dragging
a starved belly through the lichflowered
    acres,
where
burdock looses the arks of its seed
and thistle holds up its lost blooms
and rosebushes in the wind scrape their dead
    limbs
for the forced-fire
of roses.

106

# Judson Jerome

## EVE: NIGHT THOUGHTS

Okay, so the wheel bit was a grinding bore
and fire a risk in the cave, never mind the dogs
he brings home, and cows; but I can endure
his knocking rocks for sparks and rolling logs.
It's his words that get on my nerves, his incessant naming
of every bird or bug or plant, his odd
smirk as he commits a syllable, taming
Nature with categories—as though the Word were God.

Okay, so statements were bad enough,
and accusations crossing, spoiling digestion.
But then he invented the laugh.
Next day he invented the question.
I see it: he's busy building a verbal fence
surrounding life and me. But already I
counterplot: I'll make a poem of his sense.
By night, as he dreams, I am inventing the lie.

**JUDSON JEROME**

Born on February 8, 1927, in Tulsa, Oklahoma, Judson Jerome attended the University of Oklahoma and later took an M.A. from the University of Chicago and a Ph.D. from Ohio State University in Columbus. Since 1953 he has been a professor of literature at Antioch College, with two years on leave to serve as chairman of the Division of Humanities, College of the Virgin Islands (1963–1965). In 1960–1961 he was the Amy Lowell Travelling Scholar and in 1967 and 1968 was a member of the Bread Loaf Writers' Conference poetry staff. For several years he has written a column entitled "Poetry: How and Why" for *Writer's Digest*. He has written and produced four verse dramas and has written a novel and a textbook on poetry. He lives with his wife, Martha-Jane Pierce, and their son and four daughters in Columbia, Maryland, where, in addition to his teaching, he directs the Center for Documentary Arts, Antioch Columbia.

## DEER HUNT

Because the warden is a cousin, my
mountain friends hunt in summer when the deer
cherish each rattler-ridden spring, and I
have waited hours by a pool in fear
that manhood would require I shoot or that
the steady drip of the hill would dull my ear
to a snake whispering near the log I sat
upon, and listened to the yelping cheer
of dogs and men resounding ridge to ridge.
I flinched at every lonely rifle crack,
my knuckles whitening where I gripped the edge
of age and clung, like retching, sinking back,
then gripping once again the monstrous gun—
since I, to be a man, had taken one.

# W. S. Merwin

**W. S. MERWIN**

W. S. Merwin was born in New York City on September 30, 1927, and grew up in Union City, New Jersey, and Scranton, Pennsylvania. Much of his life has been spent abroad, traveling and doing a number of other things, including stints as tutor to the children of the Princess de Braganza of Portugal and to the household of Robert Graves in Majorca. He was poetry editor of *The Nation* for a while in 1961. His first book of poems was published in the Yale Younger Poets Series in 1952, and he has since won numerous other honors, including the Pulitzer Prize in 1971 for *The Carrier of Ladders*. Aside from his own poetry, Merwin has published distinguished translations of the work of a number of other poets. His most recent publication in this field, *Selected Translations*, won the 1969 P.E.N. Prize for Translation. His first collection of prose pieces, *The Miner's Pale Children*, was published in 1971.

## FLY

I have been cruel to a fat pigeon
Because he would not fly
All he wanted was to live like a friendly old man

He had let himself become a wreck filthy and confiding
Wild for his food beating the cat off the garbage
Ignoring his mate perpetually snotty at the beak
Smelling waddling having to be
Carried up the ladder at night content

*Fly* I said throwing him into the air
But he would drop and run back expecting to be fed
I said it again and again throwing him up
As he got worse
He let himself be picked up every time
Until I found him in the dovecote dead
Of the needless efforts

So that is what I am

Pondering his eye that could not
Conceive that I was a creature to run from

I who have always believed too much in words

## AVOIDING NEWS BY THE RIVER

As the stars hide in the light before daybreak
Reed warblers hunt along the narrow stream
Trout rise to their shadows
Milky light flows through the branches
Fills with blood
Men will be waking

In an hour it will be summer
I dreamed that the heavens were eating the earth
Waking it is not so
Not the heavens
I am not ashamed of the wren's murders
Nor the badger's dinners
On which all worldly good depends
If I were not human I would not be ashamed of anything

## THE LAST ONE

Well they'd made up their minds to be everywhere because
  why not.
Everywhere was theirs because they thought so.
They with two leaves they whom the birds despise.
In the middle of stones they made up their minds.
They started to cut.

Well they cut everything because why not.
Everything was theirs because they thought so.
It fell into its shadows and they took both away.
Some to have some for burning.

Well cutting everything they came to the water.
They came to the end of the day there was one left
   standing.
They would cut it tomorrow they went away.
The night gathered in the last branches.
The shadow of the night gathered in the shadow on the
   water.
The night and the shadow put on the same head.
And it said Now.

Well in the morning they cut the last one.
Like the others the last one fell into its shadow.
It fell into its shadow on the water.
They took it away its shadow stayed on the water.

Well they shrugged they started trying to get the shadow
   away.
They cut right to the ground the shadow stayed whole.
They laid boards on it the shadow came out on top.
They shone lights on it the shadow got blacker and clearer.
They exploded the water the shadow rocked.
They built a huge fire on the roots.
They sent up black smoke between the shadow and the sun.
The new shadow flowed without changing the old one.
They shrugged they went away to get stones.

They came back the shadow was growing.
They started setting up stones it was growing.
They looked the other way it went on growing.
They decided they would make a stone out of it.
They took stones to the water they poured them into the
   shadow.
They poured them in they poured them in the stones
   vanished.
The shadow was not filled it went on growing.
That was one day.

The next day was just the same it went on growing.
They did all the same things it was just the same.
They decided to take its water from under it.
They took away water they took it away the water went
   down.
The shadow stayed where it was before.
It went on growing it grew onto the land.
They started to scrape the shadow with machines.
When it touched the machines it stayed on them.
They started to beat the shadow with sticks.
Where it touched the sticks it stayed on them.
They started to beat the shadow with hands.
Where it touched the hands it stayed on them.
That was another day.

Well the next day started about the same it went on
   growing.
They pushed lights into the shadow.
Where the shadow got onto them they went out.
They began to stomp on the edge it got their feet.
And when it got their feet they fell down.
It got into eyes the eyes went blind.

The ones that fell down it grew over and they vanished.
The ones that went blind and walked into it vanished.
The ones that could see and stood still
It swallowed their shadows.
Then it swallowed them too and they vanished.
Well the others ran.

The ones that were left went away to live if it would let
   them.
They went as far as they could.
The lucky ones with their shadows.


## FOR THE ANNIVERSARY OF MY DEATH

Every year without knowing it I have passed the day
When the last fires will wave to me
And the silence will set out
Tireless traveller
Like the beam of a lightless star

Then I will no longer
Find myself in life as in a strange garment
Surprised at the earth
And the love of one woman
And the shamelessness of men
As today writing after three days of rain
Hearing the wren sing and the falling cease
And bowing not knowing to what


## THE COLD BEFORE THE MOONRISE

It is too simple to turn to the sound
Of frost stirring among its
Stars like an animal asleep
In the winter night
And say I was born far from home
If there is a place where this is the language may
It be my country

# James Wright

**JAMES WRIGHT**

James Wright was born on December 13, 1927, in Martin's Ferry, Ohio. He took a B.A. from Kenyon College, where he studied with John Crowe Ransom, and his M.S. and Ph.D. from the University of Washington, working under Theodore Roethke. Later, in 1952 and 1953, he studied in Vienna under a Fulbright Scholarship. Other honors for his work include a *Kenyon Review* Fellowship, grants from the National Institute of Arts and Letters and the Guggenheim Foundation, and the Oscar Blumenthal Award given by *Poetry*. Wright is also keenly interested in verse translation and has published four volumes, including most recently, with Robert Bly, *Twenty Poems of Pablo Neruda*. He now teaches English at Hunter College, The City University of New York.

## ON MINDING ONE'S OWN BUSINESS

Ignorant two, we glide
On ripples near the shore.
The rainbows leap no more,
And men in boats alight
To see the day subside.

All evening fins have drowned
Back in the summer dark.
Above us, up the bank,
Obscure on lonely ground,
A shack receives the night.

I hold the lefthand oar
Out of the wash, and guide
The skiff away so wide
We wander out of sight
As soundless as before.

We will not land to bear
Our will upon that house,
Nor force on any place
Our dull offensive weight.

Somebody may be there,
Peering at us outside

Across the even lake,
Wondering why we take
Our time and stay so late.

Long may the lovers hide
In viny shacks from those
Who thrash among the trees,
Who curse, who have no peace,
Who pitch and moan all night
For fear of someone's joys,
Deploring the human face.

From prudes and muddying fools,
Kind Aphrodite, spare
All hunted criminals,
Hoboes, and whip-poor-wills,
And girls with rumpled hair,
All, all of whom might hide
Within that darkening shack.
Lovers may live, and abide.
Wherefore, I turn my back,
And trawl our boat away,
Lest someone fear to call
A girl's name till we go
Over the lake so slow
We hear the darkness fall.

## COMPLAINT

She's gone. She was my love, my moon or more.
She chased the chickens out and swept the floor,
Emptied the bones and nut-shells after feasts,
And smacked the kids for leaping up like beasts.
Now morbid boys have grown past awkwardness;
The girls let stitches out, dress after dress,
To free some swinging body's riding space
And form the new child's unimagined face.
Yet, while vague nephews, spitting on their curls,
Amble to pester winds and blowsy girls,
What arm will sweep the room, what hand will hold
New snow against the milk to keep it cold?
And who will dump the garbage, feed the hogs,
And pitch the chickens' heads to hungry dogs?
Not my lost hag who dumbly bore such pain:
Childbirth and midnight sassafras and rain.
New snow against her face and hands she bore,
And now lies down, who was my moon or more.

A CENTENARY ODE: INSCRIBED TO LITTLE
CROW, LEADER OF THE SIOUX REBELLION IN
MINNESOTA, 1862

I had nothing to do with it. I was not here.
I was not born.
In 1862, when your hotheads
Raised hell from here to South Dakota,
My own fathers scattered into West Virginia
And southern Ohio.
My family fought the Confederacy
And fought the Union.
None of them got killed.
But for all that, it was not my fathers
Who murdered you.
Not much.

I don't know
Where the fathers of Minneapolis finalized
Your flayed carcass.
Little Crow, true father
Of my dark America,
When I close my eyes I lose you among
Old lonelinesses.
My family were a lot of singing drunks and good carpenters.
We had brothers who loved one another no matter what they
    did.
And they did plenty.

I think they would have run like hell from your Sioux.
And when you caught them you all would have run like hell
From the Confederacy and from the Union
Into the hills and hunted for a few things,
Some bull-cat under the stones, a gar maybe,
If you were hungry, and if you were happy,
Sunfish and corn.

If only I knew where to mourn you,
I would surely mourn.

But I don't know.

I did not come here only to grieve
For my people's defeat.
The troops of the Union, who won,
Still outnumber us.
Old Paddy Beck, my great-uncle, is dead
At the old soldiers' home near Tiffen, Ohio.
He got away with every last stitch
Of his uniform, save only
The dress trousers.

Oh all around us,
The hobo jungles of America grow wild again.
The pick handles bloom like your skinned spine.
I don't even know where
My own grave is.

MUTTERINGS OVER THE CRIB
OF A DEAF CHILD

"How will he hear the bell at school
Arrange the broken afternoon,
And know to run across the cool
Grasses where the starlings cry,
Or understand the day is gone?"

Well, someone lifting cautious brows
Will take the measure of the clock.
And he will see the birchen boughs
Outside the sagging dark from the sky,
And the shade crawling upon the rock.

"And how will he know to rise at morning?
His mother has other sons to waken,
She has the stove she must build to burning
Before the coals of the night-time die,
And he never stirs when he is shaken."

I take it the air affects the skin,
And you remember, when you were young,
Sometimes you could feel the dawn begin,
And the fire would call you, by and by,
Out of the bed and bring you along.

"Well, good enough. To serve his needs
All kinds of arrangements can be made.
But what will you do if his finger bleeds?
Or a bobwhite whistles invisibly
And flutes like an angel off in the shade?"

He will learn pain. And, as for the bird,
It is always darkening when that comes out.
I will putter as though I had not heard,
And lift him into my arms and sing
Whether he hears my song or not.

# Gene Frumkin

**GENE FRUMKIN**

Gene Frumkin was born on January 29, 1928, in New York City. He writes: I began writing poetry at the age of 4, in Yiddish. By the time I was 7, this language had lost its charm for me, since by then I had come across a few words of Bronxese. Because I am slow at learning new languages, it was not until I was 25 that I resumed my poetic career, now writing in what I continue to think of as English, which I absorbed at UCLA, where I took my B.A. My youthful Yiddish poems have been lost, but a small group of my later poems were published by Alan Swallow in 1963 under the title *The Hawk and the Lizard*. This book is now an item for unfastidious collectors. Three more volumes followed, by three different presses. At the moment, several large New York publishing houses are totally uninterested in my work. I think this is because they don't understand me. I am not understood in New Mexico, either, which may be why I hold a job as Director of Creative Writing at the University of New Mexico in Albuquerque. Yiddish probably sounds like Navajo.

## SOME KIND OF TOUGHGUY

Some kind of toughguy
remote      a darkness
A man of some nobility though
with a good left hook
willing to risk
an outpost in the shadows
Through the fog
tall and phallic
his head a lamp emitting
a slightly green light
As he comes toward me
I feel stronger      I'm prepared
to defend myself
though I know he won't attack
I want to be his equal
to see through his animal eyes

           He's almost here

The fallen leaves in the yard
crowd together

## ON A WINDY DAY

On a windy day
    in the park the sun
        pale lemon on the grass
beside us
    on the bench a basket
        holding a thermos of coffee
some macaroons a book
    on DeKooning

          As the child
    catches leaves
for the building
    of a house we discuss
        the daily problem
of how to continue

On a lawn
    some fifty yards
        before us boys
are playing football
    in flimsy shirts
        ignoring the wind and us
There is Hermes
    and there Sammy Baugh
        —who can say how their names

will change
          I played football too
    on the grass of my time
        never predicting
this park

## SOME DAYS THE BLOOD IS WARM AND CERTAIN

Some days the blood is warm and certain,
the fingers touch all objects kindly.
I step from behind my usual curtain
and smile, unnecessarily, at the desks
and cease to be that strange self
who answers the telephone warily
as if the caller might be a bomb.
Those days there is no sense of doom,
no one says anything unkindly,
and I seem to be profoundly witty.
When someone asks,
I know;
nothing is left behind
wherever I go.
What happens then around me
—a death, a birth, a breath of wind—
becomes the mind, the flesh, the bone:
that clear, intuitive self
that is all I need ever completely own.

## THE MAGDALENA SILVER MINE

Word has reached us here
at the Magdalena silver mine
that you do not love women

'Love' is merely another word
in the American language

But women exist and the word
has gone out that you
don't love them

On my side, I have heard
the Magdalena silver mine exists
but I have never seen it

We could show you photographs

I have photographs of women
(sexually exposed at that)
but I'm not convinced
I have even seen a woman

What proof do you need?

Only to see a woman

If you saw her
would you love her?

Of course

But if love is, as you said
merely a word. . .

If I ever saw a woman
I would erase the word 'love'
and the Magdalena silver mine
would vanish at the same time

We insist the mine is here
in Magdalena     we have photographs
I have never been in Magdalena

Why don't you simply drive down
from Albuquerque. . .

Not without a woman

# Dave Etter

**DAVE ETTER**
Dave Etter writes: I was born in Huntington Park, California, March 18, 1928. In college, I majored in English and History, graduating from the University of Iowa in 1953. For a number of years I travelled about the United States working at odd jobs. Since 1964 I have lived with my wife and two children in a 120-year-old house in Geneva, Illinois, and have worked in Chicago as an editor for Encyclopaedia Britannica. I am also poetry editor of the literary magazine *December*. I received the Midland Poetry Award for *Go Read the River* and the Chicagoland Poetry Award for *The Last Train to Prophetstown*. In 1967, I was a Bread Loaf Writers' Conference Fellow in Poetry.

## GREAT NORTHERN

### 1

What is it about a GREAT NORTHERN boxcar
standing on a cold siding in West Chicago
that fills me with such a nameless joy?

### 2

Wave, boy, that's the WINNIPEG LIMITED!

### 3

Inarticulate, lacking paper words,
I celebrate the railroads in my blood.

### 4

Through the snowfields of central Minnesota
the EMPIRE BUILDER plunges into the night
and I shake by the thundering tracks,
crying hoarsely: love love love.

## AUTUMN ON THE WABASH

In shadows fishing sycamores
a gold leaf seeds the river.

Red dogs round up the rabbit holes.
(Let me hear that old guitar.)

In a lean sun that saps our days
my brown boat farms the Wabash.

113

# Donald Hall

**DONALD HALL**

Donald Hall was born on September 20, 1928, in New Haven, Connecticut. After preparatory schooling at Phillips Exeter Academy, he took a B.A. from Harvard in 1951 and a B.Litt. from Oxford in 1953. He has lived twice in England and edited the England section of *New Poets of England and America* (Meridian: 1957, 1962). He was poetry editor of the *Paris Review* from 1953 to 1962 and a member of the editorial board of poetry for Wesleyan University Press from 1958 to 1964. He won the Newdigate Prize for Poetry from Oxford in 1952, the Lamont Poetry Selection Prize in 1955, the Edna St. Vincent Millay Memorial Prize in 1956, and a Guggenheim Fellowship in 1963. He is currently a professor of English at the University of Michigan.

## THE DAYS

Ten years ago this minute, he possibly sat
in the sunlight, in Connecticut, in an old chair:
a car may have stopped in the street outside;
he may have turned his head; his ear may have itched.
Since it was September, he probably saw
single leaves dropping from the maple tree.
If he was reading, he turned back to his book,
and perhaps the smell of roses in a pot
came together with the smell of cheese sandwiches
and the smell of a cigarette
smoked by his brother who was not dead then.

The moments of that day dwindled
to the small notations of clocks,
and the day busily became another day,
and another, and today, when his hand moves
from his ear which still itches
to rest on his leg, it is marked with the passage
of ten years. Suddenly he has the idea
that thousands and thousands of his days
lie stacked into the ground
like leaves, or like that pressure of green
which turns into coal in a million years.

Though leaves rot, or leaves burn in the gutter;
though the complications of this morning's breakfast
dissolve in faint shudders of light
at a great distance, he continues to daydream
that the past is a country under the ground
where the days practice their old habits
over and over, as faint and persistent
as cigarette smoke in an airless room.
He wishes he could travel there like a tourist
and photograph the unseizable days
in the sunlight, in Connecticut, in an old chair.

## MY SON, MY EXECUTIONER

My son, my executioner,
  I take you in my arms,
Quiet and small and just astir,
  And whom my body warms.

Sweet death, small son, our instrument
  Of immortality,
Your cries and hungers document
  Our bodily decay.

We twenty-five and twenty-two,
  Who seemed to live forever,
Observe enduring life in you
  And start to die together.

114

## THE MAN IN THE DEAD MACHINE

High on a slope in New Guinea
the Grumman Hellcat
lodges among bright vines
as thick as arms. In 1942,
the clenched hand of a pilot
glided it here
where no one has ever been.

In the cockpit the helmeted
skeleton sits
upright, held
by dry sinews at neck
and shoulder, and webbing
that straps the pelvic cross
to the cracked
leather of the seat, and the breastbone
to the canvas cover
of the parachute.

Or say that the shrapnel
missed him, he flew
back to the carrier, and every
morning takes his chair, his pale
hands on the black arms, and sits
upright, held
by the firm webbing.

## THE REPEATED SHAPES

I have visited Men's Rooms
in several bars
with the rows
of urinals like old men
and the six-sided odor

of disinfectant.
I have felt the sadness
of the small white tiles,
the repeated shapes
and the unavoidable whiteness.

They are my uncles,
these old men
who are only plumbing,
who throb with tears all night
and doze in the morning.

# Anne Sexton

## FOR GOD WHILE SLEEPING

Sleeping in fever, I am unfit
to know just who you are:
hung up like a pig on exhibit,
the delicate wrists,
the beard drooling blood and vinegar;
hooked to your own weight,
jolting toward death under your nameplate.

Everyone in this crowd needs a bath.
I am dressed in rags.
The mother wears blue. You grind your teeth
and with each new breath
your jaws gape and your diaper sags.
I am not to blame
for all this. I do not know your name.

Skinny man, you are somebody's fault.
You ride on dark poles—
a wooden bird that a trader built
for some fool who felt
that he could make the flight. Now you roll
in your sleep, seasick
on your own breathing, poor old convict.

**ANNE SEXTON**

Anne Sexton writes: Born, Newton, Mass., November 9, 1928; married 1948, two daughters. No visible education. Started writing in 1957; attended Boston Adult Center for Education. Studied at Boston University in 1959 and at Brandeis University in 1960. Held the Robert Frost Fellowship in 1960 at Bread Loaf Writers' Conference. Scholar at Radcliffe Institute for Independent Study from 1961–63, teaching a creative writing course at Harvard and Radcliffe during 1961. Awarded the first traveling fellowship of the American Academy of Arts and Letters (1963–64), a grant from the Ford Foundation in 1964–65 (for residence with the Charles Playhouse in Boston), and in 1965 was awarded the first literary magazine travel grant under The Congress for Cultural Freedom. Elected a Fellow of The Royal Society of Literature in London. Pulitzer Prize for Poetry in 1967 for *Live or Die*. Honorary Phi Beta Kappa, Harvard University Chapter, 1968, Honorary Phi Beta Kappa, Radcliffe Chapter, 1969. Awarded a Guggenheim Grant for 1969–70. Honorary Doctor of Letters, Tufts University, 1970. Poems have appeared in such magazines as *The New Yorker, Harper's, Hudson Review, Yale Review, Partisan Review, The Nation, Saturday Review, Poetry, Sewanee Review* and *Encounter*. Play "Mercy Street" was the first production of the American Place Theatre in New York in 1969. Taught at Wayland High School, McLean Hospital, Oberlin College (Independent Study) and currently teaching at Boston University.

## THE FARMER'S WIFE

From the hodge porridge
of their country lust,
their local life in Illinois,
where all their acres look
like a sprouting broom factory,
they name just ten years now
that she has been his habit;
as again tonight he'll say
honey bunch let's go
and she will not say how there
must be more to living
than this brief bright bridge
of the raucous bed or even
the slow braille touch of him
like a heavy god grown light,
that old pantomime of love
that she wants although
it leaves her still alone,
built back again at last,
mind's apart from him, living
her own self in her own words
and hating the sweat of the house
they keep when they finally lie
each in separate dreams
and then how she watches him,
still strong in the blowzy bag
of his usual sleep while
her young years bungle past
their same marriage bed
and she wishes him cripple, or poet,
or even lonely, or sometimes,
better, my lover, dead.


## THE TRUTH THE DEAD KNOW

*for my mother, born March 1902, died March 1959
and my father, born February 1900, died June 1959*

Gone, I say and walk from church,
refusing the stiff procession to the grave,
letting the dead ride alone in the hearse.
It is June. I am tired of being brave.

We drive to the Cape. I cultivate
myself where the sun gutters from the sky,
where the sea swings in like an iron gate
and we touch. In another country people die.

My darling, the wind falls in like stones
from the whitehearted water and when we touch
we enter touch entirely. No one's alone.
Men kill for this, or for as much.

And what of the dead? They lie without shoes
in their stone boats. They are more like stone
than the sea would be if it stopped. They refuse
to be blessed, throat, eye, and knucklebone.


## THE MOSS OF HIS SKIN

*Young girls in old Arabia were often buried alive
next to their dead fathers, apparently as sacrifice
to the goddesses of the tribes . . .*
HAROLD FELDMAN, "Children of the Desert"
*Psychoanalysis and Psychoanalytic Review, Fall 1958*

It was only important
to smile and hold still,
to lie down beside him
and to rest awhile,
to be folded up together
as if we were silk,
to sink from the eyes of mother
and not to talk.
The black room took us
like a cave or a mouth
or an indoor belly.
I held my breath
and daddy was there,
his thumbs, his fat skull,
his teeth, his hair growing
like a field or a shawl.
I lay by the moss
of his skin until
it grew strange. My sisters
will never know that I fall
out of myself and pretend
that Allah will not see
how I hold my daddy
like an old stone tree.

# William Dickey

## VOYAGE TO THE MOON

Of that world, having returned from it, I may say
There is no romance there, no air being present
To carry the sound of compliment. The inhabitants
Cannot smell one another, even when the sun
At long midday heats them beyond our temperature.

It is therefore a nation of pure philosophy
Without sin or absolution. The swift works
Of their brains show through their crystal faces
With absolute consonance. The pattern of their thoughts
Is like that of pleased clocks agreeing on an hour.

They are advanced in mathematics. The closest thing
To affection I could observe among them was
The appreciation of a theorem shared by two
Investigators. The emotion was expressed
By a formal, rapid exchanging of prime numbers.

The air of earth would surely be fatal to them,
Our sounds shatter, our perfumes corrode them. But
What would bring them, I think, most entirely to a stop
Would be to watch our explosions of hate and love
Which may serve as armament for the next expedition.

**WILLIAM DICKEY**
William Dickey was born on December 15, 1928, in Bellingham, Washington. He writes: Raised in small towns near Canada and the Pacific. Education Reed College, Harvard University, University of Iowa and Jesus College, Oxford; Woodrow Wilson and Fulbright Fellow. Worked as journalist and editor, then teaching at Cornell University, San Francisco State College, where now Professor of English and Creative Writing. Special interests: the eighteenth century, calligraphy, and cooking.

## LESSON OF THE MASTER

As much as he could learn has done no good.
Where the complexities started, there he stands,
Looking attentively at his two hands
That ought to point the way out of the wood.
They point to nothing. They curl in and rest.

Around him in the thicket bird and beast
Give birth or die in a repeated way;
God moulds the human animal out of clay.
The animal takes breath, then does its best.
Its best is good enough. Its bones decay.

The animal put by, how will he know—
Lacking that murderous heart—the innocent track?
Who knows enough to walk forward or walk back?
Generations of chattering mannikins sprout and grow
While he stand reasoning for the first attack.

As much as he could learn has done no good.
Logic of Aristotle fills his brain;
Non-Aristotelian monkey noises reign
Carnal and bloody in that primitive wood
Where his hands twitch and then curl in again.

## MEMORANDA

The scars take us back to places we have been,
Cities named Masochism or Innacuracy,
This little one between the finger and the thumb
Is something that my brother did to me
On a hot Washington's Birthday in the past,
When we were young and cruelly competent;
In a miniature world like a glass fishing float
He was the total image of intent.

Who stuck the pencil point into my palm?
It is so long ago that I cannot say,
But the black stick of graphite under the skin—
Some friend, some enemy put it there that way
To succeed in calling himself always to mind.
Action has consequence, and though his face
Has faded into the city of the lost,
I look at my hand and see the injured place.

Like hasty marks on an explorer's chart:
This white stream bed, this blue lake on my knee
Are an angry doctor at midnight, or a girl
Looking at the blood and trying not to see

What we both have seen. Most of my body lives,
But the scars are dead like the grooving of a frown,
Cannot be changed, and ceaselessly record
How much of me is already written down.

## RESOLVING DOUBTS

She:    If to demands of others I agree,
        Then I will be another, but not me.

He:    If their inquiring voices shake your ear,
        How will your very spirit help but hear?

She:    It will, a bird, desert its builded nest,
        And in the virgin cloudbank only rest.

He:    If they have wings like other birds of prey,
        How will it from those raptors keep away?

She:    It will seek out the ocean's whitest curl,
        And sink within it, and become a pearl.

He:    But when they dive as glittering fishes dive,
        Will they not take your luster all alive?

She:    Venue shall make no difference to disguise,
        Nor shall my center open to their eyes.

He:    But if by chance, by force, by God knows how,
        You all unguarded should some night allow
        Another there beside you in your bed,
        Body is body, and cannot lie dead.

She:    Body is body, but the heart stays true,
        And should that happen, I will think him you.

**ADRIENNE RICH**

Adrienne Rich writes: Born in Baltimore, May 16, 1929. Southern-Victorian-Gothic milieu. Wrote poems as a child, but became serious about it while a student at Radcliffe. When I was 21, precocious and ignorant, my first book won the Yale prize. Travelled abroad on a Guggenheim Fellowship, 1952–53, came home to marry the economist Alfred Conrad. Lived in Cambridge for about 13 years, raising three sons, trying to write poems. In 1962 I got a second Guggenheim, this one to buy time to shut myself in a room and write. Spent 15 months in Holland and did some translations of Dutch poetry. We moved to Manhattan in 1966 and I began teaching, first poetry workshops at Swarthmore and Columbia, then basic writing in the SEEK program at City College, where I have remained. My husband died suddenly in 1970. Of my six books, four are in print.

# Adrienne Rich

## AT A BACH CONCERT

Coming by evening through the wintry city
We said that art is out of love with life.
Here we approach a love that is not pity.

This antique discipline, tenderly severe,
Renews belief in love yet masters feeling,
Asking of us a grace in what we bear.

Form is the ultimate gift that love can offer—
The vital union of necessity
With all that we desire, all that we suffer.

A too-compassionate art is half an art.
Only such proud restraining purity
Restores the else-betrayed, too-human heart.

## PICNIC

Sunday in Inwood Park
               the picnic eaten
the chicken bones scattered
                  for the fox we'll
                    never see
the children playing in the caves
My death is folded in my pocket
                   like a nylon
                  raincoat
What kind of sunlight is it
              that leaves the
              rocks so cold?

## NOT LIKE THAT

It's so pure in the cemetery.
The children love to play up here.
It's a little town, a game of blocks,
a village packed in a box,
a pre-war German toy.
The turf is a bedroom carpet:
heal-all, strawberry flower
and hillocks of moss.
To come and sit here forever,
a cup of tea on one's lap
and one's eyes closed lightly, lightly,
perfectly still
in a nineteenth-century sleep!
it seems so normal to die.

Nobody sleeps here, children.
The little beds of white wrought iron
and the tall, kind, faceless nurse
are somewhere else, in a hospital
or the dreams of prisoners of war.
The drawers of this trunk are empty,
not even a snapshot
curls in a corner.

In Pullmans of childhood we lay
enthralled behind dark-green curtains,
and a little lamp burned blue
all night, for us. The day
was a dream too, even the oatmeal
under its silver lid, dream-cereal
spooned out in forests of spruce
skirting the green-black gorges,

thick woods of sleep, half prickle,
half lakes of fern.
To stay here forever
is not like that, nor even
simply to lie quite still,
the warm trickle of dream
staining the thick quiet.
The drawers of this trunk are empty.
They are all out of sleep up here.


## SIDE BY SIDE

Ho! in the dawn
how light we lie

stirring faintly as laundry
left all night on the lines.

You, a lemon-gold pyjama,
I, a trousseau-sheet, fine

linen worn paper-thin in places,
worked with the maiden monogram.

Lassitude drapes our folds.
We're slowly bleaching

with the days, the hours, and the years.
We are getting finer than ever,

time is wearing us to silk,
to sheer spiderweb.

The eye of the sun, rising, looks in
to ascertain how we are coming on.

**ROBERT PACK**

Robert Pack writes: I was born May 19, 1929 in New York City and spent my early childhood in the Hunts Point section of the Bronx where my father served as State Senator until his death. Later I was educated at the Ethical Culture Schools, Dartmouth College and Columbia University. After a grim two years in business, I returned to school and subsequently became a teacher—a career that has brought me continual satisfaction. For me teaching has the drama of familial emotions and also their rewards. In 1961 I married Patricia Powell, and in 1964 we moved to Vermont where I am now Professor of English at Middlebury College. We have three children and live in a house we built on a 100 acre farm, overlooking the Green Mountain Range (which is usually blue or purple). We cherish our privacy and are happier than perhaps one has the right to be in these times. It is from my sense of the goodness of private life, the ties of family and friendship, and the inexorable drift toward apocalypse, that I write my poems, hopefully more out of compassion than anger.

# Robert Pack

## THE PACK RAT

Collector of lost beads, buttons, bird bones,
Catalogue-maker with an eye for glitter,
Litter-lover, entrepreneur of waste—
Bits of snail-shell, chips of jugs, red thread,
Blue thread, tinfoil, teeth; fair-minded thief
(Leaving in my pocket when I slept,
A pine-cone and two nuts for the dime you stole);
Reasonable romancer, journeying more
Than half a mile to get a mate, split-eared
Lover with a bitten tail (your mate mates rough),
You last all courtship long, you stick around
When the brood comes, unlike most other rats;
Payer of prices, busy with no dreams,

But brain enough to get along; moderate
Music maker with moderate powers, thumping
The drum of the frightened ground with both hind feet
Or scraping dry leaves till the still woods chirp;
Simple screamer seized by the owl's descent,
One scream and one regret, just one; fellow,
Forebear, survivor, I have lost my way.

---

## IN A FIELD

Here, in a field
Of devil's paintbrushes,
The circle of far trees
Tightens, and near bushes
Hump like ruins
When the moon floats loosely
Past the desolation
Owl moans wake. Here,
As if the world's
Last lovers, we
Have rung from the ruins
The whippoorwill's

Thrust of melody.
You have fallen asleep,
Breathing as the wind breathes
Among the wetted thistle,
The scented vine,
And, listening, I move
My body toward you,
When a small convulsion
Shakes your hand,
The moonlight flashes
On your teeth.
I am afraid to kiss you.
Never have I wished more
Not to die.

---

## MY DAUGHTER

The odor of limp leaves

     from the drenched (November) lawn

Reminds me there is time

     to stop (inside) to pause

Watching you (by the window)

     gathering in all I need

To go on.

     Wrapped (for an instant only)

In your self

     you hold your green stuffed bird

As still as he

     believing he can fly

(That you can fly)?

     Only for an instant

I pause limp

     in your second year

As the leaves lie

     in the November morning mist

Their odor thickening

     (perhaps I imagine it)

Pouring in the window

     filling my mouth my breath

As I watch your breathing

     as I go on watching.

I am pouring out of myself

     my wounds open

But I am not hurt—

     what cure is this

What shall I do with my hands

     (shall I put them

In the fountain

     shall I heal the trees)?

Twitching his tail feathers the green bird

     scratches the leaves

The leaves fly up into the trees

     the fountain (where you sit)

Is singing

     angels are there

They pause to drink

       and the water pleases them.

My daughter what have you done

       I cannot go on watching

My hands are limp

       they would fly from me

To you

       as birds fly (as angels fly).

Do you see them in your hair

       Do you know who I am

Who must turn away

       as you rise (with your stuffed bird)

As your second year goes on

       and I go on

Though I am healed

       and all others (in November)

Who believe me.

---

## APOCALYPSE IN BLACK AND WHITE

When all the rubble of our fears was piled
Smoke upon dust, white silence upon smoke,
And one black horse reined loose by one white child
Broke by as black the bleating white waves broke,
Amid the first, the last, the dying dead,
All burning voices burned into my head.

One silenced cry, one charred black mouth, was all,
Its voices cinders searing my white eyes.

We wailed together at the wailing wall,
Blood from our hands and hearts smoking the skies,
And all the dead with all that dying spent
Cried out this death was more than death had meant.

Into the rubbled wall, the smoke, the waves,
Rode one black child spurred free on his white horse,
The white-charred men burned down in their black graves,
Fear of white death had finished its black course;
One hope, one fate, one death, one brotherhood
Was all I saw, and all I understood.

---

## LOVE

It's not that I usually try for much
The very first time I'm with a girl, and though
She was attractive, nice breasts especially,
Full but with a good lilt to them,
Still it wasn't as if I was smitten
Or really out of control. So when I eased my hand
On that fine left breast and she seemed
To like it and slipped me a look that might mean
Uncertainty or confusion or you-belong-to-me-now,
I figured what-the-hell and started unbuttoning her.
But when my hand wiggled inside, I found
A rabbit. "Keep it," she said, quite openly I thought,
Not teary or wistful as if to indicate
That's-far-enough. So I coolly fingered back (was she
Putting me on?), but it was a book I found this time—
One, as a matter of fact, that I hadn't read.
"Thank you," I said, and I wasn't merely
Being polite; after all, what *can* you say
To a girl? Another try: this time I found
A necktie. At first I gussed she might be
Criticizing my taste, but no— it was exactly my style
And quite expensive. My birthday's not till June;
Consider, what could I feel but gratitude?
And is man ever able to hold himself back
When a good thing comes his way? I was getting
Excited, and in I plunged again: a potted plant,
A wallet, a pair of gloves, theater tickets, binoculars,
Another tie, another rabbit, more books, and then—
A breast! My god, did I do something wrong?
Is she getting tired of me?

# George Garrett

## GEORGE GARRETT

George Garrett writes: So? So Real Life leaves something to be desired. I try to cultivate a full rich fantasy life and, more or less, behave myself. The poems are like postcards from that trip. The facts? Born 11 June 1929 in Orlando, Florida. Went to Princeton because they wore stripes on the arms of their football jerseys. Was in U.S. Army. Did any number of dumb jobs. Took up teaching. Have taught at Wesleyan, Rice, Virginia, Princeton, Hollins, and now South Carolina. Have written little-known novels, stories, some plays & movies of same category (man, it's *hard* to write a little-known *movie!*). Have beautiful wife and 3 neat, smart, amazing kids, who're willing to put up with my bad habits and hobbies. Speaking of which I'm real pleased you picked some little-known examples of same for this anthology. Sorry about the photograph. It's not the Real Me, of course. Just a disguise. . . .

## SALOME

I had a dream of purity.

From weight of flesh and cage of bone,
it was I who was set free
and that other me like a blown weed
was scattered by the wind. Frail bones
(They were so small and light to carry
so much hunger and fury.)
crumbled into finest dust
and the wind took that away too.
And last of all my mouth, my lips,
a red yawn, a taut shriek, my tongue
fluttered like a dead leaf and vanished.
And then it was I who was free,
flying lonely above the ruins,
the slight debris of all the fires
I had lived with, wholly consumed by.
All my dust was gone for good,
and that part of me, the breath of God,
glowed without burning, shone with dark
  light,
danced like fountains at the weightless peak
of pure delight and fell. . . .

I woke up gnashing my teeth.
—Is anything wrong? they asked.
—Did you have a bad dream?
—Do you have a fever?

—I have had a dream of purity, I said.
And then they all laughed
and my mouth stretched with laughter too,
red and white, obscene,
and my tongue was as sweet as a fresh plum
  again.
And I . . . I was on fire as before.

I have known other dreams,
the ordinary ones:
Myself naked,
riding bareback on a horse
across a country like the moon.
Something is chasing us
(or *me* anyway)
and my little whip sings
and the horse gnaws at the bit.
The wind is like ice water.
*Then suddenly the horse is riding me!*
I wake up screaming my name.

Another:
Myself with feathers and wings.
But I can't fly. I am caught.
They start to pluck me.
Now each feather is a single hair
yanked by the tender roots.
I try to cry but no sound comes.
My mouth is full of fur.
I wake up and find
I have fallen out of my cold bed.

I tell you all this
not for the pennies of your pity.
Save those coins to cover your eyes.
Nor for your eyebrows
to chevron my rank of shame.
Nor for you to whisper about me
behind your cupped palms.
But that you may know
what a thing it is to be chosen.

I had every right to love and hate holiness.

—What is flesh? you ask.
I have been called sweet,
a hive of dark honey,
worthy of worship
from roots of hair to toes.
I have been called cruel,
the tormentor of dreams,
a dancer of the abstract fancy.
All of which is a dirty lie.
The plain truth is
I was a creature that sweats,
excretes, sags, ages, wrinkles. . . .
My bones were weary of me.

The soul, then?
I think I dreamed it once.

—And the other dreams?
They weren't me. Not me! Not me!
I was not the one who was dreaming.

Bring on the wild man,
bearded like black sky before a storm,
eyes all alight like white water,
wrapped in rags,
skin and bones corrupted by neglect,
a mouth of ruined teeth and bitter breath,
a cripple cursing every dancer.

—How have you come from my dream?
I wanted to say. —Bless me!
I longed to kiss
but my lips spat for me.

Understand this:
I loved him as myself.
God must love His creatures so.

But I was caged.
My skin and bones hated me.
My thoughts hooded me like a wild bird.

The Dance?
Believe what you care to.
Picture it any way you want to.
All the world knows
truth is best revealed
by gradual deception.
It was a striptease pure and simple.

My tongue cried for his head.
But it was my mouth that kissed him
and was damned.

Then I was free and able to rejoice.

A bad marriage from the beginning,
you say, a complete mismatch.
Flesh and spirit wrestle
and we call it love.

We couple like dogs in heat.
We shudder and are sundered.
We pursue ourselves,
sniffing, nose to tail
a comic parade of appetites.

That is the truth,
but not the whole truth.
Do me a little justice.
I had a dream of purity
And I have lived in the desert ever since.

## TIRESIAS

Speak to us who
are also split.
Speak to the two
we love and hate.

You have been both
and you have known
the double truth
as, chaste, obscene,

you were the lover
and the loved.
You were the giver
who received.

Now tell us how
we can be one
another too.
Speak to us who

in single wrath
cannot be true
to life or death.
Blinder than you.

## ROMANTIC

I have heard some jealous women say
that if your skin were cut away
and tacked upon a public wall
it would not please the eyes at all.

They say your bones are no great prize,
that hanging in the neutral breeze,
your rig of ribs, your trim of thighs
would catch no fetching harmonies,

but tinkle like a running mouse
over piano keys. They hold
that, stripped, your shabby soul
would whimper like a vacant house

you are so haunted. "Ask
her," they say, "if she'll unmask.
Let her shed beauty like the trees.
Time will bring her to her knees."

Still, I must have you as you are,
all of a piece, beautiful and vain,
burning and freezing, near and far,
and all my joy and all my pain.

And if you live to scrub a floor
with prayer, to weep like a small ghost,
which of us will suffer more?
Who will be wounded most?

## AFTER BAD DREAMS

Let holy saints, now safely out
of skin and bones, arise in unison
to tip their hats and halos of pure light.
Let angels dip their wings in flight,
scattering brightness like confusion
of ice and snow. Let poor ghosts shout,

sinners and losers, gray as smoke,
notorious and nameless in this glint
of morning, shout hosanna.
In sleep I walked the desert. Manna
did not fall. I lusted for a hint
of water, tasted dust. A dirty joke

troubled my tongue when I tried to pray.
Now there's light enough to swim in
and every stone smells freshly baked.
I drink the wine of morning for my shadow's sake,
he who has suffered and must suffer once again,
who now falls victim to a perfect day.

**X. J. KENNEDY**

X. J. Kennedy writes: Born (August 21, 1929) and brought up in Dover, New Jersey, the late and only child of a Roman Catholic clerk in a boiler factory, a gentle man given to rising at dawn to feed birds, and a Methodist ex-nurse, who set me to scribbling early. Through puberty I lived in a world of fantasy, publishing mimeographed science-fiction fan magazines called *Vampire* and *Terrifying Test-tube Tales.* After college (Seton Hall) and an M.A. (Columbia), I fled the draft and high-school teaching by enlisting in the Navy (highest rating attained: journalist second class). I was sent on cruises aboard destroyers, to take pictures of the crew for their home town newspapers. Began writing verses in my bunk, keeping out of the way of the deck force. Then came a year in Paris on the GI bill and six years in Ann Arbor, Michigan, not finishing a doctorate. Michigan swarmed with young poets: Keith Waldrop, Don Hall, James Camp, Dallas Wiebe, Donald Hope, and Snodgrass in nearby Detroit. There, too, I met my wife, Dorothy Mintzlaff, and gathered a first book. Nowadays I teach for my bread, at Tufts, and have written a schoolbook. In 1969 there was a second book of verse, and in 1971 an English selected poems. We live in Bedford, Mass., with a girl, three boys, and a little magazine, *Countermeasures.* I try to write close-mouthed stuff that has rimes and beats, and sometimes tunes.

# X. J. Kennedy

## NOTHING IN HEAVEN FUNCTIONS AS IT OUGHT

Nothing in Heaven functions as it ought:
Peter's bifocals, blindly sat on, crack;
His gates lurch with the cackle of a cock,
Not turn with a hush of gold as Milton had thought;
Gangs of the slaughtered innocents keep huffing
The nimbus off the Venerable Bede
Like that of an old dandelion gone to seed;
And the beatific choir keep breaking up, coughing.

But Hell, sleek Hell hath no freewheeling part:
None takes his own sweet time, none quickens pace.
Ask anyone, How come you here, poor heart?—
And he will slot a quarter through his face,
You'll hear an instant click, a tear will start
Imprinted with an abstract of his case.

## NATIONAL SHRINE

Sanctioned by eagles, this house. Here they'd met,
Undone their swordbelts, smoked awhile and posed
Gazes that could not triumph or forget,
And held their jowls set till a shutter closed.

Kentucky rifle now, and Parrot gun
Cohabit under glass. Connecticut
And Alabama, waxed sleek in the sun,
Reflect like sisters in the parking lot.

Lee's troops led home to gutted field and farm
Mules barely stumbling. Borne off in each car,
The wounded sun and instant Kodachrome
Render our truces brighter than they are.

## FIRST CONFESSION

Blood thudded in my ears. I scuffed,
  Steps stubborn, to the telltale booth
Beyond whose curtained portal coughed
  The robed repositor of truth.

The slat shot back. The universe
  Bowed down his cratered dome to hear
Enumerated my each curse,
  The sip snitched from my old man's beer,

My sloth pride envy lechery,
  The dime held back from Peter's Pence
With which I'd bribed my girl to pee
  That I might spy her instruments.

Hovering scale-pans when I'd done
  Settled their balance slow as silt
While in the restless dark I burned
  Bright as a brimstone in my guilt

Until as one feeds birds he doled
  Seven Our Fathers and a Hail
Which I to double-scrub my soul
  Intoned twice at the altar rail

Where Sunday in seraphic light
  I knelt, as full of grace as most,
And stuck my tongue out at the priest:
  A fresh roost for the Holy Ghost.

**DONALD FINKEL**

**Donald Finkel was born on October 21, 1929. He writes: Due to an uncanny sense of timing DF was born in the Year of the Crash, in NYC. He would prefer to forget his childhood. He awoke from that dream at the age of 21 washing dishes in a coffeehouse in Greenwich Village. Since then he has produced five books and, with the help of his wife, the poet Constance Urdang, three children and a Volkswagen bus. Like too many of his kind he has resorted to teaching in order to support his habits (at Iowa, Bard, Bennington and Washington University in St. Louis, where he is now poet-in-residence). John Simon Guggenheim once gave him a year off for good behavior.**

## CROSS TIES

Out walking ties left over from a track
Where nothing travels now but rust and grass,
I could take stock in something that would pass
Bearing down Hell-bent from behind my back:
A thing to sidestep or go down before,
Far-off, indifferent as that curfew's wail
The evening wind flings like a sack of mail
Or close up as the moon whose headbeam stirs
A flock of cloud to make tracks. Down to strafe
The bristled grass a hawk falls—there's a screech
Like steel wrenched taut till severed. Out of reach
Or else beneath desiring, I go safe,
Walk on, tensed for a leap, unreconciled
To a dark void all kindness.
                    When I spill
The salt I throw the Devil some and, still,
I let them sprinkle water on my child.

# Donald Finkel

## KING MIDAS HAS ASSES' EARS

Under his careful crown he keeps
His psyche safe, and every day
In a kingdom of eyes he makes his way.
Only at midnight when his subjects sleep
In easy ignorance he stands before
His mirror, running his soft ears
Through his hands. Below the stairs
Servants like recriminations stir
In their beds, and the night birds
Scream Ears, ears! in mounting minor thirds.

Nobody hears, but yet he royally must
Be shaved in the mornings, nightly undressed;
Sunlight through his window-blind commands
The drawing near of strange impolitic hands.
His valet knocks: now like a whore he suffers
The hands, the eyes, of an untimely lover.

The barber stands behind his chair
And works the secrets from his hair;
As in a dim confessional,
The secular professional
Passive uncomprehending ear
Hears more than it was meant to hear.

I am a king who tells you this. Just so,
I keep them under my hat, all day
My kingdom course, between the hands and eyes;
At night before my mirror watch them grow
Softer and taller. Yet cannot keep
My peace: it is not servants merely
Who run and tell. I tell them daily
When they cut my hair, drag up my steep
Stair ice, my laundry. I confide
To urchins in the street who clean my shoes,
Stretch on a couch each morning and accuse
Myself of murder, mayhem, fratricide.
I am a king who tells you this: they know
Us better than we know ourselves, and rightly so.

---

## THEY

are at the end of our street now cutting down the trees
a scream like a seven foot locust they have cut off another
neatly at the pavement     never again will the pin-oak threaten
a taxi will the ash lie in wait to fall on a child     it is
a good time for this the sun is bright     the plane has only
just begun to sprout little shoots from under her fingernails
never again will she dance her terrible saraband in the tornado
the sweet gum trembles bristling with tiny mines like brown
sea urchins     never again will she drop them on the walk
to menace the sensible shoes of mailmen     they have brought
a machine that eats trees that shits sawdust     they cut off
their limbs to feed it     snarling it chews the pale green fingers
of the plane the pin-oak's wrinkled elbows and knees     they
fill truck after truck with the dust     in the schoolyard
now they are cutting down the children I can hear their screams
first at the ankles     it is nothing at all then to sever
their soles from the asphalt     there is no danger their
falling on the school and crushing it     I have invented
a machine that shoots words I type faster and faster I cannot
keep up with them in front of the house now they are cutting
the rosebush vainly she scratches their faces like a drowning
kitten they are cutting the grass scythes in their wheels
they race over our lawn flashing in the sun like the chariots
of the barbarians     the grass-blades huddle whimpering
there is no place to go     it is spring and the street
is alive with the cry of mowers     the laughter of saws.

# John Hollander

## THE GREAT BEAR

Even on clear nights, lead the most supple children
Out onto hilltops, and by no means will
They make it out. Neither the gruff round image
From a remembered page nor the uncertain
Finger tracing that image out can manage
To mark the lines of what ought to be there,
Passing through certain bounding stars, until
The whole massive expanse of bear appear
Swinging, across the ecliptic; and, although
The littlest ones say nothing, others respond,
Making us thankful in varying degrees
For what we would have shown them: "There it is!"
"I see it now!" Even "Very like a bear!"
Would make us grateful. Because there is no bear

We blame our memory of the picture: trudging
Up the dark, starlit path, stooping to clutch
An anxious hand, perhaps the outline faded
Then; perhaps could we have retained the thing
In mind ourselves, with it we might have staged
Something convincing. We easily forget
The huge, clear, homely dipper that is such
An event to reckon with, an object set
Across the space the bear should occupy;
But even so, the trouble lies in pointing
At any stars. For one's own finger aims
Always elsewhere: the man beside one seems
Never to get the point. "No! The bright star
Just above my fingertip." The star,

If any, that he sees beyond one's finger
Will never be the intended one. To bring
Another's eye to bear in such a fashion
On any single star seems to require
Something very like a constellation
That both habitually see at night;
Not in the stars themselves, but in among
Their scatter, perhaps, some old familiar sight
Is always there to take a bearing from.
And if the smallest child of all should cry
Out on the wet, black grass because he sees
Nothing but stars, though claiming that there is
Some bear not there that frightens him, we need
Only reflect that we ourselves have need

Of what is fearful (being really nothing)
With which to find our way about the path
That leads back down the hill again, and with
Which to enable the older children standing
By us to follow what we mean by "This
Star," "That one," or "The other one beyond it."

But what of the tiny, scared ones?—Such a bear,
Who needs it? We can still make do with both
The dipper that we always knew was there
And the bright, simple shapes that suddenly
Emerge on certain nights. To understand
The signs that stars compose, we need depend
Only on stars that are entirely there
And the apparent space between them. There

Never need be lines between them, puzzling
Our sense of what is what. What a star does
Is never to surprise us as it covers
The center of its patch of darkness, sparkling
Always, a point in one of many figures.
One solitary star would be quite useless,
A frigid conjecture, true but trifling;
And any single sign is meaningless
If unnecessary. Crab, bull, and ram,
Or frosty, irregular polygons of our own
Devising, or finally the Great Dark Bear
That we can never quite believe is there—
Having the others, any one of them
Can be dispensed with. The bear, of all of them,

Is somehow most like any one, taken
At random, in that we always tend to say
That just because it might be there; because
Some Ancients really traced it out, a broken
And complicated line, webbing bright stars
And fainter ones together; because a bear
Habitually appeared—then even by day
It is for us a thing that should be there.
We should not want to train ourselves to see it.
The world is everything that happens to
Be true. The stars at night seem to suggest
The shapes of what might be. If it were best,
Even, to have it there (such a great bear!
All hung with stars!), there still would be no bear.


THE NINTH OF JULY

In 1939 the skylark had nothing to say to me
As the June sunset splashed rose light on the broad
   sidewalks
And prophesied no war after the end of that August;
Only, midway between playing ball in Manhattan and
   Poland
I turned in my sleep on Long Island, groped in the dark of
   July,
And found my pillow at last down at the foot of my bed.
Through the window near her bed, brakes gasped on
   Avenue B
In 1952; her blonde crotch shadowed and silent
Astonished us both, and the iced gunpowder tea grew warm,

Till the last hollow crust of icecube cracked to its death in
   the glass.
The tea was hot on the cold hilltop in the moonlight
While a buck thrashed through the gray ghosts of burnt-out
   trees
And Thomas whispered of the S.S. from inside his sleeping-
   bag.
Someone else told a tale of the man who was cured of a
   hurt by the bears.
The bathtub drain in the Old Elberon house gucked and
   snorted
When the shadows of graying maples fell across the lawn:
The brown teddybear was a mild comfort because of his
   silence,
And I gazed at the porthole ring made by the windowshade
String, hanging silently, seeing a head and shoulders emerge
From the burning *Morro Castle* I'd seen that afternoon.
The rock cried out "I'm burning, too" as the drying heat
Entered its phase of noon over the steep concrete
Walls along Denver's excuse for a river: we read of remote
Bermudas, and gleaming Neal spat out over the parapet.
In the evening in Deal my b.b. rifle shattered a milkbottle
While the rhododendrons burned in the fading light. The tiny
Shot-sized hole in the bathhouse revealed the identical twats
Of the twins from over the hill. From over the hill on the
   other
Side of the lake a dark cloud turreted over the sunset;
Another lake sank to darkness on the other side of the hill,
Lake echoing lake in diminishing pools of reflection.
A trumpet blew Taps. While the drummer's foot boomed on
   the grandstand
The furriers' wives by the pool seemed to ignore the
   accordion
Playing "Long Ago and Far Away." None of the alewives
Rose to our nightcrawlers, wiggling on the other side of the
   mirror.
She was furrier under the darkness of all the blanketing heat
Than I'd thought to find her, and the bathroom mirror
   flashed
White with the gleam of a car on seventy-second street.
We lay there just having died; the two of us, vision and flesh,
Contraction and dream, came apart, while the fan on the
   windowsill
Blew a thin breeze of self between maker and muse, dividing
Fusing of firework, love's old explosion and outburst of
   voice.

This is the time most real: for unreeling time there are no
Moments, there are no points, but only the lines of memory
Streaking across the black film of the mind's night.
But here in the darkness between two great explosions of
   light,
Midway between the fourth of July and the fourteenth,
Suspended somewhere in summer between the ceremonies

Remembered from childhood and the historical conflagrations
Imagined in sad, learned youth—somewhere there always
    hangs
The American moment.
                          Burning, restless, between the deed
And the dream is the life remembered: the sparks of Concord
    were mine
As I lit a cherry-bomb once in a glow of myth
And hurled it over the hedge. The complexities of the Terror
Were mine as my poring eyes got burned in the fury of
    Europe
Discovered in nineteen forty-two. On the ninth of July
I have been most alive; world and I, in making each other
As always, make fewer mistakes.
                          The gibbous, historical moon
Records our nights with an eye neither narrowed against the
    brightness
Of nature, nor widened with awe at the clouds of the life of
    the mind.
Crescent and full, knowledge and touch commingled here
On this dark bed, window flung wide to the cry of the city
    night,
We lie still, making the poem of the world that emerges from
    shadows.

Doing and then having done is having ruled and commanded
A world, a self, a poem, a heartbeat in the moonlight.

To imagine a language means to imagine a form of life.

**ALVIN AUBERT**

Alvin Aubert was born on March 12, 1930, in Lutcher, Louisiana. He writes: I teach Afro-American literature at State University College, Fredonia, New York, where I live with my wife, Bernadine, and our two daughters, Mimi and Debbie. Before coming to Fredonia I taught for ten years at my alma mater, Southern University in Baton Rouge, Louisiana, forty-five miles from my hometown. I was a 1959 Woodrow Wilson Fellow at the University of Michigan and a 1968 Bread Loaf Scholar in Poetry. My poems have appeared in *The Journal of Black Poetry, Negro Digest, Prairie Schooner, The New Orleans Review, Motive, Jeopardy, Discourse,* the *New South Quarterly, Anon,* and *Analecta.*

# Alvin Aubert

## NAT TURNER IN THE CLEARING

                    Ashes, Lord—
But warm still from the fire that cheered us,
Lighted us in this clearing where it seems
Scarcely an hour ago we feasted on
Burnt pig from our tormentor's unwilling
Bounty and charted the high purpose your
Word had launched us on. And now, my comrades
Dead, or taken; your servant, pressed by the
Bloody yelps of hounds, forsaken, save for
The stillness of the word that persists quivering
And breath-moist on his tongue; and these faint coals
Soon to be rushed to dying glow by the
Indifferent winds of miscarriage—What now,
My Lord? A Priestess once, they say, could write
On leaves, unlock the time-bound spell of deeds
Undone. I let fall upon these pale remains
Your breath-moist word, preempt the winds, and give
Them now their one last glow, that some dark child
In time to come might pass this way and, in
This clearing, read and know.

**GREGORY CORSO**

Gregory Corso was born in New York City on March 26, 1930. Much of his education was gained in an orphanage, in Bellevue, and in jail before he was old enough to be out of high school. He worked as a laborer, a reporter, and a merchant seaman before becoming a central figure in the Beat Movement. In addition to his poetry, which has brought him the Longview Award and a Poetry Foundation Award, he has also written drama and fiction. He continues his own special education, traveling where his travels take him.

## BESSIE SMITH'S FUNERAL

The brief procession.
The crude gray church that pegs the bend
Of a river. After brisk December air

Smoke-white walls,
An artless trim of brown,
Windows unadorned
Except for what of fields beyond
The eye can trace on dusty panes.

Chafed by fiery oration
That rains on salamandered ears,
Naked bulbs retreat
From slaking so much darkness, turn
To dalliance with lilies and a casket
Textured to the dime-store toy that reins
The impish hands of a child close by.

Spirits are abroad in the splintery pews,
Restless in the drafty aisles, will not
Give way to order of service, to such
Superfluous mourning;

One, a burly chantress with a song,
Balks the yokeless choir that grates
The lily-scented air;
Her song is news, begins the dispensation
Of the blues.

## LAST WILL AND TESTAMENT

Something is happening.
Before it gets the upper hand
I write my will.
I do it without benefit of counsel.
Who needs that kind of advice.
To my daughter, age four, I leave
An egg.
To my wife,
Instruction to destroy
The incubator.

## CODICIL

Nothing is happening after all.
But keep the egg, daughter.
By right it's yours.
When there's time
From keeping my other things whole
We'll have a look at it
Together.
As for the incubator, my
Patient wife,
That part still holds.

# Gregory Corso

## MARRIAGE

Should I get married? Should I be good?
Astound the girl next door with my velvet suit and faustus
   hood?
Don't take her to movies but to cemeteries
tell all about werewolf bathtubs and forked clarinets
then desire her and kiss her and all the preliminaries
and she going just so far and I understanding why
not getting angry saying You must feel! It's beautiful to
   feel!
Instead take her in my arms lean against an old crooked
   tombstone
and woo her the entire night the constellations in the
   sky —

When she introduces me to her parents
back straightened, hair finally combed, strangled by a tie,
should I sit knees together on their 3rd degree sofa
and not ask Where's the bathroom?
How else to feel other than I am,

often thinking Flash Gordon soap—
O how terrible it must be for a young man
seated before a family and the family thinking
We never saw him before! He wants our Mary Lou!
After tea and homemade cookies they ask What do you do
    for a living?

Should I tell them? Would they like me then?
Say All right get married, we're losing a daughter
but we're gaining a son—
And should I then ask Where's the bathroom?

O God, and the wedding! All her family and her friends
and only a handful of mine all scroungy and bearded
just wait to get at the drinks and food—
And the priest! he looking at me as if I masturbated
asking me Do you take this woman for your lawful wedded
    wife?
And I trembling what to say say Pie Glue!
I kiss the bride all those corny men slapping me on the back
She's all yours, boy! Ha-ha-ha!
And in their eyes you could see some obscene honeymoon
    going on—

Then all that absurd rice and clanky cans and shoes
Niagara Falls! Hordes of us! Husbands! Wives! Flowers!
    Chocolates!

All streaming into cozy hotels
All going to do the same thing tonight
The indifferent clerk he knowing what was going to happen
The lobby zombies they knowing what
The whistling elevator man he knowing
The winking bellboy knowing
Everybody knowing! I'd be almost inclined not to do
    anything!
Stay up all night! Stare that hotel clerk in the eye!
Screaming: I deny honeymoon! I deny honeymoon!
running rampant into those almost climactic suites
yelling Radio belly! Cat shovel!
O I'd live in Niagara forever! in a dark cave beneath the Falls
I'd sit there the Mad Honeymooner
devising ways to break marriages, a scourge of bigamy
a saint of divorce—

But I should get married I should be good
How nice it'd be to come home to her
and sit by the fireplace and she in the kitchen
aproned young and lovely wanting my baby
and so happy about me she burns the roast beef
and comes crying to me and I get up from my big papa chair
saying Christmas teeth! Radiant brains! Apple deaf!
God what a husband I'd make! Yes, I should get married!
So much to do! like sneaking into Mr Jones' house late at
    night

and cover his golf clubs with 1920 Norwegian books
Like hanging a picture of Rimbaud on the lawnmower
like pasting Tannu Tuva postage stamps all over the picket
    fence
like when Mrs Kindhead comes to collect for the Community
    Chest
grab her and tell her There are unfavorable omens in the sky!
And when the mayor comes to get my vote tell him
When are you going to stop people killing whales!
And when the milkman comes leave him a note in the bottle
Penguin dust, bring me penguin dust, I want penguin dust—

Yet if I should get married and it's Connecticut and snow
and she gives birth to a child and I am sleepless, worn,
up for nights, head bowed against a quiet window, the past
    behind me,
finding myself in the most common of situations a trembling
    man
knowledged with responsibility not twig-smear nor Roman
    coin soup—
O what would that be like!
Surely I'd give it for a nipple a rubber Tacitus
For a rattle a bag of broken Bach records
Tack Della Francesca all over its crib
Sew the Greek alphabet on its bib
And build for its playpen a roofless Parthenon

No, I doubt I'd be that kind of father
not rural not snow no quiet window
but hot smelly tight New York City
seven flights up, roaches and rats in the walls
a fat Reichian wife screeching over potatoes Get a job!
And five nose running brats in love with Batman
And the neighbors all toothless and dry haired
like those hag masses of the 18th century
all wanting to come in and watch TV
The landlord wants his rent
Grocery store Blue Cross Gas & Electric Knights of
    Columbus
Impossible to lie back and dream Telephone snow, ghost
    parking—
No! I should not get married I should never get married!
But—imagine If I were married to a beautiful sophisticated
    woman
tall and pale wearing an elegant black dress and long black
    gloves
holding a cigarette holder in one hand and a highball in the
    other
and we lived high up in a penthouse with a huge window
from which we could see all of New York and even farther
    on clearer days
No, can't imagine myself married to that pleasant prison
    dream—

O but what about love? I forget love
not that I am incapable of love
it's just that I see love as odd as wearing shoes—
I never wanted to marry a girl who was like my mother
And Ingrid Bergman was always impossible
And there's maybe a girl now but she's already married
And I don't like men and—
but there's got to be somebody!
Because what if I'm 60 years old and not married,
all alone in a furnished room with pee stains on my
    underwear
and everybody else is married! All the universe married but
    me!

Ah, yet well I know that were a woman possible as I am
    possible
then marriage would be possible—
Like SHE in her lonely alien gaud waiting her Egyptian lover
so I wait—bereft of 2,000 years and the bath of life.


## THE LAST GANGSTER

Waiting by the window
my feet enwrapped with the dead bootleggers of Chicago
I am the last gangster, safe, at last,
waiting by a bullet-proof window.

I look down the street and know
the two torpedoes from St. Louis.
I've watched them grow old
. . . guns rusting in their arthritic hands.


## I AM 25

With a love a madness for Shelley
Chatterton    Rimbaud
and the needy-yap of my youth
        has gone from ear to ear:
       I HATE OLD POETMEN!
Especially old poetmen who retract
who consult other old poetmen
who speak their youth in whispers,
saying:—I did those then
        but that was then
        that was then—
O I would quiet old men
say to them:—I am your friend
        what you once were, thru me
        you'll be again—
Then at night in the confidence of their homes
rip out their apology-tongues
        and steal their poems.


## BUT I DO NOT NEED KINDNESS

I have known the strange nurses of Kindness,
I have seen them kiss the sick, attend the old,
give candy to the mad!
I have watched them, at night, dark and sad,
rolling wheelchairs by the sea!
I have known the fat pontiffs of Kindness,
the little old grey-haired lady,
the neighborhood priest,
the famous poet,
the mother,
I have known them all!
I have watched them, at night, dark and sad,
pasting posters of mercy
        on the stark posts of despair.

2

I have known Almighty Kindness Herself!
I have sat beside Her pure white feet,
gaining Her confidence!
We spoke of nothing unkind,
but one night I was tormented by those strange nurses,
those fat pontiffs
The little old lady rode a spiked car over my head!
The priest cut open my stomach, put his hands in me,
and cried:—Where's your soul? Where's your soul!—
The famous poet picked me up
and threw me out of the window!
The mother abandoned me!
I ran to Kindness, broke into Her chamber,
and profaned!
with an unnamable knife I gave Her a thousand wounds,
and inflicted them with filth!
I carried Her away, on my back, like a ghoul!
down the cobble-stoned night!
Dogs howled! Cats fled! All windows closed!
I carried Her ten flights of stairs!
Dropped Her on the floor of my small room,
and kneeling beside Her, I wept. I wept.

3

But what is Kindness? I have killed Kindness,
but what is it?
You are kind because you live a kind life.
St. Francis was kind.
The landord is kind.
A cane is kind.
Can I say people, sitting in parks, are kinder?

# Miller Williams

**MILLER WILLIAMS**

Miller Williams writes: I was born April 8, 1930, in Hoxie, Arkansas, where my father was the Methodist preacher. I most remember gospel music and country music and Chopin on a wind-up Victrola when nobody had wind-up Victrolas anymore, tent revivals and Woodrow Wilson Grade School, Foxe's Book of Martyrs and the King James Bible and Shakespeare, and maybe the only Methodist parsonage in the country haunted by the ghosts of Joe Hill and Jimmie Rodgers and Eugene V. Debs and King Lear. After picking up degrees in science for some reason I still don't understand and teaching college biology for a few years, then quitting to sell refrigerators for Sears, I was offered a Fellowship to the Bread Loaf Writers' Conference and went and met John Ciardi and John Nims and Howard Nemerov and Robert Frost and got lost and got a job teaching English, went to live in Chile and met Nicanor Parra and then Mexico and didn't meet anybody and then came home to teach and write and live with Becky Hall and now and then three children.

## LET ME TELL YOU

how to do it from the beginning.
First notice everything:
The stain on the wallpaper
of the vacant house,
the mothball smell of a
Greyhound toilet.
Miss nothing. Memorize it.
You cannot twist the fact you do not know.

Remember
The blonde girl you saw in the spade bar.
Put a scar on her breast.
Say she left home to get away from her
    father.
Invent whatever will support your line.
Leave out the rest.

Use metaphors: The mayor is a pig
is a metaphor
which is not to suggest

it is not a fact.
Which is irrelevant.
Nothing is less important
than a fact.

Be suspicious of any word you learned
and were proud of learning.
It will go bad.
It will fall off the page.

When your father lies
in the last light
and your mother cries for him,
listen to the sound of her crying.
When your father dies
take notes
somewhere inside.

If there is a heaven
he will forgive you
if the line you found was a good line.

It does not have to be worth the dying.

## THE CATERPILLAR

Today on the lip of a bowl in the backyard
we watched a caterpillar caught in the circle
of his larval assumptions

my daughter counted
27 times he went around
before rolling back and laughing
*I'm a caterpillar, look*
she left him
measuring out his slow green way to some
    place
there must have been a picture of inside him

After supper
coming from putting the car up
we stopped to look
figured he crossed the yard
once every hour
and left him
when we went to bed
wrinkling no closer to my landlord's leaves
than when he somehow fell to his private
    circle

Later I followed
barefeet and doorclicks of my daughter
to the yard          the bowl
a milkwhite moonlight eye
in the black grass

*it died*

I said honey they don't live very long

In bed again
re-covered and re-kissed
she locked her arms and mumbling love to
    mine
until turning she slipped
into the deep bone-bottomed dish
of sleep

Stumbling drunk around the rim
I hold
the words she said to me across the dark

*I think he thought he was*
*going in a straight line*

133

# Gary Snyder

**GARY SNYDER**

Born in San Francisco on May 8, 1930, Gary Snyder was reared in Seattle and educated in Portland, Bloomington, Berkeley, San Francisco, and Kyoto. He says, "My poetic mentors were Tu Fu, Archilochus, Rexroth, Duncan, Mila Repa, Buson, Blake, Lawrence, Jeffers, Whitman, Pound, Williams, Whalen and Graves (but not as a poet). One more: the unknown Makers of devotional Tantric Songs, and the ancient Singers of Turtle Island." He hopes to finish *Mountains & Rivers Without End* soon and then commence a series of Hymns to Logic and Ecstasy in their play with the inter-relatedness of myriad phenomena.

## ONCE ONLY

almost at the equator
almost at the equinox
   exactly at midnight
     from a ship
      the full

    moon

in the center of the sky.

*Sappa Creek near Singapore*
*March 1958*

## AFTER WORK

The shack and a few trees
float in the blowing fog

I pull out your blouse,
warm my cold hands
    on your breasts.
you laugh and shudder
peeling garlic by the
    hot iron stove.
bring in the axe, the rake,
the wood

we'll lean on the wall
against each other
stew simmering on the fire
as it grows dark
    drinking wine.

## LOOKING AT PICTURES TO BE PUT AWAY

Who was this girl
In her white night gown
Clutching a pair of jeans

On a foggy redwood deck.
She looks up at me tender,
Calm, surprised,

What will we remember
Bodies thick with food and lovers
After twenty years.

## SOME GOOD THINGS TO BE SAID FOR THE IRON AGE

A ringing tire iron
    dropped on the pavement

Whang of a saw
brusht on limbs

    the taste
    of rust.

# Milton Kessler

## ROUTE 40—OHIO, U.S.A.

It is dark now.

Nets of snow
Tumble about us.

We slide like fish,
The road dissolving.

And in the fields
The farmlights chant:

You have no land—
You have no land.

## THE LYNCHING

Dragged through doorways of fragrance
Dense as embalmer's perfume, Parker,
Wounds deep as blossoms,
Died beneath magnolia.
He fell; than sky was
Grass, and the flash of quartz in stone.
Blood soured; the cage was not enough.
They hacked the white bones through.

Tonight, in Poplarville,
The rain dies at the eaves;
Leaves fall face-downward;
The hill-shacks breathe on their stones;
Porches sag like lips
Tasting blood in their corners;
And three men sit on a fence
Only their odors alive.

But it happened, then, there,
With flowers: jasmine, lily, magnolia;
And by the smell of flowers
He knew the place.
Now, beneath birds,
Licked by the water's drifting mold,
Parker, skin bleaching white,
Swells in the Pearl River.

## BEYOND ANGUISH

At dawn, caught beneath the rim of light,
it fled into a place still black,
tore its side upon a nail,
and bled small robes upon the snow.
Then rain came, and fever, then cold
and the long cool drowse.
It slept to death within the cling of ice,
curled on its side in fetal dreaming.

At evening, when cobblestones shiver,
and every path has a figure,
the dead leaves jump in a flash of wind,
the trees are black with holding on.
And here in the snow he finds it,
under a window of laughing faces.
He thinks it is a child stillborn.
In anguish, he follows his own breath home.

But this night, the air changes, the bird
    comes,
men gather to smell the springtime.
And warm with thaw the gray fur shifts
equal in wind with the yellow grass.

**MILTON KESSLER**

Milton Kessler writes: Born in Brooklyn, May 9, 1930. Origins in Lithuania and Russia. My father, an athlete and singer, worked the graveyard shift at the General Post Office in Manhattan. I left high school at 15. Had many jobs: optician, shipping clerk, Roxy Theater usher, law clerk, freight loader, retailer. Studied to be a singer. Began college late, then taught literature at universities from Seattle to Boston; since 1965, at the State University of New York in Binghamton. Soon I'll take my wife and three children to Israel, where we will live in the Negev. Since '65, I've given many readings, made some recordings, and traveled in this country, Canada, and Europe. I continue to write very slowly, finding and losing myself again each time. The title of my third collection, *Woodlawn North,* comes from the Woodlawn section of the Bronx, where I lived during and after World War II. That's where the apartment houses end and the cemetery and some open land begin. Lately, I've been enjoying the poems of Lorine Niedecker; I've been translating ancient Egyptian songs, and I've been to England, where, in the Morden Tower and elsewhere, I read my work.

**BARRY SPACKS**

Barry Spacks writes: I was born (Feb. 21, 1931) and raised in Philadelphia; went to Central High School, where I debated, won an oratorical contest, acted in plays; then to the University of Pennsylvania, English Major, founding editor of the literary magazine, that sort of thing. The army supplied fourteen months in Korea; I returned to the School of Letters at Indiana University, and stayed on to teach at I.U., to take an M.A., to marry. Next there came a Fulbright year at Cambridge, then English teaching at the U. of Florida, and since 1960 at M.I.T. Meanwhile I'd been publishing poems, stories, essays, reviews, in various magazines. A first collection of poems appeared in 1969; a second now, *The Conscience of the Tide,* is almost ready. I've also brought forth a novel, *The Sophomore, and* adapted it for the movies, although the script was shelved. A second novel, *A Summer Soldier,* has reached its final stages, and meanwhile I teach, help to raise a daughter, hunt mushrooms, play pool, am very much the teacher-writer, reading my poems here and there, doing some politics when my conscience hurts, a committed commuter, a family man. Recently I won a prize, the St. Botolph's Arts Award for 1970. I paint a little. I also sing.

# Barry Spacks

## FRESHMEN

My freshmen
settle in. Achilles
sulks; Pascal consults
his watch; and true
Cordelia—with her just-washed hair,

stern-hearted princess, ready to defend
the meticulous garden of truths in her highschool notebook—
uncaps her ballpoint pen.
And the corridors drum:
give us a flourish, fluorescence of light, for the teachers
   come,

green and seasoned, bearers
of the Word, who differ
like its letters; there are some
so wise their eyes
are birdbites; one,

a mad, grinning gent with a golden tooth, God knows
he might be Pan, or the sub-
custodian; another
is a walking podium, dense
with his mystery—high

priests and attachés
of the ministry; kindly
old women, like unfashionable watering places;
and the assuming young, rolled tight as a City
umbrella;

thought-salesmen with samples cases,
and saints upon whom
merely to gaze is like Sunday—
their rapt, bright,
cat-licked faces!

And the freshmen wait;
wait bristling, acned, glowing like a brand,
or easy, chatting, munching, muscles lax,
each in his chosen corner, and in each
a chosen corner.

Full of certainties and reasons,
or uncertainties and reasons,
full of reasons as a conch contains the sea,
they wait: for the term's first bell;
for another mismatched wrestle through the year;

for a teacher who's religious in his art,
a wizard of a sort, to call the roll

and from mere names
cause people
to appear.

The best look like the swinging door
to the Opera just before
the Marx Brothers break through.
The worst—debased,
on the back row,

as far as one can go
from speech—
are walls where childish scribbling's been erased;
are stones
to teach.

And I am paid to ask them questions:
Dare man proceed by need alone?
Did Esau like
his pottage?
Is any heart in order after Belsen?

And when one stops to think, I'll catch his heel,
put scissors to him, excavate his chest!
Watch, freshmen, for my words about the past
can make you turn your back. I wait to throw,
most foul, most foul, the future in your face.


## THE OUTRAGEOUSLY BLESSED

The gods would have us chastened through confusion,
so those who tempt the skies' outrage are blessed.
Though Zeus might be a cupboy for the thanks he gets
from these,
the pretty boys who'd fall asleep
disputing with slow Socrates,
they're still the ones who catch the key equations
and laugh to straw the schoolmen and the schools;
they win the game by changing all the rules.

Small comfort to the sane, who do their best,
to find we cherish maddening exceptions:
the lines that need not scan; the gulfs in nature;
the odds and irritants our cosmic oyster
cannot digest
as the pearl grows precious in its queer success.


## AN EMBLEM OF TWO FOXES

Simply to breathe
can make him bleed,
the fox whose leg
is trapped, whose will
awaits the kill.
Why should he flail?
Moving hurts,
so he lies still.

Around him walks
a prouder fox,
his severed leg
a homily
on going free,
as if to say
it hurts, it hurts
either way.

# Robert Wallace

**ROBERT WALLACE**

Robert Wallace writes: I was born on January 10, 1932 in Springfield, Missouri, where my father ran a small factory that made cherry and walnut furniture, which he designed. Springfield was a small-town sort of city with lots of trees, pleasant even in the Depression. For a time my Uncle Clarence lived with us and I sat on the porch before the sun was up listening to his stories about Alaska or bootlegging or playing *Macbeth* in a traveling company with Lon Chaney, Sr., in Texas before World War I. Later, he sent me a crazy, bent-up, antique typewriter from somewhere. My father wrote long, illustrated doggerel poems about people he knew, and I must have got the verse-itch from him. Robert W. Service was the only poet we owned, but I found others, Poe, James Whitcomb Riley, Ogden Nash; and I was ready for Marvell and Pope and Williams when I went to Harvard in 1949. Thereafter: a Fulbright to St. Catharine's College at Cambridge; two years of army; teaching at Bryn Mawr, Sweet Briar, Vassar, then Case Western Reserve University. My wife, Jan, is a philosopher of science.

## IN A SPRING STILL NOT WRITTEN OF

This morning
with a class of girls outdoors, I saw
how frail poems are
in a world burning up with flowers,
in which, overhead,
the great elms
—green, and tall—
stood carrying leaves in their arms.

The girls listened equally
to my drone, reading, and to the bees'
ricocheting
among them for the blossom on the bone,
or gazed off at a distant mower's
astronomies of green
and clover, flashing,
threshing in the new, untarnished sunlight.

And all the while, dwindling,
tinier, the voices—Yeats, Marvell, Donne—
sank drowning
in a spring still not written of,
as only the sky
clear above the brick bell-tower
—blue, and white—
was shifting toward the hour.

Calm, indifferent, cross-legged
or on elbows half-lying in the grass—
how should the great dead
tell them of dying?
They will come to time for poems at last,
when they have found they are no more
the beautiful and young
all poems are for.

## WHAT HE SAYS

Raspberries splash, redly
        in their leaves;
            squirrels

squabble in the pine-tops.
        An old man,
            wearing

a sweater in warm July,
        breathes
            the same morning as the birds,

goes, talking among flowers
        beautiful as he is,
            bending

leaves at his elbow.
        What he says,
            by himself, wandering

in the sunny garden,
        need not be true,
            nor useful.

## *AUBADE:* N. Y. C.

it is morning darling look the sun
by the fire escape comes peeping
rose on our sheets how fresh how
still oh and the roaches are sleeping

## THE PLACE

*Where to hide a leaf,* he said,
    *is in a tree.*
A starling in a flock.
    Water in the sea.

In limbs, in waves, in air—

All of them hidden there!

# Sylvia Plath

## THE COLOSSUS

I shall never get you put together entirely,
Pieced, glued, and properly jointed.
Mule-bray, pig-grunt and bawdy cackles
Proceed from your great lips.
It's worse than a barnyard.

Perhaps you consider yourself an oracle,
Mouthpiece of the dead, or of some god or other.
Thirty years now I have labored
To dredge the silt from your throat.
I am none the wiser.

Scaling little ladders with gluepots and pails of lysol
I crawl like an ant in mourning
Over the weedy acres of your brow
To mend the immense skull plates and clear
The bald, white tumuli of your eyes.

A blue sky out of the Oresteia
Arches above us. O father, all by yourself
You are pithy and historical as the Roman Forum.
I open my lunch on a hill of black cypress.
Your fluted bones and acanthine hair are littered

In their old anarchy to the horizon-line.
It would take more than a lightning-stroke
To create such a ruin.
Nights, I squat in the cornucopia
Of your left ear, out of the wind,

Counting the red stars and those of plum-color.
The sun rises under the pillar of your tongue.
My hours are married to shadow.
No longer do I listen for the scrape of a keel
On the blank stones of the landing.

**SYLVIA PLATH**

Sylvia Plath was born in Boston on October 27, 1932. After graduation from Smith College, she was awarded a Fulbright Fellowship in 1955 to study at Newnham College, Cambridge, where she met and married the English poet Ted Hughes. While at Smith she won the *Mademoiselle* fiction contest, and she later received several other prizes for her work, including the Bess Hopkins Award offered by *Poetry* and first prize at the Cheltenham Festival in England. She returned to teach at Smith for a while after her year at Cambridge and then returned to England, where she lived with her husband and their children until she committed suicide on February 11, 1963. Her novel entitled *The Bell Jar,* which was published posthumously in the United States in 1971, was a best-seller.

## SOW

God knows how our neighbor managed to breed
His great sow:
Whatever his shrewd secret, he kept it hid

In the same way
He kept the sow—impounded from public stare,
Prize ribbon and pig show.

But one dusk our questions commended us to a tour
Through his lantern-lit
Maze of barns to the lintel of the sunk sty door

To gape at it:
This was no rose-and-larkspurred china suckling
With a penny slot

For thrifty children, nor dolt pig ripe for heckling,
About to be
Glorified for prime flesh and golden crackling

In a parsley halo;
Nor even one of the common barnyard sows,
Mire-smirched, blowzy,

Maunching thistle and knotweed on her snout-cruise—
Bloat tun of milk
On the move, hedged by a litter of feat-foot ninnies

Shrilling her hulk
To halt for a swig at the pink teats. No. This vast
Brobdingnag bulk

Of a sow lounged belly-bedded on that black compost,
Fat-rutted eyes
Dream-filmed. What a vision of ancient hoghood must

Thus wholly engross
The great grandam!—our marvel blazoned a knight,
Helmed, in cuirass,

Unhorsed and shredded in the grove of combat
By a grisly-bristled
Boar, fabulous enough to straddle that sow's heat.

But our farmer whistled,
Then, with a jocular fist thwacked the barrel nape,
And the green-copse-castled

Pig hove, letting legend like dried mud drop,
Slowly, grunt
On grunt, up in the flickering light to shape

A monument
Prodigious in gluttonies as that hog whose want
Made lean Lent

Of kitchen slops and, stomaching no constraint,
Proceeded to swill
The seven troughed seas and every earthquaking continent.

---

## ALL THE DEAD DEARS

*In the Archæological Museum in Cambridge is a stone coffin of the
fourth century* A.D. *containing the skeletons of a woman, a mouse
and a shrew. The ankle-bone of the woman has been slightly gnawn.*

Rigged poker-stiff on her back
With a granite grin
This antique museum-cased lady
Lies, companioned by the gimcrack
Relics of a mouse and a shrew
That battened for a day on her ankle-bone.

These three, unmasked now, bear
Dry witness
To the gross eating game
We'd wink at if we didn't hear
Stars grinding, crumb by crumb,
Our own grist down to its bony face.

How they grip us through thin and thick,
These barnacle dead!
This lady here's no kin
Of mine, yet kin she is: she'll suck
Blood and whistle my marrow clean
To prove it. As I think now of her head,

From the mercury-backed glass
Mother, grandmother, greatgrandmother
Reach hag hands to haul me in,
And an image looms under the fishpond surface
Where the daft father went down
With orange duck-feet winnowing his hair—

All the long gone darlings: they
Get back, though, soon,
Soon: be it by wakes, weddings,
Childbirths or a family barbecue:

Any touch, taste, tang's
Fit for those outlaws to ride home on,

And to sanctuary: usurping the armchair
Between tick
And tack of the clock, until we go,
Each skulled-and-crossboned Gulliver
Riddled with ghosts, to lie
Deadlocked with them, taking root as cradles rock.

## SPINSTER

Now this particular girl
During a ceremonious April walk
With her latest suitor
Found herself, of a sudden, intolerably struck
By the birds' irregular babel
And the leaves' litter.

By this tumult afflicted, she
Observed her lover's gestures unbalance the air,
His gait stray uneven
Through a rank wilderness of fern and flower.
She judged petals in disarray,
The whole season, sloven.

How she longed for winter then!—
Scrupulously austere in its order
Of white and black
Ice and rock, each sentiment within border,
And heart's frosty discipline
Exact as a snowflake.

But here—a burgeoning
Unruly enough to pitch her five queenly wits
Into vulgar motley—

A treason not to be borne. Let idiots
Reel giddy in bedlam spring:
She withdrew neatly.

And round her house she set
Such a barricade of barb and check
Against mutinous weather
As no mere insurgent man could hope to break
With curse, fist, threat
Or love, either.

# John William Corrington

JOHN WILLIAM CORRINGTON
John William Corrington was born
in Memphis, Tennessee, on Octo-
ber 28, 1932. He writes: Living it
has been more fun than writing
it. Grew up in Shreveport, went to
Jesuit High School. Thrown out
in 1950. Here and there a trumpet-
player, a photographer, a news-
paperman (or boy). *B.A. Centenary
College, 1956.* It looked like work
ahead, so I went to graduate
school. The real thing began in
1957, when I met Joyce Hooper, a
nice Chemical Engineer. Poems
fell like rain. *M.A. Rice University,
1960.* We married that year, and
I began my first novel—still poem-
ing indecently. Baton Rouge and
a five-year sojourn at Louisiana
State University. Exceedingly easy
to forget—except for the coming
of children, Shelley, John Wesley,
Robert Edward Lee, and of books.
In 1963–64, we went to England
to get a doctoral degree. The rea-
sons were several. To get the LSU
Academic Jerkoff Squad off my
back. To scratch an itch to spend
time in a civilized country. To get
a better degree than the clowns
who nightly pet and polish theirs.
*D. Phil., The University of Sussex,
1964* (Thesis Director, Professor
David Daiches). By 1966, LSU had
become intolerable. An offer from
Loyola University in New Orleans
to be chairman of the English
Department. Since I had grown
considerably in the preceding 15
years, I presumed the Jesuits had.
I came there assuming religious
values, charity and a respect for
human beings. Unfortunately, I was
a visiting professor at Berkeley in
1968. It was great. Just after I
came back, I was commissioned
for the first screenplay Joyce and
I wrote together. Who knows what
next?—probably our youngest,
Thomas Jonathan Jackson, now
three.

## ON MY 18th BIRTHDAY

this is the sum of it:

        what i can expect
        from bones has
        succinctly arrived

  skin has done its

        part

time of gratuities is ending:
    tony's sister will ask
    for a fin; free juice is
    memory; a lump of boy
    is snuffling in my
    throat

birthday
        ends a barefoot deluge
        of
        interminable dry runs:
the next rap could be scary and adult; the
    next misstep may draw

        some of my wonderful
        blood

my analyst
    a black barber who sips
    adrenalin
    and barbecues like a god
        gave me a slip of paper
        tied with some dental
        floss:

  for birthday

it said

        —you must have learned
          you can eat almost anything
          and almost everything
          will certainly try to
        eat you
          this is for the winner
          to clean his teeth

from now on a haircut is six bits

## GUEVARA WITH MINUTES TO GO

Finally the problem is my meaning:

Out of a thousand crusty pots
amidst the moaning Andes
my face will shine like
the dead center of a silent film,
each gesture drawing sobs,
pitchmen as may be needed
cursing the purchased pigs who,
hating common art,
marched me into a yanqui road,
fired me like a needle
into the world's dumb eye.

They will barter me, a bearded
cherub from Scottsboro, amongst

the hopeless while I lurk forever
a great fingerless red star.
Posters, murals, busts, tractor
factories, a cooperative store—
all reared by the pressure of my love,
but what I mean, smiling outsize
in a Mayday parade, lithographed
like Jesus, is the problem's core.

Trotsky burning
Reed in the wall
Lenin preserved
I sprawled in a marble manger—
We are all saviors waiting for judgement.
We know
the end of what we do, we do
not know.

# THE GRAND INQUISITOR CONTINUES

*The kiss burns his cheek,*
*but the old man clings to his idea.*

## I

If it were not for these things—
these inconsistencies between your vision
of mankind and what, in fact, he is,
faith would be a tattered mask,
the simulacrum of a skull—
concealing what? A skull, of course.
That must not be. Faith is a cunning vise
to pinch our freedom into useful paths.

The myth of Godhead clinched in flesh,
mercy wedded to justice immaculately,
finding apotheosis in Golgothic slaughter
and the chill assumption on which
the mad depend—
all this requires a tension unfit
for metaphysics, bereft of human sense.

But things are not so arranged:
The universe is silent as a tomb.
We have no roots in this or any world,
no hope and hence no fear. Cosmic bastards,
strangers, castaway, and only the ship,
the sailing matters—
only a steady course. And steady courses
are the product of sailors who behave.

## II

I have seen trapped wolves survive
the unspeakable, break away from angry
peasants. But the end was known: for that
night or the next—a week at most
and your wolf was rotting in deep grass,
corrupting a water-hole. And on that
shaggy corpse the marks of its own teeth.
In its fierce crystal eyes the absolute
fulfillment of despair. All of which
it might have gotten quickly, once
the trap had sprung, by simply lying still.

## III

The fossil remnants of God remain
to be explained. That is our function.
Inventor of reason, he stepped beyond
his creature, rose in smoky glory
while disciples gawked. Out of his robe,
by accident perhaps, fell the pebble
of Rome. But through the increment
of centuries, as he drifted onward
beyond the limits of this galaxy,
eyes still warm and kind, mouth full

of figs and mustardseed, that perilous
rock has grown into an anvil upon which
hard sayings are tortured into steel.
The hammer is discipline: the product truth—
or a likeness, a graven image of it,
if you will.

There are eight sacraments. The last
is Obedience. Holiness is not intensity;
sanctity does not consist of shrieks.
The circuit of the Law is a cold road
and at its end, a dark cottage
in which the Holy Family waits
like waxen figures in a Christmas scene,
behind the house a shadowed and imponderable lane.
The trip is best made with eyes
straight ahead. Arrival is worth
the madness, the pain,
and all of the dead are sane.

# FOR A WOODSCOLT MISCARRIED

I know the barn where they got you
the night they tricked each other
and themselves.

In that season, the nights are
full of rain, the sky shakes
like a lost child and for an hour
it is cool enough to love.

Out of such cool love you came
to burgeon day by day,
carelessly made and moving darkly
like the land your most distant bending
fathers tilled, crying for Israel,
hoping for Jesus.

Your nearly mother felt trouble in her depths
where an ignorant angel stirred the waters
with his holy staff.
She sat big on the shack's long porch
watching cars dart South for Baton Rouge,
watching fingers of young pine fondle
tumid clouds above the field and shed
where you took place.

Cars throbbed toward the city. The shack
stayed where it was. And stayed
till her time came. And yours.

At the clinic they found something wrong:
her blood, his seed—your own blind weaving
of them both. They said that you were dead.
And it was so.

Some time in the sixth month you gave it up.
Maybe you heard some talk of what there was,

could feel the chill dissension in her gut:
her wanting and her fearing and her shame.
And gave it up. Collapsed, began to junk
limbs and fingers,
the tassel of your kind,
the piggish brooding something like a face.
Each cell dissolved, left off its yearning,
its moist prophecies.

In the Felicianas,
there are no coffins for what is not born
but loosed, a stewy discharge almost the
    same
as if the bowels went wrong.
Preachers, fine at birth, adroit at marriage,
inured to burial,
have no rite for those who almost were.
A near thing does not count.
A miss had just as well be fifty miles.

Just as well: no matter what they say
each coming and each leaving is a feast,
a celebration of the sun we squall to see
and weep to leave: a leaping forth,
a going down, each swings its own harsh joy
and the round of its perfection has no
    words.
But for you, what?
Who lay for a brief time within
the confines of her deep uneasy space,

your sun her heart thundering there above
red as the wounds of Jesus.
Who turned and turned amidst a tideless
inward sea as ghosts of her body
taught your spindrift hands to be
and made a tongue for speech and eyes to
    see.

For you, what?

Somewhere near in the fields your father
turns the land waiting for a first
bold thrust of green out of the earth's
confusion. Maybe relieved, as mute and
unaware as she, he will watch the stalks
and leaves spread out, will bless
the flower and the bole. Will shout and
carry the first opened fruit,
a pale victory, running down the rows
pulling its long staple through his fingers
like a sheaf of dollar bills.

And you who lost nothing that you had,
no trees or blooms or words
rising against Louisiana's sun, will stir,
if ever, in the evening breeze, a trouble
    missed,
a junction passed and never seen
like a field or shack at the edge of sight
down a highway to the Gulf.

**STUART SILVERMAN**
Stuart Silverman was born on December 21, 1933. He writes: My birthplace, and home for twenty-six years, was Brooklyn, N.Y., middle-middle class, uptight, about as far from Whitman in spirit as the Grand Canyon in fact. I've been trying to escape Brooklyn for about half my life, first via Manhattan and a job in advertising, since then through teaching in the southeast and mid-west, writing, travelling whenever funds are plentiful enough to get there and back and afford an occasional meal en route. I've never belonged to a poetic school, idolized a particular writer, or tried to develop my work in terms of a theory. As a result, I go from sonnets and sestinas to blank verse, free verse, prose poems, concrete poetry, and one-time unnamed experimental forms, and range from the personal, though rarely confessional, to literary and purely topical subjects. It makes for something of a hodgepodge, and irritates an editor here and there, but it limits monotony to the distance between the first and last line of a given poem. At the moment, my wife, Sondra Rosenberg, and I both teach in Chicago, but we would like to go southwest or northwest to get the soot out of our lungs and the sulfur trioxide out of our eyes.

# Stuart Silverman

### THE GAME

All his life, my father looked for money.
He saw it in cars, in strange women, whose eyes
Were bright as headlights, in yachts on sunny
Pages out of the Sunday paper. All lies.

In the evening he fiddled with numbers
Listening for the click that had his name
Written in script green as cucumbers,
All for the winning of a little game.

The bank was savage; the ponies, only horses,
Couldn't carry him over the gray hills;
And oh the market broke and spent his forces
To line the pockets of a hundred shills.

So at the end he drew himself within;
Strung, bitten, taken, had, he drew away,

Afraid of light itself so tender was the skin
In which he'd dared the world and seized the day.

In that dark room, he sat astride the years
Waiting for money, but it never came.
Fate found his books, as always, in arrears,
And darkness cancelled the suspended game.

---

## THE GARDEN

Where was the fault? You do not know nor can.
Time had not happened to enstructure man
When that fatality of play began.

The trees were heavy, the soil soft as lace
On softest skin, as careless as the face
Spun in the wildness of that place:

The air heavy as nectar with perfume.
The green vines insistent to assume
The texture of a tableland of spume

Hung motionless; the plum-tree great with fruit,
The tare in constant labor at the root
Brought forth, and the date and oleander followed suit.

Time was, time was not, among the trees.
Though the still drop fell from the leaves
This was no measure for the face to seize;

No birth bore brutally upon the past,
Nor death stood patiently to see the last:
The greedy minutes and the ages massed

In the incorruptible round of day and night.
Against the fullness of an evening's light
He slept, and sleep was simple, then, and right.

But in the olive wood with the round sun
Hugely above, he rested like a stone
One day, and the grove was silent, and the deed was done.

The living tissue open to desire
Found a white finger like a white fire
To draw the bone and breathe upon the wire.

And the sun failing in that perfect sky
Watched, and the beasts listened to that cry,
And the garden waited for the sound to die.

Night, and the beasts coupled, and the simple pair.
This was no wonder for the two were fair,
And made of one flesh in the garden there.

Day, and the day returned. And much the same
As it had been before the maiden came
The garden was, and Eve was made her name.

He gave her honeycomb that she might eat,
Grapes on whose dark skin the sun would beat
Until they shone like gold, and they were sweet.

He taught her berrying among the vines
And where the cold and crystal river winds,
The deeper coverts where the white-throat pines.

She called him Adam, and no childish thing
Passed ever in their understanding.
They were too old to laugh, too young to sing.

And when they passed the Tree, an ordinary day,
She nodded as he spoke, not sad, not gay,
For having been no child she could not say

What either was. And what he said, she heard
In the gray continuance of the word.
And what she did, she never would have dared.

Nor quite certain, when the moment came,
What stood between the boxwoods murmuring her name
With the insistence of a mortal thing.

Evil is only form and never act.
Unskilled to caution, she assumed the fact
Gathered before her with its drawling tact.

She was not made, of course, to understand,
Question, examine, but rather to attend.
There was an Adam who drew her by the hand.

Along the pathways overgrown with good
And in and out amid the geometric wood,
And he it was who knew. But now there stood

A greater brightness than the form of man
In the dark wood, and the first time laughter ran
Through the dry courses of the perfect plan.

And fruit she bore Adam while the false light
Shone like dull metal against the weary sight,
And he did eat of it before the night.

Where was the fault? He could not well refuse
Bone of his bone, flesh of his flesh, to lose.
There was no choice, nor was he asked to choose.

The day emptied itself against the sky.
Night, and the beasts coupled, and the pair lay by
Fingering the hard existence of the *I;*

Grown to a deep confusion of themselves
The bone and flesh lay taut upon their shelves,
And desire gaped behind the necessary valves.

Night, and the day returned, and they went out
To take their breakfast from the formal rout,
But an immense otherness lay all about.

The green leaves, like a green host that day,
Camped in the forest's arms, and the broad ray
Of the inquiring sun touched them as they lay;

The earth was full of fragrance soft as loam,
The air in columns held the light like foam
And like a warm image turned it to and fro;

The pathways glided like a living thing
Away. In the distance they heard the cuckoo sing
And when they turned she watched a moth take wing

As though for the first time. And seeing her rise
To the profound sun, he turned away his eyes
And watched the clouds make patterns through the trees.

They wandered, then, beyond the simple bounds
That had contented them, and bathed their wounds
In darker rivers of unquiet grounds.

And saying nothing, he tore a twisted leaf
From the fig-tree with the hurry of a thief,
And meeting Eve, looked down, and called her, *wife*.

And travelling, stopped when she was great with child,
Raised a low roof, broke ground, grew many-skilled,
And left the garden forever to the wild.

**DAN MASTERSON**

Dan Masterson was born on February 22, 1934. He writes: I got hooked on Shelley's poetry in high school and even wrote a few lines, but it was Norman Whitney who gave me the nudge I needed when I studied writing under him at Syracuse. After college, I worked as a disc-jockey in Buffalo—my birthplace—did some army time, and invaded Manhattan where, after two lean years, I was chosen to emcee a network quiz show. It folded before it debuted, thanks to the quiz scandal. I wrote garbage spray ads and pushed shopping carts full of film along Fifth Avenue until I hit it lucky as a publicist for a theatrical company. Five years later, my wife and I gave our belongings away and joined a missionary society. After five months, we realized we'd goofed, but also knew we didn't want New York anymore. I tried teaching and liked it. In 1966, I signed-on at New York State's Rockland Community College, where I continue to teach courses in writing and contemporary poetry. I'm publishing in places like *Esquire* and *The New Orleans Review*, touring some, and finding it possible to spend a lot of time with my wife and our son and daughter.

# Dan Masterson

## ONE-ELEVEN GRAPE STREET

*("My clock is down at the jeweler's and I don't know when
to eat or when to go to bed or get up. But anyway I live on
and on and on.")*

She was eager to be heard and nibbled on memories,
While I listened to the mournful chewing, and
Scraped the last puddle of vanilla ice cream,
From a deep-bottom dish, with a silver-black spoon.
The wool-wrapped legs barely showed but bulged
Beneath uncountable layers of arctic skirts
Safety-pinned each day against the imaginery freeze.
There were always cookies in the pickle crock
And Pepsi in jelly jars during those hours together
In that fear-fed neighborhood on the fringe of Lake Erie.

I remember her padding blindly about, in her frayed maroon
    slippers,
Pressing dustballs and giant hairpins into the silent carpet.
A copper-colored gas heater pumped itself year 'round,

**MARK STRAND**

Mark Strand writes: I was born on Prince Edward Island, Canada, on April 11, 1934. I went to Antioch College and Yale University, where I studied painting with Joseph Albers. I had a Fulbright to Italy in 1960. When I returned I taught at the University of Iowa. I've since taught at the University of Washington, Columbia and Yale, and now teach at Brooklyn College of CUNY. I've had other grants including a Rockefeller, a National Endowment for the Arts grant, and I've published three books of poetry. I live in New York with my wife and daughter.

And the temperature held to its constant eighty-five,
Having leapt there once many years before.
The sun would sear its way through two paper shades
That were drawn and tacked against the eternal glare,
As I'd read to her from the accumulated mail,
A slim stack forever staling in open envelopes.

And then the men came.
They tapped at the windows,
Took the tacks from the shades,
Broke the ice cream bowls,
Hid her slippers,
Unpinned her skirts,
Stole her mail,
And sat on the table-top to taunt her.
Only finger-tip tall, they were never seen,
But she assaulted them daily, fiercely.
In the end, they went away, leaving her alone
With the fear that they might return.
She died in her sleep without them.

## COOK-OUT

I rise from the sun-deck
to enter the thicket
in search of a bouncing ball,
and find instead a grenade
rolling toward a thatched hut.

I go deep within it:
my eyes dropping to a sling,
hung from criss-cross poles,

supporting a child, sleeping
above the settling ball.

The concussion blows the roof off
like a puff of dandelion fuzz:
gently, not to waken the infant
wrapped in flame and floating
slowly, head over heels through leaves.

I watch until he burns away in the sun.

# Mark Strand

## EATING POETRY

Ink runs from the corners of my mouth.
There is no happiness like mine.
I have been eating poetry.

The librarian does not believe what she sees.
Her eyes are sad
and she walks with her hands in her dress.

The poems are gone.
The light is dim.
The dogs are on the basement stairs and
 coming up.

Their eyeballs roll,
their blond legs burn like brush.
The poor librarian begins to stamp her feet
 and weep.

She does not understand.
When I get on my knees and lick her hand,
she screams.

I am a new man.
I snarl at her and bark.
I romp with joy in the bookish dark.

## KEEPING THINGS WHOLE

In a field
I am the absence
of field.
This is
always the case.
Wherever I am
I am what is missing.

146

When I walk
I part the air
and always
the air moves in
to fill the spaces
where my body's been.

We all have reasons
for moving.
I move
to keep things whole.

**LEWIS TURCO**
Lewis Turco writes: I was born
May 2, 1934 in Buffalo, New York,
the son of an Italian Baptist minis-
ter and a Midwestern Methodist
missionary who, four years later,
moved to Meriden, Connecticut,
taking me with them. For these
reasons, I began to write science-
fiction and horror stories in gram-
mar school. During my senior year
in high school I was given a minis-
terial scholarship to Bucknell Uni-
versity. For this reason I joined the
Navy during the last part of the
Korean War and spent four years
—two of them at sea—writing
poetry. I have been doing the
same ever since, through college
(Connecticut and Iowa) and four
teaching jobs. At present I'm Di-
rector of the Program in Writing
Arts at the State University of New
York at Oswego.

# Lewis Turco

## THE DOOR

There is a door
    made of faces
faces snakes and green moss

    which to enter is
        death or perhaps
life which to touch is

    to sense beyond the
        figures carved in
shades of flesh and emerald

    the Inhabitant at home
        in his dark
rooms his hours shadowed or

lamptouched and that door
    must not be
attempted the moss disturbed nor

    the coiling lichen approached
        because once opened
the visitor must remain in

    that place among the
        Inhabitant's couches and
violets must be that man

    in his house cohabiting
        with the dark
wife her daughter or both.

## THE FOREST BEYOND THE GLASS

    Hundreds of yards of woodland
        smashed and torn.
    They had been a long while dying,
        these great beasts;
one, of a broken neck—the lucky
        one. Thirst took
the other: even on his side he'd dug
        a dozen

    holes, deep as his hooves could delve,
        trying for
    water. It had been one of those
        tremendous
agonies. There lie the two moose still,
        locked upon
love's combat, horns fused. All is as it was.
        The bulls are

    dead; so says the placard hung
        upon the
    glass; thus they were found, silent in
        the forest.
The point and object of contention

        had long since
vanished when men happened upon these hulks
        steaming in

    a spring thaw. But it was not
        love that had
    conquered; as usual, it was
        time. Engrossed
with death's petrified grove and with the
        heart's beasts calm
in the wildwood, we stand frozen by love's
        passing glance
reflected in the forest beyond the glass.

## AN OLD ACQUAINTANCE

As we stand talking, his eye
    drops out. I am amazed.
    His socket looks funny.
    It's a nice day, I say.
His scalp is scattered on the

carpet. What's the matter with
    your nose, I ask—but it

**LAURENCE LIEBERMAN**

Laurence Lieberman was born in Detroit, Michigan, on February 16, 1935. He was educated at the University of Michigan and the University of California at Berkeley. His first book of poems was published by Macmillan in 1968, and in the same year Scott-Foresman published his critical study of James Dickey's poetry in their Modern Poets Series. His critical articles and reviews of contemporary poetry have been appearing with some regularity since 1965, and he is currently a regular poetry reviewer for *Yale Review*. After living and teaching for four years in St. Thomas, Virgin Islands, he moved in 1968 to Urbana, where he now teaches at the University of Illinois. He was granted an associate fellowship to the Center for Advanced Study of the University of Illinois for the academic year 1971–1972, and spent the fellowship year with his wife and three children in Japan and Hawaii.

is too late. He laughs. His
teeth hit something on their
way down. I must be getting

on, I suggest. But I am
too slow to catch his ear.
Can't you say something, I
inquire: he opens his
mouth to show me. That's too bad,

I say, but he shakes his head
too hard. I try looking
into his mind, but he
is thinking of nothing.
A spider is spinning her

wed in a white cave. It is
awkward. Well, it's getting
late, I say. The spider
has caught something. I smile
at him; he stands there grinning.

---

### THE PILOT

*Calais, France, May 18, 1968 (AP)—Low tide yesterday uncovered a plane, presumably of World War II, with the remains of the pilot still at the controls. Its origin could not be determined immediately.*

It has been
a long flight. Like flak,
the seagrass exploded
beneath me as I fell

out of light into
an older and a heavier air.

My planing
continued in the tide.
When the cuttlefish had
done with my flesh, I found
that still the stick would
answer, though more slowly than before.

So I flew,
and am flying still, back
to the beginning. In
my marrow direction
lay. Now the sea has
released me, and I have been constant.

But I was
wrong. You see me at death's
controls, in the primal
mud where our flight began,
but it has not been
a fleeing, as we have long supposed.

I see that
now, with these sockets where
fish have swum. You, rising
from the shore, have shown me
what the snail tried to
tell: the journey is the other way.

Turn me around. I am with you still.

---

# Laurence Lieberman

### NO ONE TO BLAME

Birds move from branch to branch
with so little emotion. I think it is easy for them.
They splash in puddles of air,

fold their wings and fall
without caring how far, and do not touch the bottom.
There are no accidents.

It has all been planned for them.
We suppose they mourn their dead, and are good at keeping
secrets. It is not a matter

of kindness. The beaks are cruel.
It is a way they have of making evil. A passion.
To fill their stomachs? Yes.

But the bird-hearts are not troubled.
Or quiet. They are filled with a kind of rapture. In the open
   air there is room for the terrible.

Do not listen for cries in the night.
One can learn to hear too well, if even the birds love
   claws. There is no one to blame.

---

## TREE ANIMALS

### I. Termites

Just inside the bark the tree's charm slides. Termites
Suck the dark. Sap is honey in their jaws.
All they destroy they love. Their faith
Is the wisdom of tiny claws
And quick teeth.
Bites

Can reduce the largest carcass of wood to sawdust. Dust.
The smallest monsters masticate the gods.
Their bodies are furious mouths. Their souls
Are pure as bubbles, soapsuds.
Their exquisite tools
Don't rust.

It is true their appetites are overlarge. They grow
From tiny to small, and scatter tons of waste.
Secretly, they are jealous of leaves
And twigs. They do not taste.
They kiss themselves
Hello.

### II. Owls

Owls
Help us to dream.
They enter our sleeping heads
And hoot. They drop some feathers. (We blame
Them on our pillows.) They call to the dead in their shrouds.
That is all. They slip from our sleep, and return to their
   tree-holes.
The eyes that stare back at you are not bats or toads.
Roosting in the tree's hollow, a tomb
In the trunk, the sultans of mood
Sulk. Tree-gloom
Moles?

Perhaps.
But they don't burrow.
They dream of moonlight, not dirt.
It takes them years to learn to mellow
And to sustain an erect dignity when they fart.
They stare. Their eyes are always open and don't need drops.
Compared to how old they think, their lives are short.
They sink deep in themselves. Not shallow,

They toil to remain alert,
But will not follow
Maps

Or clocks.
In the owl mind's-eye
The lion's roar is a cough,
The whale a goldfish in the bowl of sea,
The python's crush tickles, not firm enough
To choke a lamb, the eagle cannot scale high rocks,
The bear won't hug, nor does the hyena laugh;
All creatures halt in their lives to pray
For grace. If they do not bluff,
The owl mind's-eye
Unlocks.

---

## SKIN SONG

I cannot be a fish     sure of failure, I will try
no risk, no loss

the flippers tell my feet     flesh, be rubber
you must not bend or kick     to be
moved, lie still     to be held
let go

the mask instructs my face
mouth, stay shut     the Other
opens     be slow, nose
you will breathe
easy     eyes
do not be first, come
after     late, you will see more

Water commands:

body, be light     the will
is heaviness     ignorance
has no weight     know
nothing     give everything away     cast off
self to the deep     shed weight
lightness     grows
full     body, be light

be white, blood     be
without color     lose your red
grow lighter than water
thinner     blood, be white

skin, be empty     sleep
you will dream
a motion not your own     a motion
that is given     give
up, touch     be taken     emptiness
lifts     skin, be empty

# David R. Slavitt

**DAVID R. SLAVITT**

David R. Slavitt writes: Poems are, among other things, strategies for the management of experience. There is no simple relation between a man's work and his life —and it is silly to try to think of a life as an artifact—but still we look at poets' lives hoping to find something of their strategic knack in the crude medium of worldly coping. I seem to have done most of the wrong, conventional things, but the wrong way— so that maybe I got them right, after all. I was born on March 23, 1935, in White Plains, New York, schooled at Andover, Yale, and Columbia, and trained at *Newsweek* where I went to the movies a lot and learned how to write for a mass audience. I quit at 30 and, under a pen-name, took up the writing of best sellers as a way to support my poetry and fiction. This activity has earned me the concern and contempt of people with raddled brains who suggest that my dual career may raddle my brain. As perhaps it will. But so far I am alive and well in Miami and Cape Cod, still working, still much—dare I say?—amused.

## EPITAPH FOR GOLIATH

After so many victories, one
defeat, and that one by a stone:
but let this stone atone for that
breach of the order of combat.
He was a victim of a ruse
of the rude boy of the barbarous Jews.
Goliath shall have honor while
men yet have any use for style
or the purity of form they mean
by the accolade of Philistine.

## DAY SAILING

### 1

Distance deceives. Novelists mistake
extent for weight, their thicknesses
for acuity. Endurance rarely
endures. Chichester, Bannister,
Sisyphus sweat. Lazier,
I cannot believe that far,
go to no such lengths.
Day sailing in a small catboat in the bay
satisfies me, who have nowhere to go.

What rarity have the Indies now
but famine, cholera and war,
what riches for a new Magellan
or Drake to take from that arduous route?
The Pacific boils with testing;
Atlantis is long sunk.

Still, the mainsheet tugs,
tiller and centerboard puff.
The wind blows the hair.

I go sailing.

### 2

It is conversation of craft and force,
the wind so, and the sail and rudder so;

it is compromise between the wind
and me, a settling for that bluff, that flagpole,
and tacking back, beating up the wind,
achieving direction out of indirection;

it is balancing, my weight
to windward, heeling to leeward;

it is a triumph, for civilization is
neither writing, nor painting pictures, nor
    forging metal,
nor breeding animals, nor sowing grain,
but sailing into the wind, sailing to
    westward,
the knowing, the craft.
The cove at low tide
swarms, gulls and terns,
sandpipers, and crows
pick over the shingle,
small crabs start,
clams squirt, worms
snake in the rich reek
of sea-wrack rot.
The muck smacks soles,
oozes between my toes.

I bring to the hull a cloth, a plank, a stick,
and bring the hull to life, and it brings me
off the shingle, into the narrow channel,
and out into the bay. The fetor fades
to salt. The wind freshens.

I have my craft—a skill, a trade, duplicity,
a small boat.

### 3

The intricate maneuvering for the sake
of maneuvering, or to put myself in the sun
for my tan, or out of the sun for fear of
    burn,
or just to adjust the look of the boat is not
different from our comfortable lives ashore,
neither praiseworthy nor blameworthy,
except that sometimes when a fresh wind
    comes up
out of nowhere, out of the south, and I
have to head south to the cove, and the
    spray breaks
over the bow, and the boat slants, riding,
    riving
the water, comes about sharp, smart, to
    find
that it is, I am, seaworthy is something.
I am no sailor, but there is no virtue
wholly irrelevant. The seaman with the oar
must find the farmer willing to improvise
some use for what he carries, able to see
it could make do, perhaps, as a winnowing
    fan.

## JONAH: A REPORT

He is mad. He is filthy. He sits all day in his shack.
He says he never sleeps and never wakes,
but hangs between in a trance. His hair is white
and yet we know his age is thirty-one.
The cures are remarkable. Of course, the doctors
say he is a fake, but cannot explain
the cases, scores of them, hundreds, of small children
sick to death with fever and brought to him
at the last moment, when all other hope is lost,
and suddenly well again. And deaf made to hear
and blind to see again. The usual things.

The dream, however, is dangerous. He says
that all his powers came to him in the dream,
and he tells the dream, over and over again.
We have asked him, we have begged him to desist,
but still he tells his dream, this blasphemous dream,
which threatens our religion and our people.

**The Dream**

"I lay three days. The coffinmaker came
to make my coffin, but while he worked the wood,
I heard my sickness speak to me. It promised
that from the Lord of the Ocean I might receive
the gift of healing. Therefore I asked my father
to let my body be buried at once, in the sea.
        "They carried me to the harbour and found a ship
ready to set sail, and loaded me on.
My sickness churned the sea, and the mariners
threw me over the side and sailed away.
I fell upon the ocean in my coffin,
and the coffin was a boat which bore me, swifter
than any ship. I came, then, to an island
where the Lady of the Ocean makes her home.
Naked, she welcomed me, and gave me her teat
and suckled me, and sang to me of hardships,
of the trouble I should find, and the weariness.
I laid my head in her lap and slept a while.
        "When I woke, along, to the rushing of wings,
I saw a bird like an eagle, but larger, larger,
with feathers of iron and beak of blackest stone.
The eagle plucked me up and carried me
to the top of a mountain. There a birch tree grew,
and the Lord of the Tree bade me break a branch,
but when I touched the tree, it groaned and cried.
I broke a twig, the smallest I could find,
and felt the pain of it in my little finger,
which also broke, but when I touched the twig
to the broken finger, it healed me instantly.
The Lord of the Tree approved and told me his secrets,
the seven virtues of the seven plants,
the powers of nine stones and of nine metals.
        "I visited the tents of illness, torn,
and in a barren place. In the first tent, Syphilis

tore out my living heart. In the next, Madness
cut off my head. Leprosy peeled my skin,
and the others took my nerves, my bones, my blood.
But the eagle, who is Lord of the Sky, returned
and carried my body's pieces to a cave
where a smith with one eye beat upon an anvil
and forged me whole again. I was molten hot
and he threw me down to cool in a deep pool.
        "The pool was a part of the ocean, very deep
where all the oceans meet. The Lord of the Ocean
sulks there, in his castle. He was the Lord
of Chaos before our God created the world
and separated dry land from the water.
The Lord of the Ocean is angry, and sends the waves
to beat upon the land and wash it away,
and sends the storms to sink the ships of land
that sail upon his sea, and sends the wind
to blow down trees that men build into ships.
He fought with me and killed me many times,
but every time I lived again, and was stronger,
for the smith had forged me well. The Lord of the Ocean
at last relented and offered me his daughter,
an ugly hag with green snakes for her hair,
scales for skin, sea scallops for dugs.
I lay with her (and still I stink of fish)
and she told me her father's secrets—of the waters,
fresh and salt, and all the sacred springs,
and how to find the water when digging wells.
Then she put me inside an enormous fish
which brought me back to earth and Nineveh."

He does not insist, of course, on the literal truth
of everything in the dream, but he does repeat it,
and the people, because he cures their children, believe.
The man is remarkable, but Israel
cannot survive his kindnesses. Therefore,
the committee on heterodoxy recommends
that Jonah be stoned to death, as the law prescribes,
but privately, and at night. In a few years
if he is not forgotten, let us publish
our own, official account of his exploits.
We can make him a minor prophet, let him go
on a voyage, even let him get thrown in the sea,
and on his return he can preach something inoffensive—
virtue and reform are the usual things.
This is our report and our proposal,
submitted on the fifteenth day of Adar,
in the year 3436 of the Lord's people.

---

## SEALS

The fish
that fly,
dead, flung by
the counting keeper—

**WILLIAM MILLS**

William Mills writes: I was born in Hattiesburg, Mississippi, June 17, 1935. My father was raised on a small, red-clay farm in Richton, Mississippi, where his father was farmer-judge-mayor of the little whistle-stop, *his* father having marched off to the War Between the States and never returned. My mother, in turn, had followed her father, an Irish "tramp printer," around the country east of the Mississippi while he worked on newspapers. Maybe the travelling and the words come from that side. Anyway after a while we moved to Louisiana, because times were harder in Mississippi. I've banged about Europe and Japan and Central America, spent three years in the Army, hung around the Universities of Tübingen and Munchen, taught school and done some welding. I was farming in Louisiana and working in Nicaragua when I wrote the poems for my first book. Sylvia and I have a place to live in Baton Rouge, Louisiana, where I teach classes at L.S.U.

more to the sluggish,
fewer to the sleeker
seals—nourish
fairly, filling up
as heaven equally fills
every unequal cup.

To watch
among
them, to favor young
or elderly or sick
seals not up to catching
lunch with a trick
or to fend off the snatching
of the greedier ones requires
a number of different skills
from those the crowd admires.

And so
with seals:
youngsters take meals
in small, separate pools
where keepers throw
smelts, seal schools
where the young grow

clever, and able to compete
with adults for the flung
fish they will have to eat.

To live
in zoos,
the animals lose
natural seal sense,
and being captive,
acquire dependence,
even on imitative
children who throw balls.
The seals oblige and catch
what miscellany falls.

They bark
as they
always do, play
for a while longer,
having made of life a lark
and a game of hunger.
But later, in the dark
a seal will get sick,
get sick to death, fed up
at last with its one trick.

# William Mills

## I KNOW A SPOT JUST OVER THE HILL

I thought they stood
For good times.
Women on any Monday
My mother
Were Saturday night Circes,
Their sagging milk sacks
Adjusted to goddess shapes
By a factory in New Jersey.

The eyes look at me
And I see myself.

A patient on a weekend pass
Explains love.

Emma Jean wiggles
Believing in playboy.

Jo once
Flung her secretary hips
Over me.
For one jukeboxbeer moment
I was a Mississippi Ulysses
Passing rocks without wax
In my ears

But her tongue said no.
Her husband belched
"I taught her everything
She knows" and
With all her education
She killed him.

I was going to Mt. Carmel
But down the way
Jezebel was eaten by dogs
Ahab failed.

Their sharpened faces
Are marble,
Reflected sun
Catches my eyes.

The decadence here
Stops being literature,
Orders a doubleshot
Of sour mash.
His sister
Pulls off her shoes and shirt
And straddling the
Yellow line
Is hit by a semi
On its dark way
To Centerville.

## PITY

She asked me twice
Didn't I kill the
Catfish
Before I took the pliers
And stripped his hide.
I said no,
You'd have to break his neck.
She sat there, watching.
I, now uneasy,

Blood bright on my fingers
Saw her wince,
The whiskered fish
Twisting.
Looks like torture that way,
She said,
And I said look
If you ask that question
It leads to another.
This is the way it's done.

# Charles Wright

**CHARLES WRIGHT**

Charles Wright writes: I was born on 25 August 1935 in Pickwick Dam, Tennessee, and grew up in Tennessee and North Carolina. I graduated from Davidson College in 1957. I spent the next 4 years in the Army—in Maryland, California and Italy. It was during this first stay in Italy (in Verona) that I started writing poems, at age 25. I began by using Ezra Pound's Italian Cantos first as a guide book to out-of-the-way places, then as a reference book and finally as a 'copy' book. After the Army I went to the University of Iowa for 2 years. After Iowa I went back to Italy as a Fulbright student, living in Rome for 2 years, 1963–65. While there I worked on translations from the poems of Eugenio Montale, Cesare Pavese and Pier Paolo Pasolini. Since 1966 I have been a member of the English Department of the University of California, Irvine—except for 1 year spent in Italy again as a Fulbright teacher, in Venice. I live now in Laguna Beach, California with my wife Holly and son Luke.

## THE NEW POEM

It will not resemble the sea.
It will not have dirt on its thick hands.
It will not be part of the weather.

It will not reveal its name.
It will not have dreams you can count on.
It will not be photogenic.

It will not attend our sorrow.
It will not console our children.
It will not be able to help us.

## EPITHALAMION

The kingfisher falls through the dry air—whose eye can stop
   his falling;

The crab, her bones shut tight as a baby's fist, waits under
   water, waits to be opened;

And deer, caged in the ring of a flashlight's glare, their veins
   electric, their hearts cold fire, can neither leave nor stay—

These are geographies you must assume, and rearrange,
   drifting into the pocked dream hanging before you like
   the moon, faint as a thumbprint on a window pane,
   gathering dust . . .

# John Stone

**JOHN STONE**

John Stone writes: I was born February 7, 1936, in Jackson, Mississippi, graduated from Millsaps College in Jackson, and received my M.D. degree from Washington University in St. Louis in 1962. The next several years were spent in training in Internal Medicine and Cardiology at the University of Rochester (New York) and Emory University—Grady Memorial Hospital (Atlanta). For three summers recently I have served as Physician for the Bread Loaf Writers' Conference. When I am not busy with patients or poems or teaching medical students, I enjoy listening to classical music and playing soccer with my sons. I am Assistant Professor of Medicine and Assistant Dean of Emory University School of Medicine and Medical Director of Outpatient Services at Grady Memorial Hospital. I am married and the father of two sons.

## CADAVER

*"The initial lesion of syphilis may result over the years in a gradual weakening and dilatation (aneurysm) of the aorta. This aneurysm may ultimately rupture and lead to death of the patient". . . medical textbook*

Fitting the labels
in our books
to our own tense tendons
slipping in their sheaths

we memorized the body
and the word

stripped the toughened skin
from the stringing nerve
the giving muscle.

Ribs sprang like gates.

In the chest
like archaeologists
we found it:
clotted, swollen,
aneurysmal
sign of an old sin

the silent lust
that had buried itself
in the years

growing
in the hollow of his chest

still rounded by her arms
clinging
belly to belly
years beyond that first seed

to the rigid final fact

of a body.

## LIVING WITH A VOODOO DOLL

Hair and nose and eyes like mine,
I made you, doll, to look like me
from teak and paper, bits of twine.
I place you in your chair for tea

to tell you what my world is like.
About the phases of the moon,
the way a pin becomes a spike,
how I have danced and to what tune.

All evil signs I leave for you:
red threads of worry for your eyes,
the sleeplessness and deep tattoo
of wrinkles, the pain. You realize

that yours is mine to take or give.
And I could kill you.
                    I make you live.

## TO A 14 YEAR OLD GIRL
## IN LABOR AND DELIVERY

I cannot say it to you, Mother. Child.
Nowhere now is there a trace of the guile
that brought you here. Near the end of
    exile

I hold you prisoner, jailer, in my cage—
with no easy remedy for your rage
against him and the child. Your coming of
    age

is a time of first things: a slipping of
    latches;
of parallels like fire and the smell of
    matches.
The salmon swims upstream. The egg
    hatches.

## LINDA

Seven, frog-legged among the boys,
even now you realize
what magic holds mechanical toys

have on them. In the green sway
of a sun-burst tree you compromise
the zoom and sputter of their play.

Then you rise, shake off the grass:
you are seventeen, and wise;
their long necks bobble as you pass.

Their gaudy noise halts and garbles.
You know their automatic eyes
are rolling after you like marbles.

# James Whitehead

## THE YOUNG DEPUTY

It was Leroy Smith we meant to find
In the slough, the old river, with hooks
But didn't. It was two others, or halves
Of two, the big man's torso, the small
Man's thighs, which made the Sheriff sick
In the boat.
         It wasn't one man no matter
How hard he tried.

Eaten by fish was one answer.
Maybe gar. Drowned, with rope
Still strung from the thick wrist, and a little
Chain around the bottom's ankle.

Considering conflicting reports
Of disappearance from various places
They might have been a dozen men.

Then it got to be a joke about
The burial: one grave or two
Since they'd got fixed as a single thing
In everybody's mind.
               Smith,
He never came to light, and it seemed
To figure that the one good grave
Could somehow cover all three—and more,
Said a few with furious souls.

There'd be, I thought, if things were right,
A fine day of picknicking,
Preaching to a big mixed audience,
And, in the nearest pine, one buzzard,
Glossy, hunkering, with a confused gaze.

**JAMES WHITEHEAD**

James Whitehead was born in St. Louis, Missouri, on March 15, 1936. He attended Vanderbilt University, where he played varsity football, studied under Donald Davidson, and took a B.A. in Philosophy and an M.A. in English. At the University of Iowa, where he received an M.F.A., he studied with R. V. Cassill and Donald Justice. His novel, *Joiner,* published by Alfred A. Knopf, was named by *The New York Times* to its list of Noteworthy Books of the Year for 1971. He was recipient of the Robert Frost Fellowship in Poetry to the Bread Loaf Writers' Conference in 1967. Whitehead has also served on the staff of Bread Loaf and a number of other writers' conferences, including the famed Hollins Conference of 1970. He lives with his wife, Gen, and their seven children in Fayetteville, Arkansas, where he teaches in the M.F.A. program at the University of Arkansas.

## FIRST LECTURE

### 1

Recently I heard a friend was mad.
It seems he took to women by the score,
Went nude to teach a class of freshman boys,
Then burned the books he loved.
No doubt this fits
Some classic case concluded and almost cured
Years ago, but I won't seek a paradox
To call him sane.
He was no Christ, and his loss
Of mind might well have led to serious crime.

### 2

He was the kind we rarely understand.
He feared the voice, was pressed to complete a clause
Without a breath—
His lungs were strong, but he weighed
Each word too carefully.
He knew nine languages
By heart and tried to read each line of poetry
As if it were the last the man has said.
He wanted to know what caused a hand to push pen
Or to type, he wanted to know why any man
Felt wise enough to speak
At all. This led to his fall.

**3**

Yet now they say he rests quite well
Takes easily to therapy
Though they have no plans to let him out
And I hear he reads again for his board
He reads to children and the old
Will keep it up so long as they
Will stay and at this play all seem
To understand for none requires
The meaning of a word he reads
And his stammering has almost stopped.

**4**

Which brings to mind a thought he used to say:
*The end of style for honest men is clarity.*

---

## A LOCAL MAN REMEMBERS THE KILLING GROUND

They formed the ritual circle
Of Chevy trucks. Tracks were there,
Worn tires, the still prints in the mud
And thin grass. My light could barely suggest
The glare that fell on the men they killed.

It was an intimate thing—
All of them drawn in so close
They didn't bother with guns
Or the normal uses of the knife.
It was done with boots.

I walked around that quiet place
And tried to reclaim the energy
That must of course remain in the earth.
It keeps the truth to itself
As they will, when they stride out of court.

By then it was all grey, false dawn—
And I thought it was like stomping
A fetus in the womb, a little
Skin between the killers, the killed,
For the dead were curled in their passive way.

---

## STATEMENT AND VISION, TWO SIGNS OF HISTORY

**1**

**His Old Friend Who Sometimes Comes To Talk**

In May, his last time over, he drank too much,
Was vulgar and sick by one, then wept till three—

It was all about the end of such and such
An order, but I never follow well the free
Confusion of the graceful past not memory

And I honestly suspect mortality
In general defeats him more than Lee.

**2**

**McComb City, August 1958**

This town is silent. No wind
All day would cross the balustrade
And now in the streets the night
Dogs are gay and on parade,
Mad with an old moon.

I hear them begin to whine their thin curses
Against all signs of rain.
I watch them pad toward dawn where rage is.

---

# Diane Wakoski

## LOVE TO MY ELECTRIC HANDMIXER

*with apologies to André Breton*

My electric handmixer of 87 bloodstone finches,
my electric handmixer of a house on fire,
my electric handmixer of sunflower petals,
my electric handmixer of clenched teeth,
my electric handmixer of gold in the sea water,
my electric handmixer of carboned tunnels,
my electric handmixer of frequent metallic rain,
my electric handmixer of sugar beet oceans,
my electric handmixer of lemon ears,
I am happier with you than
lifting leather cushions and finding spongy gold.
I am happier with you than
electing a cowboy to office.
I am happier with you than
the United States Navy.
O, electric handmixer, I would put your
names on the wings of gypsy moths,
for love.

**DIANE WAKOSKI**

**Diane Wakoski writes: I was born in Whittier, California August 3, 1937; attended the University of California at Berkeley (BA in English) and came to New York City in 1960 where I've lived ever since. The exterior events of my life are not very noteworthy and all the interior events are recorded in my poems. I've published seven collections of poems. I've also published 8 "slim volumes," part of which include my long, continuing didactic poem, "Greed," now in 9 parts. In my poems, I try to speak to men and communicate what it's like to be a woman so that they could feel and know.**

## THANK YOU FOR THE VALENTINE

I leave my heart in the doorway
for you
or anyone
to trip over. This will not be Valentine
talk though,
      the lace of Chopin études that sprinkles over
my teeth, the velvet rag carnations I find whispering
suicide notes in the street.
          No, this is
to be a conversation of plasterers' dusty overalls,
and the gas meter reader's flashlight.

Look, I wear my heart on my sleeve, my arm rather,
cut in the shape of the letter "M."
Can you write a check for my rent?
Can you pay my dental bill?
Can you be a family man?
Can you give me the things I need?
You are not the man I want.
      I would have to climb a mountain in Tibet
        to cash your checks.

I would have to fill my teeth with pebbles.
I would have to have paper children.
You are six letters away from "M" in the
    alphabet.
You are not even the one who gave me this
    Valentine.
And I want to thank you,
that is,
all my friends.
      You's are as many as the facets of a fly's eye.
I wear my heart on my sleeve, sometimes a piece of it
lies sloppily in my doorway, and you gave me this Valentine,
loaned it, I should say,
a heart that is temporarily mine.
        Round
          or lumpy
or not decorative
or rusty
or full of slivers
this little tick-tock that slips through my throat
and taps under my arm pits

this clock that can be wound
only with a silver "M" shaped key.

# R. H. W. Dillard

**R. H. W. DILLARD**

R. H. W. Dillard writes: I was born October 11, 1937 in Roanoke, Virginia where for one reason or another I have lived for most of my life. I lived in Florida for a year during the war (WWII, that is) and spent six years in Charlottesville at the University of Virginia, but otherwise I am truly provincial, mountainbound and rooted in high valley soil. I took a B.A. at Roanoke College and an M.A. and a Ph.D. at the University of Virginia, and I am now an associate professor of English at Hollins College. I married Annie Doak, my sophomore student who is now the poet Annie Dillard, in 1965. Besides poetry, I have written literary criticism, film criticism, fiction, and am the co-author of a horror movie entitled *Frankenstein Meets the Space Monster*.

## MEDITATION FOR A PICKLE SUITE

Morning: the soft release
As you open a jar of pickles.
The sun through the window warm
And moving like light through brine,
The shadows of pickles swim the floor.
And in the tree, flowing down the chimney,
The songs of fresh birds clean as pickles.
Memories float through the day
Like pickles, perhaps sweet gherkins.
The past rises and falls
Like curious pickles in dark jars,
Your hands sure as pickles,
Opening dreams like albums,
Pale Polish pickles.
Your eyes grow sharp as pickles,
Thoughts as green, as shining
As rows of pickles, damp and fresh,
Placed out in the afternoon sun.

## LOOKING FOR ASIA

*You are out of the way to Japon,*
*for this is not it.*
—Captain Luke Foxe (1631)

The bay is as cold
As colored silk at night,
As smooth as colored silk.

The two small ships hang
On their anchor lines
Like paper balloons,
Easing around in the tide,
Echoed in the still water.

Well into the long day,
The sun reaches for Japan
As it crosses the bay
And points the ships' masts
Back home across the water,
Across lost Vinland, the ocean,
The familiar tides of Bristol.

Captain Foxe offers his advice,
And the two captains laugh
Like the rattle of swords,
Tear the silent air
Like paper walls, secure

In having come beyond the point
Of Frobisher's return, where
Hudson's wake lingers
In the still cold water
Like an uneasy ghost.

We find the story
In *North-West Fox*, p. 223,
(1635). The captains' laughter
Eddies in the bay, mingles
With the sound of axes
On the shore, spattering
From the slim pines
Like small arms fire.

## HATS

Annie appears, arrayed
In an amazing assortment
Of hats.

They stagger above her
Like a happy drunk
Looking for the familiar lamppost.

What a strange creature,
The Martian must think,
Taking a quick snap
From the step of his lander,
I hope this shot comes out.

All of my friends
Are astounded. They
Applaud, not really knowing
What is expected of them.
As always, they have done
The right thing.

Her walk is a dance
Taller than telephone poles.
Birds light lightly
On the brims.

The grass is alert
Underfoot for droppings.
Three small hats do fall:
The Sudanese felt tarboosh
And the two York Harbor
Paper fireman's hats.
They bounce like dervishes,
Like water drops on a hot roof.

What a strange creature,
You must think. So do I.

Odd that she should prove
So lovely. Odder still
How her eyes are friendly
Like the tracks of birds,
How her hands are safe
As the eyelids of birds.


## AMERICA IS DARKEN'D

*Washington, Franklin, Paine & Warren,*
*Gate, Hancock & Green*
—William Blake

"Now, my dear friend, what is our plan?"
Cornwallis wrote to Phillips,
Already tired of Greene and Guilford,
Soon to leave with no reply
For Yorktown and Washington,
De Rochambeau and Comte de Grasse.

How could he know how Washington
Burned in the imagination of Blake,
How red hairy Orc squeezes out of earth
Like a tough vine to bloom in Yorktown?

Children, their clothes shed
Like worn skin, ride the tamed serpent,
As relaxed as fat lambs.

The *Terrible* blazes off Cape Charles.
Pale women burn in the flames, swell

Like new grapes on the vine, spread
Their legs and fly like smoke
Across Cape Charles, across Yorktown,
Darkening the blue mountains,
The dim midwest, the Rockies
Where the sun burns down like a pyre,
Like a ship hissing down in salt water.

What could Cornwallis do?
He and his armies fared better
In India where the fire was unreal,
Where elephants kneeled on command,
Where dark men were used to Juggernaut
And could agree to the benefits of the
 wheel.

Lord North cried, "O God! It is all over!"

In American, Blake's dream burns on.
The smoke stings the eye to tears.
A lizard tongues insects in the scorched air.
Bolts and hinges are melted.
Snakes hiss from every hip and thigh.

Blake wove his FINISH in thorns
With blooms as hot as coals. Trees
Clutch each other like lust. Men
Clutch the earth and bloom like fruitful
 trees.
The eye ignites to see. The hand holds.
Blake's dream burns on.

**DABNEY STUART**

Dabney Stuart dates from November 4, 1937, in Richmond, Virginia. He writes: Dabney Stuart was born previously and resides. His principal states have been Virginia, North Carolina and Massachusetts, where he has taught and studied. He wrote his first poem after nine years of practice; after nine more years of practice he has begun to conceive poems on other than narrative bases. He has learned more from English poets than from American, and believes that any utterance should live in the history of its language as well as on various levels of perception. A poem is an organ among organs, he has often dreamed, and should be played in sympathy. A reviewer of his first book—*The Diving Bell*, from which the poems herein are taken—said he "resembled a man going slowly, but surely, to sleep." One hopes that this turns out to be true; though it was intended as a slur it remains the fondest of possibilities, for the creations of sleep are the quickest. He recommends his second book—*A Particular Place*, from which no poems herein are taken—as slower still, and more sure. Mr. Stuart is finally married. He has two incredible sons.

# Dabney Stuart

## FALL PRACTICE

Some after a night of sex, some hungover,
Some tanned, some fat, all still half asleep,
They'd sit around and give each other lip
Before padding up and cleating the summer clover
The field had grown to cover last season's dust.

"Her? Aw, man, that chick's a highway, I oughtta know,
I've driven it." "You gotta taste
That stuff, grow whiskers on your ass." "The best
I ever had was. . ." and so forth, The old show.
A bunch of scrubs bucking for first team berth.

I couldn't believe their talk. They'd cat all night
Yet next day hit the dummies, digging the turf,
Sweating, driving themselves for all they were worth
Into each other like bulls, brute against brute.
Whatever they got, girls, drunk, it wasn't enough.

It went on like that, late August through November.
Though I was the quarterback, the thinker
Who directed that beef, split ends, and set the flanker,
I worked at the center's butt, and I remember
Being primed for the big game, hungering for the cup.

**JAMES HARRISON**

James Harrison writes: I was born December 11th, 1937, in Grayling in Northern Michigan and find myself living in the same general area at present, only nearer the water on a small farm in Lake Leelanau. Between times I have lived in New York, Boston and San Francisco, taken an M.A. in Comparative Literature from MSU, taught at Stony Brook for two years, gotten married. I've published three books of poems. A novel, *Wolf—A False Memoir,* was published by Simon & Schuster in 1971. I received a grant from the National Endowment for the Arts for 1967–68 and was a Guggenheim Fellow for 1969–70. I've printed poems and reviews and articles in *Poetry, The Nation, New York Times Book Review, Partisan, Sports Illustrated, Sumac, Stony Brook Journal* and others, and have read my work aloud fairly widely though I don't care for this activity. Though I am perpetually broke I find I can't teach and write at the same time so have given up on the former which I wasn't good at anyway. I use all my spare time fishing in Michigan, Montana and Key West; if I don't fish relentlessly I go batty. Seriously.

## TIES

When I faded back to pass
Late in the game, as one
Who has been away some time
Fades back into memory,
My father, who had been nodding
At home by the radio,
Would wake, asking
My mother, who had not
Been listening, "What's the score?"
And she would answer, "Tied,"
While the pass I threw
Hung high in the brilliant air
Beneath the dark, like a star.

## THE SOUP JAR

Its metal top refused my father's twisting;
He tried warm water, a dishcloth, the heel of a shoe,
But couldn't budge its stubborn *status quo.*
It had stood its ground, longer than he, rusting.

I had to help. Gripped the jar while he cursed
Into place the tricky gadget guaranteed
To open anything, then gave it all he had.
I jerked my hand, and a hunk of glass, back when it burst.

Someone else tied my tourniquet. He paled
And had to sit down. Seven stitches later
We cleaned the floor and had another dish for supper.
Alone, he got nothing. It took us both to fail.

Weeks after, my world spun around that jar
And I saw it, and him, through angry tears.
Now it seems, recalled through these shattered years,
So small a thing—some broken glass, a scar.

## GLUCOSE

When I veined that quick syrup
The bottle hung above me
Like a sun. And now my father,
Tubed and pumped, in traction,
What sun does he see?

I call to him
Stranded six stories over
My head, *Father,*
*Stranger, I wish I were hanging*
*Above you like a sun.*

As it is, these white walls
Stare through me, an empty bottle
The nurses take pains
Not to break.

# James Harrison

## A SEQUENCE OF WOMEN

### I

I've known her too long:
we devour as two mirrors,
opposed,
swallow each other a thousand
times at midpoints,
lost in the black center
of the other.

### II

She sits on the bed,
breasts slack,
watching a curl of dust
float through a ray of sun,
drift down to a corner.
So brief this meeting
with a strange child—
Do I want to be remembered?
Only as a mare might know

the body of her rider,
the pressure of legs
unlike any other.

### III

The girl who was once my mistress,
is dead now, I learn, in childbirth.
I thought that long ago women ceased
dying this way.

To set records straight, our enmity
relaxes, I wrote a verse for her—

to dole her by pieces, ring finger
and lock of hair.

But I'm a poor Midas to turn her golden,
make a Helen, grand whore, of this graceless
girl; the sparrow that died was only
a sparrow:

*Though in the dark, she doesn't sleep.*
*On cushions, embraced by silk, no lover*
*comes to her. In the first light when birds*
*stir she does not stir or sing. O eyes can't*
*focus to this dark.*

---

## BELLEVUE

John in the desert
mixed honey with blood.
Three white birds surround me
and my voice is in my feet—
How beautiful with shoes, O Redeemer.
From a lightbulb a drop of blood emerges
and floats
softly down toward my head,
the room whines O Redeemer,
this is my baptism.

This is cold salt
a pulled tooth
the freshly set bone:
the girl who left my bed this morning,
who smiled last night as her slip
floated to the floor,
my Roselita,
today up on Amsterdam Avenue
I saw her with her Manuelo.

---

## MOVING

Not those who have lived here and gone
but what they have left: a worn-out broom,
coat hangers, the legs of a doll,
errors of possession to remind us of
    ourselves;
but for drunkenness or prayers the walls
collapse in boredom, or any new ecstasy
could hold them up, any moan or caress
or pillow-muffled laugh;

leaving behind as a gift seven rooms of air
once thought cathedral, those imagined
beasts at windows,
her griefs hung from the ceiling for spectacle.

But finally here I am often there
in its vacant shabbiness,
standing back to a window in the dark,
carried by the house as history, a boat,
deeper into a year, into the shadow
of all that happened there.

---

## SEQUENCE

### I

The mad have black roots in their brains
around which vessels clot and embrace
each other as mating snakes.

The roots feed on the brain until the brain
is all root— now the brain is gray
and suffocates in its own folds.

The brain grows smaller and beats
against its cage of bone
like a small wet bird.

Let us pity the mad we see every day,
the bird is dying without air and water
and growing smaller,
the air is cold, her beak is sharp,
the beating shriller.

### 2

He loves her until
tomorrow or until 12:15 AM
when again he assumes the firedrake,
ricochets from the walls
in the exhaustion of kingship;

**JOYCE CAROL OATES**

Joyce Carol Oates writes: I was born in Lockport, New York, on June 16, 1938. I've received degrees from Syracuse University and the University of Wisconsin; I've taught so far at two universities—the University of Detroit and the University of Windsor, in Ontario, Canada. My husband is Raymond Smith, also a professor at Windsor who specializes in the 18th century and modern poetry. My stories have been anthologized in various books, mainly the *O. Henry Prize Stories* and *The Best American Short Stories*. In 1967 I was awarded a Guggenheim Grant; I received the Rosenthal Award from the National Academy of Arts and Letters and, in 1970, the National Book Award for fiction (for *Them*). These are the facts and while they do not represent me at all, while they seem in some bizarre way to misrepresent me, the real world seems put together by facts and it is necessary at times to honor that world.

somewhere in skull the Bible's leaves
seem turned by another's hand.

The pool table's green felt is earth,
ivory balls, people cracked toward leather
    holes.
Christ's blood is whiskey. Light is dark.
And light from a cave in whose furnace
three children continue their burning.

**3**

The dead haloed in gladiolas
and electric organs,
those impossible hurts, trepanations,
the left eye punctured with glass;
he'll go to Canada with his dog,
a truly loved and loving creature—
fish in the water, bear in his den.

Not fox shrinking before foxhound
snaps its neck, horse cowered before crop.

**4**

In the woods the low red bridge;
under it and above the flowing water
spiders roost in girder's
rust and scale, flaking to touch.
Swift clear water. Soiled sand,
slippery green moss on rock face.
From the red bridge, years back
he dove into an eddy catching
the river's backward bend and swirl,
wishing not to swim on or in
as a duck and fish
but to be the water herself,
flowing then and still.

# Joyce Carol Oates

## LINES FOR THOSE TO WHOM TRAGEDY IS DENIED

These women have no language and so they chatter
In the rhythm of stereotype that is won
After certain years and certain money.
Or perhaps they once rose naked from the sea
And the stereotype rose from them, like a snapshot
Snapped by envious fingers, an act of love
They never noticed.
The ladies are metronomes or pendulums
As their laments swing from one to the other
Around the heavy oak table, rooted to the floor
Like many another oak: here the roots are bolts.
The floor is parquet, polished and indifferent
To the tappings of expensive feet.
No matter what these ladies say, no matter,
It is crime to listen to the language of ladies
Who have no language.

> *Fifteen years ago when we were first married*
> *we lived on an army base; we had no money;*
> *we saved to go to the camp movies, which cost*
> *a dime. We saved all week . . . for the movies.*

The army has cleared out, marched away, the soldiers are
Grown out of their boys' uniforms and some are
Rotted entirely out of them and some, like your husbands,
Are important now and very expensive.

> *The car broke down in Kansas City, on our*
> *way to his mother in Texas. And I broke*
> *down, with the baby and all, and he sat*
> *talking to me and kidding in the car, in*
> *the rain . . . in Kansas City . . . . That was*
> *nineteen years ago.*

Of sorrow their diamonds are stereotypes, again,
And no tears can quite equal their brilliance.
Bloated out of themselves like corpses in water
Such suburban ladies stare upon their former bodies,
Girls' bodies, and it is the innocence of plant and algae
They seem to taste, and not human guise.

> *Then Michael was born, and then I got pregnant*
> *again and we were afaid to write home;*
> *between his family and mine what choice did*
> *we have? I had the baby, that's Perry at*
> *Yale. He's going to Italy this summer . . . .*

There are five ladies here and two are divorced and
Sad to say divorce awaits the others, like death.
Their husbands never dream away time in Kansas City.
Never do they dream of khaki and mud and never youth
Without power, never the submersion in shapes
Unshaped like the good silky leather gloves
Tangled around the straps of leather purses.
Their husbands account for the success of airlines
And the thick red carpets of certain restaurants.
Ah, manly men!—and stripped clean of the garments
Of tawdry questions: What am I?
The latest light-toned lipstick cannot quite disguise
The bitter bitter set of your skulls' teeth, ladies.
And you are educated, or were.
Your milk-curdled glands stir
At the fate of adolescent children, your children,
Who will not obey. No fur to your bodies, ladies,
But the pelts of animals killed for you.
These pelts gleam and glisten

In the five o'clock light of the Oak Room
Of the club. We are very wealthy here and
Very liberal about Negroes.

> *We never argued, never fought.*
> *Then that night he told me, before*
> *guests, that the house was sold; he*
> *said, "Your taste was never good."*
> *It seemed to begin then . . . .*

In the depths of the table over which they lean
Their younger selves dream and drown
And the gold of their trinkets which is real
And heartbreaking in beauty, and the pink
Of their gentle besieged ears, and the perfumed wires
They wear as hair, and the droning question of
Their chatter grow heavy, heavy
In the absence of men and the absence of sky and
Cloudy wet mornings in other cities, minor cities,
And the rapid jerky heartbeat of youth with no
Gold to it but youth.
Do the ribbed wonders of the brain still hold
In terraces without nerves the outlines
Of faces, of love? And what was love? And who were
Those boy husbands, those wives; and who were those babies
So loved and feared? When they were real were they real?
Now it is certain that the time of day is real.
The table, the floor, the panelled walls are real
And real the density of bodies and
The images, like angels, of ladies settled and bizarre
As certain birds bred for color and song and beyond
Their youth's charm.

---

# A GIRL AT THE CENTER OF HER LIFE

There may be some way back
she thinks, past familiar homes
that will look painful now
and the hammer of cries in her blood,
past the unchanged sky that is any sky—
"What time is it?" is her mind's question.

This field is any field beyond the town,
and twenty miles from her parents' house.
Twenty miles takes you anywhere.
In the country you must curve
and calculate to get
where you're going, accounting for great
blocks of farms selfish with land, and creeks,
and uncrossable boneyards of rock and junk.
This is any field, then, being so far.

Its silence and its indifferent rustling
of mice and birds of any field
make her want to cry in a delirum:
"Let me be off to soak in hot water,
bright hot water, or to brush my hair

in a girl's fury drawing the hairs out
onto the gold-backed brush—"
At the place of her heart is
a hot closed fist.
It is closed against the man who waits
for her at the car . . . .

How to release to the warm air
such a useless riot of hate?
Lacking love, her casual song
fell swiftly to hate, a dark vengeance
of no form, and unpracticed—
A dragonfly skims near, like metal.
Into her eyesight burns the face
of this man, half a boy,
who stands puzzled
on one shore, she on another.
Her brain pounds . . . . Who will not see
what she has become? Who will not know?
There is no confronting this blunder
of pains and lusts opened
like milkweed, scattered casually with wind,

soft and flimsy, adhesive to human touch
and delicate as a pillow's suffocation.
A hypnosis of milkweed!
A young girl, in terror not young,

is no colt now but a sore-jointed cow
whose pores stutter for help, help,
and whose sweaty skin has gathered
seeds upon it, and tiny dry bits of grass.

**DICK ALLEN**

Dick Allen, who was born on August 8, 1939, in Troy, New York, describes himself as perhaps the only American "science fiction" poet in captivity, "working heavily with SF subjects, future-casting, surrealistic satire, war and ecology politics." One of Allen's main concerns in poetry, in addition to "extending the human vision beyond Rilke," is to "bring back to American poetry the story-telling quality, the dramatic poem, in order to explore the myth and wonder of the *average* American's experience." Allen is the winner of an Academy of American Poets Prize, the Hart Crane Memorial Fellowship for Poetry, and *Poetry*'s Union Arts and Civic League Prize. Formerly the editor of *Mad River Review*, he is now director of creative writing at the University of Bridgeport. He lives in Fairfield, Connecticut, with his wife, Lori, a son, Ricky, and a daughter, Tanya.

# Dick Allen

PODUNK, 1941

John Doe and Mary Smith
live here and
and they're of course proud
and insane.

After work, they meet
in the post-office lobby—
if one of them is late
the other reads posters:

the troublemakers leer
at Mary's knees.
She memorizes scars
and interesting habits.

Often on their walk
to Woolworth's or Grant's
they watch for license plates
and sawed-off shotguns,

for legend has it Pretty
Boy Floyd
thought this
the ideal knockoff.

They walk down Main Street where
ten parking meters have
just been installed.
The mayor's progressive.

John lingers by
the haberdashery—
his eye
on a hat with a brim

while Mary Smith leans
her well-washed five and ten
unpadded cotton
bosom on him.

He grins
and takes her hand
in his—
they talk of the weather,

money, the weather, money,
his and her friends,
and what shall they do
that is "different, exciting, new."

Maybe explore
the haunted mansion where
a millionaire lived
for a reason

or maybe John
can talk her into taking
a swim in the nude.
But he doubts it.

Or maybe they should try
to invent
a new invention that
has always been needed.

But Mary hides
her dreams like underclothes
inside
a pillowslip

and John Doe waits
until the kids next door
have gone to bed
before he'll pour

his kitchen table glass
of ice-cold beer.
Both of them are sure
they are evil and dull.

And let me tell you something
that's true
as the rain:
there isn't any Podunk, anymore.

## TO A WOMAN HALF A WORLD AWAY

Just about now
you will be dusting the flowers
or changing from your bathrobe into something nice.

The kids will all be out
oiling their bikes, and thinking of birthdays.
The mailman will take his time up the hill.

Maybe this is the morning you will go shopping
to buy a percolator, or a yellow blouse.
Drive, darling, careful.

That book you mean to read
if nothing on the set is well worth watching,
I bet is something with an ending really happy.

Now you are dressed
and walk around the house with your blood pressure up,
looking for something, anything, not in its place.

The mailman comes, and this letter
of course is not there.
You worry just a little as you close the door.

And then you turn, and your face
is just so beautiful it makes me stop
and wonder why I thought I would remember your body.

Here, you will remember, I am in night
beside a river that seems to flow through every field,
learning I am sentimental past my wildest fears.

**AL YOUNG**

Al Young writes: I was born a classic Gemini 1939 (May 31) in Mississippi, Ocean Springs by the Gulf of Mexico. My father was a jazz musician who, after serving with the Navy during World War II, gave up playing for steadier work at the Chevrolet plant in Detroit. The eldest of seven children, I grew up in both the South & the Midwest. In grade school & junior high I wrote detective, cowboy & sci-fi fantasies, discovering poetry around the 9th grade. At the University of Michigan, preparing to major in anthropology, I studied writing with the late novelist Allan Seager & with J. Radcliffe Squires, later taking a degree in Spanish at UC Berkeley. I have traveled widely in the U.S., Mexico, the Azores, Portugal, Spain & France, working at a variety of jobs, sometimes as a professional musician. Poetry, like blues, is my favorite way of crying out loud & laughing at myself & the world at the same time. Sound (people-talk, language, music), since much of my life revolves around it, is a force that I'm addicted to & writing provides a means for expressing my love of it. I have taught writing for the San Francisco Museum of Art, the Neighborhood Youth Corps &, most recently, as Jones Lecturer in Creative Writing at Stanford. Work of mine has appeared in a number of magazines & anthologies both in this country & abroad, including *Essence, Massachusetts Review, The American Literary Anthology, The New Black Poetry, Chicago Review, New Directions, Evergreen* & my own occasional review *Loveletter.*

2 takes from
LOVE IN LOS ANGELES

A potted fern
in a Vine St apartment
spreads its green delicate tentacles
like my cousin Cynthia
does her fingers
at the piano
in the window
West 27th St
the colored district
where almost everybody
has a REpublic or a 73-
telephone number;
no maps sold
to the homes of these stars:

my Uncle James
game to the end

in his rickety walkup
room on the 2nd floor
with low-rent view
of rooftops & parkinglots
neon liquor messages
where you watch
a dude out of Texas
with a process
& a redhead
turn left
on a red light &
barely miss
getting his jag
smashed to pieces;
Unc is imagining
how many nickel numbers
he'd have to hit
back in Detroit
to get his used car
overhauled again—

James
Cynthia
Richard
Toni
Marti
Inez
Desi
Pierre,
their blood my blood
in this other kind of colony

way out west

where the Indians are real
& train for equal opportunity positions,

where the young Chicanos
whip ass
& wig behind
soul music &
Brown is Beautiful,
where lithe &
lipsticked Chinese girls
avoid Japanese advances
maintaining that cool
by any means necessary,

where the keeper of dreams
is solemn &
wears a whole body dickey
from odious head
to fabulous toe
to entice the young women
& other boys

In one dream
the third world ghosts
of Charlie Chan &
Mantan Moreland
in the gentle sting
of a gasoline twilight
take turns
kissing on
an unidentified starlet
with a natural &
a bankamericard

Even the flourishing nazi
whose children smoke opium
& inject themselves
for laughs
in Orange County
has his angeleno mistresses,
intelligent negresses
in auburn wig
& shades;
strange thin-lipped aryans

whose underwear glitters,
new Marilyn Monroes
in colorfast fashion knits
parking their cars
in puddles of quicksilver
who wink at spooks
propped next to palmtrees

Love licks its lip
at no one

_____

## PARIS

I couldnt ever tell you
just what might have been going on,
the gray brick nowhereness
of certain gendarmes
if you can dig it

But for now
you follow me into ice cream places
where they push hamburgers
& beer too
where nothing seems to have changed
since Worcester,
where I can feel the flirtiness
of meat heat rising in the streets,
a european princess
easing herself up next to me
dead on the Champs Elysees

I buy my *jetons*
& make phonecalls like a nice fellow
to whom directions are mapped out sweetly
by tender old ladies born in Rue La Bruyere
as all the african brothers
hop on & off the metro
jammed up with birds & algerians

England no
this is France
another colonial power environment
far from Richard Wright's
or my own wrong Mississippi

Encircled by luminous space
I lay my woolly head
against your tan belly of Italy
& listen to the fat cars in the streets
hometown of the bourgeoisie
& clean creamy ladies & you
sparkle darkly
where I too
am pregnant
with astonishment

## POEM FOUND EMPTYING OUT MY POCKETS

*for Ron & Taffy Dabl*

It is a normal day.
I rise just as the room's filling up again
with light
feeling myself to be the award winning
   goof-off
who wanted to practice yoga
& write the world a thousand good books
simultaneously,
whose lady is slumbering in Massachusetts
lit up & pounding with dream horses.

An orange fur creature taps me naked
purring for breakfast
(groaning for roast fowl or ocean fish).

Re-washing
I think things over
then re-dress & re-comb with my African
   woodcomb.
I consume oranges bananas & cold milk
yearning to know more about fruits &
   animals.

Out in the streets I know everybody
but I dont know anything.
I dont know these blind buildings.
I dont know what people are doing.

I dont even know what I'm doing.
I arrive at my job,
the sun makes its round,
at noon if it's warm I sleep under a tree,
at midnight sometimes trees sleep under me,
angels beckon from books & at stop/lights,
the mouths of warmongers work overtime
to convince me I am what I'm not,
fingers touch my palm making change
or I stutter
greeting somebody I havent seen.

Behind everyone's eye
I can sense the steady stream of dreams
or temporary malice
rippling & flickering helplessly.
Who needs television?
I could tell everything
if there werent so many of us.

A little dinner
a little nourishment
a little remembrance of things to come
a considerate voice against my cheek &
I too am willing to continue
wearily inspired by this strange change
called love
that keeps coming
like death
to everybody

---

## FOR KENNETH & MIRIAM PATCHEN

Here
I am cutting you
these fresh healthy flowers
from my sick bed
where I toss with nickel illuminations.
Time is a fever
that burns in the pores
consuming everything the mind creates.
I send you
this cool arrangement of dream blossoms
these tender stems & shining leaves
while I shiver
& detect in your own eyes

of gentle remove
a similar disgust with what has come
to our fat cancerous land
of the sensual circus
& the disembodied broadcast wave,
swallowing in sorrow
to hear the old hatred
& undercover selfishness
rumbling back up from the bosoms of men
out into the good open air.
May these new flowers
from the forest of my heart
bring you a breath of the joy
men must believe they are going to recover
by moving again & again
against one another.

---

# David Steingass

**DAVID STEINGASS**

David Steingass writes: I was born 12 July 1940 in Elyria, Ohio, the first child of Katherine Lutsch and Herbert Steingass, and grew up one county from Lake Erie in Geauga on a sixty acre poultry farm, to whose detail and reality I owe the bulk of my knowledge. I went to Capital University (a Lutheran denominational college in Columbus) and the universities of Maine and California at Irvine, where I was awarded an M.F.A. degree in 1968 from the Writing Program. My thesis, *Body Compass*, was one of four books of poetry published in the University of Pittsburgh Press poetry series in 1969. The book won an endowment from the National Council for the Arts. I have supported myself, my wife Susan, and my son Brook by teaching college English, in Maine, Louisiana, California, and most recently Wisconsin State University in Stevens Point. I've published short stories, and am working on subsequent books of poems, and a novel.

## LOVE POEM BEGINNING WITH I

I am drunk
And you have locked me out,
Barring the double doors with slabs
Of marble. Children and animals
Are there with you, knives and leather.

I fire the place with pine
Chips and my torch.
The flame crashes off my steel
Headpiece and the snow,
Vanishing in my bearskins.

I will withdraw in this warmth
To a cold and distant mountain
If you choose to stay.

## A BEGINNING

When it stood, my town was small
Enough to fill a single
Snapshot. Memorial days
Packed-in a cozy graveyard,
Where even the dead could hear
Without amplification.

It grew each year a century
Old, by preserving horse-hitch
Bars in concrete, donating
Rope so the moron could dance
Out his eyes, stoning the girl
Who finally chose her horse over
The boy she met in bushes.

Buckeyes kept the roads busy
So they couldn't stretch, where hounds
Shambled before horns, slowly,
And lost themselves in a ditch.
So slow a boy could tell time
By bullheads, so quiet he heard
Voices on the party line.

It felt like a cavity
After cake, in the end, twice
Bigger than its nightmare stall.
I think of traveling back,
Marking the roads have narrowed,
My gas tank full to the top.

## THE SLAUGHTER-ROOM PICTURE

Every two hours they broke
Because the big houses did, fearing
Blood fixation, and once
The mother took a picture.

"Would it help to smile," she wondered,
And caught the proud half-leers
Of husband and son,
Alike in arctics and denim, brown rubber
Aprons spotted with feathers and blood,
Hands puffed and pink as babies'.

The father's hooded picker behind,
Where turkeys flew from their feathers
On a drum of hollow, rubber fingers.
Cooling vats glazed with ice;
The stainless-steel eviscerating table;
The tendon puller on the wall.

Loose in the son's hand, a pencil-
Thin killing knife. Blood and cold
Have deadened his hand. The killing
Funnels beside him on the wall;
The empty scalder cage open
Over threads of steaming water.

He dreams of slaughter: rhythm
Packs the room like steam from the scalder.
Groping for a turkey upside down,
Its grape-full wattles pale after the jugular
Slash, blood squirting up his arm.
The snap of his wrist pops the neck:
A tumult in the funnel
Exactly as if the turkey were running.
On and on, soaked in blood, a smooth
    machine.

Then the break again, and the son
Wakes in the dark, groping
With his left hand, his right
Clenched thin as a pencil.

# Jonathan Price

Nine meshes of the net enclose
The school of carp

          a narrow ring
          draws the nets
          into a bundle

          you sense
          already
          what I am doing to you

          yet you are the boat, and I the fish; for you
          each moment, each turning of the page,
          deceive yourself, conceiving of your eye
          seeing, not seeing, but knowing

          expert
          the lie                       over here
          the ease of movement within known barriers    the quick
                                             small

flip, fish!                                         fish
                                          skitter away

      we ignore that
      you ignore it                      even the sunfish
      I too, in writing in such orderly fashion     gets through
      get to it only after a while             this hole

---

         The glaze. You try to see
         What is beneath the glassy surface, and
         You see the white, and you try to see how far,
         But it is one with the glass, no depth, all white,
         It draws you in, and then your eye discovers
         You have been outside all along

Consider our coffee pot.

         The oily grit inside

         The heating coil at the bottom, stainless steel,
         And the rod rising up the side,
         To the connection

         The spout

         The handle, black, attached by a steel hoop
         To the ceramic pot

    You do not see it in pieces
    No one can describe
    Without resorting to the eye,
    And the mind's
    Impression
    For it is not coffee pots we tell each other about
    In this we are solipsists; we announce
    And our listeners only really care about
    What went on inside of us.
    The glaze keeps us out, and in ourselves, and we may be content with that.

**JONATHAN PRICE**

Jonathan Price writes: I was born October 19th, 1941, in Boston, and bred by New England teachers. My father's family is Welsh—they fought with the Tories in the Revolution, and left for Canada. My grandfather, a writer, fled Canada to become a world traveller. My mother's family is English, French, and Dutch, mingled from the 17th century, and fought from New England on the American side in all those wars. I feel typically American: mixed. I like proud beautiful women, I love one in particular, I love making love: and I like being stoned: I also like Sicilian pizza, steak, the Stones, Robin Hood, Dionysius, Christmas carols, Claes Oldenburg, John Cage, Tina Turner, Jane Fonda, Rembrandt, Vergil, Homer, Grendel, George Washington, and Samuel Adams. I have written a book on the theater around us, with John Lahr, called *Life Show.* I have exhibited my poems in museums and art galleries, and on balloons. My poems may be read in several directions: as you will: but of late I have been branching out, and I now take commissions for wall poems. My permanent address is care of Newell Farm, West Newbury, Mass., but I currently live in New York, here and there, working on a novel about Lincoln Hospital.

## EZRA POUND

in the first
in the beginning, in a genesis
almost as muscular as a whale's burst

Keats  Merwin  Shakespeare remember me

in the first, as I say,
de los cantares

he spoke like Homer, and he was Homer, and Homer was in him

a boast.  a vow.  a truth.

He knew it,
And he resisted it.

The history of the land of Ch'ing ming

Always his mind ran off.

The economics

Why is it that some men

John Quincy Adams

Can grow, when they run off, into alleys
Like Shakespeare, like Homer,
But others get lost.
Why is it he

Such promise     Such stone

He created Stonehenge,
He put each Druid in his work,
And made a circle of them,
Solid, singing

Why is it he could not find his way back?
The tenor of the man
Suddenly leaked out, like a vibration of music
No longer heard.

At the loss, we feel an anguish like that of Job:
We ask God: How can this happen? How can a man like that
Break, under his own brain's buffeting?
It was an Armada
Unbelievably gone down. I still do not believe.

---

## TEST

test
Hit it on the rock                test
Like a wet towel                  test
test
test test
test
test

test test test test test test test test test test test

a test

how much will it bear?
test   test   test
I have confidence in men, and therefore in their ability to speak;
I have some confidence in words, but, like men,
Each must be put to the test
test   test   test

Pope is a test of sorts
Swift. Fielding. Pound.
Each word gives under the weight we put on it.            You must
Test.
Yet something of the courage of these men
Comes through.                                    Test?

**CALVIN FORBES**

Calvin Forbes was born on October 6, 1944. He writes: There's not much information about me. I was born in Newark, New Jersey, the seventh son in a family of ten. I went to high school there, college also, and since then I have lived in various places: New York, San Francisco, Honolulu, Yugoslavia. I wish to write poems as well as Charlie Parker played music. I read all of it and I hope it all becomes homogenized. At present, I teach at Emerson College in Boston.

        test        test        test

                        test

This is a test                     test

          test

     Not of you                test

     Of the word itself            test

               each moment
                              test
        test        test        test

        Test?    There is nothing left in the word.
               There is much left in me, and in you.
               test it
               test test test test test test test

# Calvin Forbes

## MY FATHER'S HOUSE

*1908-1970*

I live quietly and go nowhere
And this house shakes like a tree.
Open the door, jesus is the hinge
Squeaking from the rusty rain.

Deadheart, this house wasn't built
By human hands, and no bricks will
You find, wood or glass. This house
Stands like a skeleton inside the worst

Possible skin. Knock and enter afraid
Your shadow rigid as the brass laid
Across your coffin. Come closer and see
Broken beams, a sacred slum, no mystery

Except memory. Rise and make ends meet,
My tenant. Safe in its vastness, retreat
To a hidden corner; without mercy guard
Its three edges as if a fortune were yours.

## THE HOURS

In the morning cool and slender, you
Haunt the hours I'm blind in; you shoot
The night. I'm on a diet of beer, I'm
Cold, the weather tutors me with the dry
Smell of cow dung that lights me when
I fantasize I'm foreign. Your grey eyes

Dull the crayon sun. How crazy I am today!
This pasture isn't home but the months
Go on like an elephant's skin. The weight

Of my sleep makes me stumble to smooth
My exploding bones; the hot water of beer
Rises like a fire torn from me again where
I broke you in your belly. Daily you knock
Like a bandit, a ghost beating my heart.

**GARY MARGOLIS**

Gary Margolis was born on May 24, 1945. He writes: Leaving college, Middlebury, the country, and a major, to do what we are promised we can, took me to Buffalo, the State University, a doctorate, and a position counseling at Buffalo State College, thence to Middlebury College in Vermont. Over ice and recent summers I have served an army of Bloody Marys at the Bread Loaf Writer's Conference. Some of my poems have appeared in *The American Scholar, Tri-Quarterly,* and *The New Orleans Review.* Holt, Rinehart, and Winston will be publishing *Poetry and the Promise of Self,* the use of poems in counseling theory and practice.

# Gary Margolis

## REARRANGEMENT FOR THE BRAIN

Make this assumption:
There is no difference between good and
  bad
right and wrong.
Then, all things being equal, begin.
First, exercise freedom.
Taking hold of your right ear,
rip upwards.
As the canals fill with blood,
expect to lose your balance.
Second, display power.
Insert any object close at hand—
letter opener, tuning fork,
master key or ice cream scoop—
being careful not to use discretion.
Pry apart as much as you can,
working day in and day out.
Make sure the corpus callosum is cut,
that is to say, the connection between
  hemispheres,
using history as your guide.
Third, reserve judgement.
Anticipate the appointment
made for your heart,
by pronouncing death yourself.
Use this form:
I, the undersigned, assume full responsibility
for the disappearance of pulse and hope.
And finally, be temperate.
Listen to the clatter of sighs, rites, and
  stretchers,
strung together like wooden police lines,
as permeable as silk stockings.
Know that your ghost will elude them,
like an amoeba hiding at the edges of a slide.

## KEEP IT UNDER YOUR HAT

Leave it for the papers
and the politicians,
shouting the words in boldface,
mouth to mouth.
Don't let the cat out of the bag.
Save it for later when you
will not have to share it with outsiders,
who will demand a piece for themselves.
Don't give it away.
Make a tight fist,
squeezing the confetti
until the colors dye your hand,
and then, when you can see
the stars on his shoulders,
let some go, piece by piece,
commemorating
an unconditional surrender
fifty years from now—
a treaty signed half-way
between here and there.
Remember, no matter how much you wish
  to lose,
this is important.

# Ralph Adamo

**RALPH ADAMO**

Ralph Adamo writes: I was born in New Orleans on April 28, 1948. New Orleans is a beautiful city and it is my home, though I am living and working in Arkansas now. My undergraduate degree is from Loyola University. I taught one year in a girl's high school and was fired during the Cambodia-Kent State-Jackson State offensive for my own small part in our war effort. I've done an assortment of odd jobs as well. My poems have appeared in many magazines, big and little. Needless to say, my writing style is still undergoing considerable change; by the time this anthology goes to press, these poems won't represent what I'm doing anymore, but that's part of what writing is about.

## EASTER SUNDAY: NOT THE ARTIST

**1**

The unmade girl on my bed
crawls beneath herself to find sleep.
I search her face
for a line to put in my poem.
There are no lines.

Last night she wore
a scarf of rayon flowers
at midnight vigil mass
and asked me
*How are you doing*
*at forgetting*
*what you are not?*
And when the priest
consumed the blood
and didn't spill a drop
she said
*I could stand a drink.*

**2**

Any movement now
would be indiscreet;
my thick-fingered heart
does not want to feel her deeper.
There is no life in meaning.

After mass
she said
she was an honorary virgin
and when I told her
*Time is what stands between us*
she said *Shut up*
then remade my bed
in someone else's likeness:
*We'll sleep together soundly*
*since I have no place to go;*
*tomorrow*
*you can help me look.*

**3**

She stirs now with open lips,
eyes open slowly.
Mine close.
I hear her sit
and feel her looking at me.

Somewhere is a secret she knows
too true for dreaming
dark in the room of her thoughts.
I feel like screaming
but her fingers seal my lips.
And when I look
I see her laughing,
leaning close:
*You didn't touch me. Why didn't you*
*touch me?*
I say *You drew the line.*
She settles back and smiling says
*There are no lines.*

## LOW ALONG THE RIVER

**I**

Low along the river where the morning
comes down half-whiskered like a catfish
swimming the brown river, the morning
brown as the catfish caught ten feet down
by a touch of sun
                    They crouched low
along the river
and when the east came up
and when the river moved to the sky
where it wound by the deep mud
and the river dogs looked up
from their fishbones and growled
like last night's sky
                    They stuck
unstuck their thick steps in the mud
and waited by the dumped car
for the man who comes with the sun
on a good day, the golden man

**II**

Here we have dreams, we are dreams;
our city is a fly city in a toy time.

**III**

Pull the tongue from your eyes; eyes
are for looking
and nothing else. Grow yourself over
and come down to me. I am the next fire
to burn here. You are my beautiful thorns,
my love and my crawling things.

**JOHN BIGUENET**

John Biguenet writes: I was born on March 9, 1949 in New Orleans. I have been a construction worker, a teacher, a mailman, a swimming instructor, mostly a student, and lately a writer. My poetry and fiction have appeared in a number of journals. In 1970 I won a *Harper's* writing award. With the prize money I went to Mexico and learned more than I wanted to. I was advised to put "Poet" on my visa as my occupation. When I crossed into Mexico, the Mexican custom officials shook my hand and didn't even check my bags. As I was coming back into America, however, a U.S. agent took one look at my visa and invited me to join him in the interrogation room. He took my driver's license number. It was good to be home. I haven't the slightest idea what the future holds.

IV

And when the east comes up
we will be waiting in our false pastoral
imagining what is too near to hold;
we will call ourselves by other times
and do, with our closing world, our particular
river city, as we are told.

The dogs that return wild together,
lost with all hope from the hands of children
and blue women, have got their teeth
into something still, or growing, warm.
And what is torn or eaten and what
moves in small gestures still
seems to be walking out of the river.

# John Biguenet

## ONE-DAY DIARY

So we lay down and made our love
and fell asleep and woke. She got up
and cooked some food. I rolled a joint to
 smoke.

We ate our meal and cleaned the place
and then went back to bed, and made more
 love
and talked awhile till everything was said.

Then she did kiss me all about
my body with no shame, and I lay down
between her legs and played until she came.

Oh, we were tired and bruised and sore
and had no dope to smoke, so we lay down
and made our love and fell asleep and woke.

## EVERYONE BEGS FOR MERCY

Everyone begs for mercy.

The small woman tells the police
her niece smokes pot. She does

this for the good of the niece
who lately was embraced by young men
and soon will crack the heads of dolls.

The insurance man in bed with
his hollow wife, remembers that
he was a virgin on his wedding night.

Everyone begs for mercy.

The student marching past
the White House in the rain, takes
acid. He is not afraid. The man
dressed in blue is a friend to me
and a friend to you. Mary had
a little lamb. Jack, jump.
Greetings: Jack. The candle melts
away. A girl holds the head of a boy
in her red lap. She does not scream
at the cops.

The old man squats at the corner
selling pencils. He spits at
the people. They think he is blind.
They do not notice that one hand
holds green pencils and the other blue.

Everyone begs for mercy.

# Bibliography

A number of the poets have published works of fiction, criticism, translations, and so forth. For the purposes of this anthology, only volumes of poetry (excluding children's verse) are listed. Also, when a poet has published his complete poems, books previous to that publication are not listed.

**Allen, Dick**
*Anon and Various Time Machine Poems.* New York: Delacorte, 1971.

**Ammons, A. R.**
*Ommateum.* Philadelphia: Dorrance, 1955.
*Expressions of Sea Level.* Columbus: Ohio State University Press, 1964.
*Corsons Inlet.* Ithaca, N. Y.: Cornell University Press, 1965.
*Tape for the Turn of the Year.* Ithaca, N. Y.: Cornell University Press, 1965.
*Northfield Poems.* Ithaca, N. Y.: Cornell University Press, 1966.
*Selected Poems.* Ithaca, N. Y.: Cornell University Press, 1968.

**Aubert, Alvin**
*Against the Blues.* Detroit: Broadside Press, 1972.

**Berryman, John**
and others. *Five Young American Poets.* New York: New Directions, 1940.
*Poems.* New York: New Directions, 1942.
*The Dispossessed.* New York: William Sloane, 1950.
*Homage to Mistress Bradstreet.* New York: Farrar, Straus & Giroux, 1956.
*His Thoughts Made Pockets and the Plane Buckt.* New York: C. Fredericks, 1958.
*77 Dream Songs.* New York: Farrar, Straus & Giroux, 1964.
*Berryman's Sonnets.* New York: Farrar, Straus & Giroux, 1967.
*Short Poems.* New York: Farrar, Straus & Giroux, 1967.
*His Toy, His Dream, His Rest.* New York: Farrar, Straus & Giroux, 1968.
*The Dream Songs.* New York: Farrar, Straus & Giroux, 1970.

**Bishop, Elizabeth**
*The Complete Poems.* New York: Farrar, Straus & Giroux, 1969.

**Bly, Robert**
*Silence in the Snowy Fields.* Middletown, Conn.: Wesleyan University Press, 1962; and London: Jonathan Cape, 1967.
*The Light Around the Body.* New York: Harper & Row, 1967; and London: Rapp and Whiting, 1968.
*The Morning Glory.* San Francisco: Kayak Books, 1969.

**Brooks, Gwendolyn**
*A Street in Bronzeville.* New York: Harper & Row, 1945.
*Annie Allen.* New York: Harper & Row, 1949.
*Selected Poems.* New York: Harper & Row, 1963.
*In the Mecca.* New York: Harper & Row, 1968.
*Riot.* Detoit: Broadside Press, 1969.

**Bukowski, Charles**
*Flower, Fist and Bestial Wall.* Eureka, Calif.: Hearse Press, 1959.
*Longshot Poems for Broke Players.* New York: 7 Poets Press, 1961.
*Run with the Hunted.* Chicago: Midwest Poetry Chapbooks, 1962.
*It Catches My Heart in Its Hands . . . (New and Selected Poems, 1955-63).* New Orleans: Loujon Press, 1963.
*Cold Dogs in the Courtyard.* Chicago: Chicago Literary Times, 1965.
*Crucifix in a Deathhand.* New Orleans: Loujon Press, 1965.
*At Terror Street and Agony Way.* Los Angeles: Black Sparrow Press, 1968.
*Poems Written Before Jumping Out of an 8-Story Window.* Berkeley, Calif.: Litmus, 1968.
and Philip Lamantia and Harold Norse. *Penguin Modern Poets 13.* Harmondsworth, Middlesex: Penguin, 1969.
*The Days Run Away Like Wild Horses Over the Hills.* Los Angeles: Black Sparrow Press, 1970.

**Canzoneri, Robert**
*Watch Us Pass.* Columbus: Ohio State University Press, 1968.

**Ciardi, John**
*Homeward to America.* New York: Holt, Rinehart and Winston, 1940.
*Other Skies.* Boston: Little, Brown, 1947.
*Live Another Day.* New York: Twayne, 1949.
*From Time to Time.* New York: Twayne, 1951.
*As If.* New Brunswick, N. J.: Rutgers University Press, 1955.
*I Marry You: A Sheaf of Love Poems.* New Brunswick, N. J.: Rutgers University Press, 1958.
*Thirty-Nine Poems.* New Brunswick, N. J.: Rutgers University Press, 1959.

*In the Stoneworks.* New Brunswick, N. J.: Rutgers University Press, 1961.

*In Fact.* New Brunswick, N. J.: Rutgers University Press, 1962.

*Person to Person.* New Brunswick, N. J.: Rutgers University Press, 1964.

*This Strangest Everything.* New Brunswick, N. J.: Rutgers University Press, 1966.

*An Alphabestiary.* New York: Lippincott, 1967.

*Lives of X.* New Brunswick, N. J.: Rutgers University Press, 1971.

---

**Cooper, Jane**

*The Weather of Six Mornings.* New York: Macmillan, 1969.

---

**Corrington, John William**

*Where We Are.* Washington, D. C.: Charioteer Press, 1962.

*The Anatomy of Love.* Fort Lauderdale, Fla.: Roman Books, 1964.

*Mr. Clean and Other Poems.* San Francisco: The Amber House Press, 1964.

*Lines to the South.* Baton Rouge: Louisiana State University Press, 1965.

---

**Corso, Gregory**

*The Vestal Lady on Brattle.* Cambridge, Mass.: Richard Brukenfeld, 1955.

*Gasoline.* San Francisco: City Lights, 1958.

*Bomb.* San Francisco: City Lights, 1958.

*The Happy Birthday of Death.* New York: New Directions, 1960.

*Long Live Man.* New York: New Directions, 1962.

*Selected Poems.* London: Eyre and Spottiswoode, 1962.

and Lawrence Ferlinghetti and Allen Ginsberg, *Penguin Modern Poets 5.* Harmondsworth, Middlesex: Penguin, 1963.

*The Mutation of the Spirit.* New York: Death Press, 1964.

*Elegiac Feelings American.* New York: New Directions, 1970.

---

**Creeley, Robert**

*Poems, 1950-1965.* London: Calder and Boyars, 1966.

*Words: Poems.* New York: Scribner, 1967.

*The Charm: Early and Uncollected Poems.* Mount Horeb, Wis.: Perishable Press, 1968.

*The Finger.* Los Angeles: Black Sparrow Press, 1968.

*Divisions and Other Early Poems.* Mount Horeb, Wis.: Perishable Press, 1969.

*5 Numbers.* New York: Poets Press, 1969.

*St. Martin's.* Los Angeles: Black Sparrow Press, 1971.

---

**Cunningham, J. V.**

*The Helmsman.* San Francisco: Colt Press, 1942.

*The Judge Is Fury.* New York: William Morrow, 1947.

*Doctor Drink.* Cummington, Mass.: Cummington Press, 1950.

*The Exclusions of a Rhyme: Poems and Epigrams.* Denver, Colo.: Alan Swallow, 1960.

*To What Strangers, What Welcome.* Denver, Colo.: Alan Swallow, 1964.

*Some Salt.* Madison, Wis.: Perishable Press, 1967.

---

**Dickey, James**

*Poems 1957-1967.* Middletown, Conn.: Wesleyan University Press, 1967.

*The Eye-Beaters, Blood, Victory, Madness, Bulkhead and Mercy.* New York: Doubleday, 1970.

---

**Dickey, William**

*Of the Festivity.* New Haven, Conn.: Yale University Press, 1959.

*Interpreter's House.* Columbus: Ohio State University Press, 1964.

*Rivers of the Pacific Northwest.* San Francisco: Twowindows Press, 1969.

*More Under Saturn.* Middletown, Conn.: Wesleyan University Press, 1972.

---

**Dillard, R. H. W.**

*The Day I Stopped Dreaming About Barbara Steele.* New York: Knopf, 1966.

*News of the Nile.* Chapel Hill: University of North Carolina Press, 1971.

---

**Dugan, Alan**

*Collected Poems.* New Haven, Conn.: Yale University Press; and London: Faber and Faber, 1969.

---

**Eberhart, Richard**

*Collected Poems 1930-1960.* New York: Oxford University Press; and London: Chatto and Windus, 1960.

*The Quarry.* New York: Oxford University Press; and London: Chatto and Windus, 1964.

*Selected Poems 1930-1965.* New York: New Directions, 1965.

*Thirty One Sonnets.* New York: Eakins Press, 1967.

*Shifts of Being.* New York: Oxford University Press; and London: Chatto and Windus 1968.

---

**Etter, Dave**

*Go Read the River.* Lincoln: University of Nebraska Press, 1966.

*The Last Train to Prophetstown.* Lincoln: University of Nebraska Press, 1968.

*Strawberries.* La Crosse, Wis.: Northeast/Juniper Books, 1970.

---

**Everson, William**
(as William Everson)
*These Are the Ravens.* San Leandro, Calif.: Greater West
    Publishing Company, 1935.
*San Joaquin.* Los Angeles: Ward Ritchie Press, 1939.
*The Masculine Dead.* Prairie City, Ill.: Decker Press, 1942.
*The Waldport Poems.* Waldport, Oreg.: Untide Press, 1943.
*War Elegies.* Waldport, Oreg.: Untide Press, 1944.
*The Residual Years.* Waldport, Oreg.: Untide Press, 1944;
    and New York: New Directions, 1948 and 1968.
*Poems MCMXLII.* Waldport, Oreg.: Untide Press, 1945.
*A Privacy of Speech.* Berkeley, Calif.: Equinox Press, 1949.
*Triptych for the Living.* Oakland, Calif.: Seraphim Press,
    1951.
*The Year's Declension.* Berkeley, Calif.: Berkeley Albion,
    1961.
*The Blowing of the Seed.* New Haven, Conn.: Henry W.
    Wenning, 1966.
*Single Source.* Berkeley, Calif.: Oyez Press, 1966.
*In the Fictive Wish.* Berkeley, Calif.: Oyez Press, 1967.
*The Springing of the Blade.* Reno, Nev.: Black Rock Press,
    1968.
(as Brother Antoninus)
*The Crooked Lines of God.* Detroit: University of Detroit
    Press, 1959.
*The Hazards of Holiness.* New York: Doubleday, 1962.
*The Poet Is Dead.* San Francisco: Auerhahn Press, 1964.
*The Rose of Solitude.* New York: Doubleday, 1967.
*A Canticle to the Waterbirds.* Berkeley, Calif.: Eizo Press,
    1968.
*The City Does Not Die.* Berkeley, Calif.: Oyez Press, 1969.
*The Last Crusade.* Berkeley, Calif.: Oyez Press, 1969.

**Ferlinghetti, Lawrence**
*Pictures of the Gone World.* San Francisco: City Lights, 1955.
*A Coney Island of the Mind.* New York: New Directions,
    1958.
*Tentative Description of a Dinner Given to Promote the
    Impeachment of President Eisenhower.* San Francisco:
    Golden Mountain, 1958.
*One Thousand Fearful Words for Fidel Castro.* San Francisco:
    City Lights, 1961.
*Starting from San Francisco.* New York: New Directions,
    1961.
and Gregory Corso and Allen Ginsberg. *Penguin Modern
    Poets 5.* Harmondsworth, Middlesex: Penguin, 1963.
*Where Is Vietnam?* San Francisco: City Lights, 1965.
*After the Cries of the Birds.* San Francisco: Dave Haslewood
    Books, 1967.
*An Eye on the World: Selected Poems.* London: MacGibbon
    and Kee, 1967.
*Moscow in the Wilderness, Segovia in the Snow.* San
    Francisco: Beach Books, 1967.
*The Secret Meaning of Things.* New York: New Directions,
    1969.

*Tyrannus Nix?* New York: New Directions, 1969.
*Back Roads to Far Towns.* San Francisco: City Lights, 1970.
*Mexican Night.* New York: New Directions, 1970.

**Finkel, Donald**
*The Clothing's New Emperor.* New York: Scribner, 1959.
*Simeon.* New York: Atheneum, 1964.
*A Joyful Noise.* New York: Atheneum, 1966.
*Answer Back.* New York: Atheneum, 1968.
*The Garbage Wars.* New York: Atheneum, 1970.

**Frumkin, Gene**
*The Hawk and the Lizard.* Denver, Colo.: Alan Swallow,
    1963.
*The Orange Tree.* Chicago: Cyfeeth Press, 1965.
*The Rainbow Walker.* Albuquerque, N. M.: The Grasshopper
    Press, 1969.
*Dostoyevsky and Other Nature Poems.* San Luis Obispo,
    Calif.: Solo Press, 1972.
*Locust Cry.* Cerrillos, N. M.: San Marcos Press, 1972.

**Garrett, George**
*The Reverend Ghost: Poems.* New York: Scribner, 1957.
*The Sleeping Gypsy and Other Poems.* Austin: University
    of Texas Press, 1958.
*Abraham's Knife: Poems.* Chapel Hill: University of North
    Carolina Press, 1961.
*For a Bitter Season: New and Selected Poems.* Columbia:
    University of Missouri Press, 1967.

**Ginsberg, Allen**
*Howl.* San Francisco: City Lights, 1956.
*Empty Mirror: Early Poems.* New York: Corinth Books,
    1961.
*Kaddish and Other Poems, 1958-1960.* San Francisco: City
    Lights, 1961.
*Reality Sandwiches.* San Francisco: City Lights, 1963.
and Lawrence Ferlinghetti and Gregory Corso. *Penguin
    Modern Poets 5.* Harmondsworth, Middlesex: Penguin,
    1963.
*T. V. Baby Poems.* New York: Grossman; and London:
    Cape Goliard Press, 1967.
*Ankor-Wat.* London: Fulcrum Press, 1968.
*Planet News: 1961-1967.* San Francisco: City Lights, 1968.
*Airplane Dreams.* San Francisco: City Lights and Anansi
    Press, 1969.
*Indian Journals.* San Francisco: Dave Haselwood Books
    with City Lights, 1969.

**Hall, Donald**
*Exiles and Marriages.* New York: Viking, 1955.
*The Dark Houses.* New York: Viking, 1958.

*A Roof of Tiger Lilies.* New York: Viking; and London: André Deutsch, 1964.
*The Alligator Bride: Poems New and Selected.* New York: Harper & Row, 1969.
*The Yellow Room.* New York: Harper & Row, 1971.

**Harrison, James**
*Plain Song.* New York: Norton, 1965.
*Locations.* New York: Norton, 1968.
*Outlyer.* New York: Norton, 1971.

**Hayden, Robert**
*Heartshape in the Dust.* Detroit: Falcon Press, 1940.
and Myron O'Higgins. *The Lion and the Archer.* Nashville, Tenn.: The Counterpoise Press, 1948.
*Figure of Time.* Nashville, Tenn.: The Counterpoise Press, 1954.
*A Ballad of Remembrance.* London: Paul Bremen, 1962.
*Selected Poems.* New York: October House, 1966.
*Words in the Mourning Time.* New York: October House, 1971.

**Hecht, Anthony**
*A Summoning of Stones.* New York: Macmillan, 1954.
*The Seven Deadly Sins.* Northampton, Mass.: Gehenna Press, 1958.
*The Hard Hours.* New York: Atheneum, 1968.

**Hollander, John**
*Crackling of Thorns.* New Haven, Conn.: Yale University Press, 1958.
*Movie-Going and Other Poems.* New York: Atheneum, 1962.
*Visions from the Ramble.* New York: Atheneum, 1966.
*Philomel.* London: Turret Books, 1968.
*Types of Shape.* New York: Atheneum, 1969.

**Howes, Barbara**
*The Undersea Farmer.* Pawlet, Vt.: Banyan Press, 1948.
*In the Cold Country.* New York: Bonacio and Saul with Grove Press, 1954.
*Light and Dark.* Middletown, Conn.: Wesleyan University Press, 1959.
*Looking Up at Leaves.* New York: Knopf, 1966.

**Huff, Robert**
*Colonel Johnson's Ride.* Detroit: Wayne State University Press, 1959.
*The Course.* Detroit: Wayne State University Press, 1966.
*The Ventriloquist.* Chicago: Swallow Press, 1972.

**Hughes, Langston**
*The Weary Blues.* New York: Knopf, 1926.
*Fine Clothes to the Jew.* New York: Knopf, 1927.
*Shakespeare in Harlem.* New York: Knopf, 1942.
*Fields of Wonder.* New York: Knopf, 1947.
*One-Way Ticket.* New York: Knopf, 1948.
*Montage of a Dream Deferred.* New York: Holt, Rinehart and Winston, 1951.
*Laughing to Keep from Crying.* New York: Holt, Rinehart and Winston, 1952.
*Selected Poems of Langston Hughes.* New York: Knopf, 1959.
*Ask Your Mama: 12 Moods for Jazz.* New York: Knopf, 1961.

**Jarrell, Randall**
*The Complete Poems.* New York: Farrar, Straus & Giroux, 1969.

**Jerome, Judson**
*Light in the West.* Francestown, N. H.: Golden Quill Press, 1962.
*The Ocean's Warning to the Skin Diver and Other Love Poems.* Point Richmond, Calif.: Crown Point Press, 1964.
*Serenade.* Point Richmond, Calif.: Crown Point Press, 1968.

**Justice, Donald**
*The Summer Anniversaries.* Middletown, Conn.: Wesleyan University Press, 1960.
*A Local Storm.* Iowa City, Iowa: Stone Wall Press, 1963.
*Night Light.* Middletown, Conn.: Wesleyan University Press, 1967.
*Sixteen Poems.* Iowa City, Iowa: Stone Wall Press, 1970.

**Kennedy, X. J.**
*Nude Descending a Staircase.* New York: Doubleday, 1961.
*Growing into Love.* New York: Doubleday, 1969.

**Kessler, Milton**
*A Road Came Once.* Columbus: Ohio State University Press, 1963.
*Called Home.* New York: Black Bird Press, 1967.
*Heart Stones.* Boston: Impressions Workshop, 1970.

**Kinnell, Galway**
*What a Kingdom It Was.* Boston: Houghton Mifflin, 1960.
*Flower Herding on Mount Monadnock.* Boston: Houghton Mifflin, 1964.
*Poems of Night.* London: Rapp and Carroll, 1968.
*Body Rags.* Boston: Houghton Mifflin, 1968; and London: Rapp and Whiting, 1969.
*The Book of Nightmares.* Boston: Houghton Mifflin, 1971.

**Kumin, Maxine**
*Halfway.* New York: Holt, Rinehart and Winston, 1961.
*The Privilege.* New York: Harper & Row, 1965.
*The Nightmare Factory.* New York: Harper & Row, 1970.

**Levertov, Denise**
*The Double Image.* London: Cresset Press, 1946.
*Here and Now.* San Francisco: City Lights, 1957.
*Overland to the Islands.* Highlands, N. C.: Jargon Press, 1958.
*With Eyes at the Back of Our Heads.* New York: New Directions, 1960.
*The Jacob's Ladder.* New York: New Directions, 1962; and London: Jonathan Cape, 1965.
*O Taste and See.* New York: New Directions, 1964.
*The Sorrow Dance.* New York: New Directions, 1967; and London: Jonathan Cape, 1968.
and Kenneth Rexroth and William Carlos Williams. *Penguin Modern Poets 9.* Harmondsworth, Middlesex: Penguin, 1967.
*Embroideries.* Los Angeles: Black Sparrow Press, 1969.
*Relearning the Alphabet.* New York: New Directions, 1970.

**Lieberman, Laurence.**
*The Unblinding.* New York: Macmillan, 1968.

**Logan, John**
*Cycle for Mother Cabrini.* New York: Grove Press, 1955.
*Ghosts of the Heart.* Chicago: University of Chicago Press, 1960.
*Spring of the Thief.* New York: Knopf, 1963.
*The Zig-Zag Walk.* New York: Dutton, 1969.
*New and Selected Poems.* New York: Dutton, 1972.

**Lowell, Robert**
*The Land of Unlikeness.* Cummington, Mass.: Cummington Press, 1944.
*Lord Weary's Castle.* New York: Harcourt Brace Jovanovich, 1946.
*Poems, 1938-1949.* London: Faber and Faber, 1950.
*The Mills of the Kavanaughs.* New York: Harcourt Brace Jovanovich, 1951.
*Life Studies.* New York: Farrar, Straus & Giroux; and London: Faber and Faber, 1959.
*For the Union Dead.* New York: Farrar, Straus & Giroux, 1964; and London: Faber and Faber, 1965.
*Near the Ocean.* New York: Farrar, Straus & Giroux; and London: Faber and Faber, 1967.
*Notebooks, 1967-68.* New York: Farrar, Straus & Giroux, 1969.

**Margolis, Gary**
*Rearrangement for the Brain.* New York: Holt, Rinehart and Winston, 1972.

**Meredith, William**
*Love Letter from an Impossible Land.* New Haven, Conn.: Yale University Press, 1944.
*Ships and Other Figures.* Princeton, N. J.: Princeton University Press, 1948.
*The Open Sea and Other Poems.* New York: Knopf, 1958.
*The Wreck of the Thresher and Other Poems.* New York: Knopf, 1964.
*Earth Walk: New and Selected Poems.* New York: Knopf, 1970.

**Merrill, James**
*The Black Swan.* Athens: Icaros, 1946.
*First Poems.* New York: Knopf, 1951.
*Short Stories.* Pawlet, Vt.: Banyan Press, 1954.
*The Country of a Thousand Years of Peace.* New York: Knopf, 1959.
*Selected Poems.* London: Chatto and Windus, 1961.
*Water Street.* New York: Atheneum, 1962.
*Nights and Days.* New York; Atheneum; and London: Chatto and Windus, 1966.
*The Thousand and Second Night.* Athens: Editions 8 1/2, 1966.
*The Fire Screen.* New York: Atheneum, 1969.

**Merwin, W. S.**
*A Mask for Janus.* New Haven, Conn.: Yale University Press, 1952.
*The Dancing Bears.* New Haven, Conn.: Yale University Press, 1954.
*Green with Beasts.* London and New York: Rupert Hart-Davis, 1956.
*The Drunk in the Furnace.* New York: Macmillan; and London: Rupert Hart-Davis, 1960
*The Moving Target.* New York: Atheneum, 1963; and London: Rupert Hart-Davis, 1967.
*The Lice.* New York: Atheneum; and London: Rupert Hart-Davis, 1967.
*Animae.* San Francisco: Kayak Books, 1969.
*The Carrier of Ladders.* New York: Atheneum, 1970.

**Miles, Josephine**
*Poems, 1930-1960.* Bloomington: Indiana University Press, 1960.
*Kinds of Affection.* Middletown, Conn.: Wesleyan University Press, 1967.

**Miller, Vassar**

*Adam's Footprint*. New Orleans: New Orleans Poetry Journal, 1956.

*Wage War on Silence*. Middletown, Conn.: Wesleyan University Press, 1960.

*My Bones Being Wiser*. Middletown, Conn.: Wesleyan University Press, 1963.

*Onions and Roses*. Middletown, Conn.: Wesleyan University Press, 1968.

---

**Nemerov, Howard**

*The Image and the Law*. New York: Holt, Rinehart and Winston, 1947.

*Guide to the Ruins*. New York: Random House, 1950.

*The Salt Garden*. Boston: Little, Brown, 1955.

*Mirrors and Windows*. Chicago: University of Chicago Press, 1958.

*New and Selected Poems*. Chicago: University of Chicago Press, 1960.

*The Next Room of the Dream: Poems and Two Plays*. Chicago: University of Chicago Press, 1962.

and others; edited by Thom Gunn and Ted Hughes. *Five American Poets*. London: Faber and Faber, 1963.

*The Blue Swallows*. Chicago: University of Chicago Press, 1967.

*The Winter Lightning: Selected Poems*. London: Rapp and Whiting, 1968.

---

**Nims, John Frederick**

and others. *Five Young American Poets: Third Series*. New York: New Directions, 1944.

*The Iron Pastoral*. New York: William Sloane, 1947.

*Knowledge of the Evening*. New Brunswick, N. J.: Rutgers University Press, 1960.

*Of Flesh and Bone*. New Brunswick, N. J.: Rutgers University Press, 1968.

---

**Oates, Joyce Carol**

*Anonymous Sins and Other Poems*. Baton Rouge: Louisiana State University Press, 1969.

*Love and Its Derangements*. Baton Rouge: Louisiana State University Press, 1970.

---

**O' Hara, Frank**

*The Collected Poems of Frank O' Hara*. New York: Knopf, 1971.

---

**Olson, Charles**

*To Corrado Cagli*. New York: Knoedler Gallery, 1947.

*Y and X*. Washington, D. C.: Black Sun, 1950.

*Letter for Melville*. North Carolina: Black Mountain College, 1951.

*This*. North Carolina: Black Mountain College, 1952.

*In Cold Hell, in Thicket*. Majorca: Divers Press; and Dorchester, Mass.: Origin, 1953.

*The Maximus Poems 1-10*. Highlands, N. C.: Jargon Press, 1953.

*The Maximus Poems 11-22*. Highlands, N. C.: Jargon Press, 1956.

*O' Ryan*. San Francisco: White Rabbit Press, 1958.

*Projective Verse*. New York: Totem Press, 1959.

*The Distances*. New York and London: Grove Press, 1960.

*The Maximus Poems*. New York: Corinth Books; and London: Centaur Press, 1960.

*Maximus, From Dogtown I*. San Francisco: Auerhahn Press, 1961.

*O' Ryan 1 2 3 4 5 6 7 8 9 10*. San Francisco: White Rabbit Press, 1965.

*Proprioception*. San Francisco: Four Seasons, 1965.

*Charles Olson Reading at Berkeley*. San Francisco: Coyote Books, 1966.

*Selected Writings*. New York: New Directions, 1967.

*The Maximus Poems, IV, V, VI*. London: Cape Goliard Press, 1968.

---

**Pack, Robert**

*The Irony of Joy*. New York: Scribner, 1955.

*A Stranger's Privilege*. New York: Macmillan, 1959.

*Guarded by Women*. New York: Random House, 1963.

*Selected Poems*. London: Chatto and Windus, 1965.

*Home From the Cemetery*. New Brunswick, N. J.: Rutgers University Press, 1969.

---

**Patchen, Kenneth**

*Collected Poems*. New York: New Directions, 1969.

*Aflame and Afun of Walking Faces*. New York: New Directions, 1970.

*Wonderings*. New York: New Directions, 1971.

---

**Plath, Sylvia**

*Colossus*. New York: Knopf, 1960.

*Ariel*. New York: Harper & Row, 1966.

---

**Rich, Adrienne**

*A Change of World*. New Haven, Conn.: Yale University Press, 1951.

*The Diamond Cutters*. New York: Harper & Row, 1955.

*Snapshots of a Daughter-in-Law*. New York: Harper & Row, 1963; and London: Chatto and Windus, 1970.

*Necessities of Life*. New York: Norton, 1966.

*Selected Poems*. London: Chatto and Windus, 1967.

*Leaflets*. New York: Norton, 1969.

*The Will to Change*. New York: Norton, 1971.

---

**Roethke, Theodore**
*Open House.* New York: Knopf, 1941.
*The Lost Son and Other Poems.* New York: Doubleday, 1948.
*Praise to the End!* New York: Doubleday, 1951.
*The Waking: Poems 1933-1953.* New York: Doubleday, 1953.
*The Collected Verse of Theodore Roethke: Words for the Wind.* New York: Doubleday, 1958; and Bloomington: Indiana University Press, 1961.
*Sequence, Sometimes Metaphysical.* Iowa City, Iowa: Stone Wall Press, 1963.
*The Far Field.* New York: Doubleday, 1964.

**Sexton, Anne**
*To Bedlam and Part Way Back.* Boston: Houghton Mifflin, 1960.
*All My Pretty Ones.* Boston: Houghton Mifflin, 1962.
*Selected Poems.* London and New York: Oxford University Press, 1964.
*Live or Die.* Boston: Houghton Mifflin, 1966; and London: Oxford University Press, 1967.
*Love Poems.* Boston: Houghton Mifflin; and London: Oxford University Press, 1969.

**Shapiro, Karl**
*Poems.* Baltimore: Waverly Press, 1935.
*Poems, 1940-1953.* New York: Random House, 1953.
*Poems of a Jew.* New York: Random House, 1958.
*The Bourgeois Poet.* New York: Random House, 1964.
*Selected Poems.* New York: Random House, 1968.
*White Haired Lover.* New York: Random House, 1968.

**Simpson, Louis**
*The Arrivistes.* New York: Fine Editions Press, 1949.
*Good News of Death.* New York: Scribner, 1955.
*A Dream of Governors.* Middletown, Conn.: Wesleyan University Press, 1959.
*At the End of the Open Road.* Middletown, Conn.: Wesleyan University Press, 1963.
and others. *Five American Poets.* London: Faber and Faber, 1963.
*Selected Poems.* New York: Harcourt Brace Jovanovich, 1965.
*Adventures of the Letter I.* New York: Harper & Row, 1971.

**Slavitt, David R.**
*Poets of Today VIII.* New York: Scribner, 1961.
*The Carnivore.* Chapel Hill: The University of North Carolina Press, 1965.
*Day Sailing.* Chapel Hill: The University of North Carolina Press, 1969.

*Child's Play.* Baton Rouge: Louisiana State University Press, 1972.

**Smith, William Jay**
*Poems 1947-1957.* Boston: Little, Brown, 1957.
*The Tin Can and Other Poems.* New York: Delacorte, 1966.
*New and Selected Poems.* New York: Delacorte, 1970.

**Snodgrass, W. D.**
*Heart's Needle.* New York: Knopf, 1959; and Hull, Yorkshire: Marvell Press, 1960.
*After Experience: Poems and Translations.* New York: Harper & Row, 1968; and London: Oxford University Press, 1969.

**Snyder, Gary**
*Riprap.* Kyoto, Japan: Origin Press, 1959.
*Myths and Texts.* New York: Totem Press, 1960.
*The Firing.* R. L. Ross, 1964.
*Hop, Skip, and Jump.* Berkeley, Calif.: Auerhahn Press, for Oyez Press, 1964.
*Nanoa Knows.* San Francisco: Four Seasons, 1964.
*Six Sections of Mountains and Rivers Without End.* San Francisco: Four Seasons, 1965; and London: Fulcrum Press, 1967.
*A Range of Poems.* London: Fulcrum Press, 1966.
*The Black Country.* London: Fulcrum Press, 1967; and New York: New Directions, 1968.
*Regarding Wave.* New York: New Directions, 1970.

**Spacks, Barry**
*The Company of Children.* New York: Doubleday, 1969.

**Stafford, William**
*West of Your City.* Georgetown, Calif.: Talisman Press, 1960.
*Traveling Through the Dark.* New York: Harper & Row, 1962.
and others. *Five American Poets.* London: Faber and Faber, 1963.
and others. *Five Poets of the Pacific Northwest.* Seattle: University of Washington Press, 1964.
*The Rescued Year.* New York: Harper & Row, 1966.
*Eleven Untitled Poems.* Mount Horeb, Wis.: Perishable Press, 1968.
*Allegiances.* New York: Harper & Row, 1970.

**Steingass, David**
*Body Compass.* Pittsburgh: University of Pittsburgh Press, 1969.

**Stone, John**
*The Smell of Matches.* New Brunswick, N. J.: Rutgers University Press, 1972.

**Strand, Mark**
*Sleeping with One Eye Open.* Iowa City, Iowa: Stone Wall Press, 1964.
*Reasons for Moving.* New York: Atheneum, 1968.
*Darker.* New York: Atheneum, 1970.

**Stuart, Dabney**
*The Diving Bell.* New York: Knopf, 1966.
*A Particular Place.* New York: Knopf, 1969.

**Summers, Hollis**
*The Walks Near Athens.* New York: Harper & Row, 1959.
*Someone Else.* Philadelphia: Lippincott, 1962.
*Seven Occasions.* New Brunswick, N. J.: Rutgers University Press, 1965.
*The Peddler and Other Domestic Matters.* New Brunswick, N. J.: Rutgers University Press, 1967.
*Sit Opposite Each Other.* New Brunswick, N. J.: Rutgers University Press, 1970.

**Turco, Lewis**
*Day After History.* Arlington, Va.: privately printed, 1956.
*First Poems.* Francestown, N. H.: Golden Quill Press, 1960.
*The Sketches of Lewis Turco and Livevil: A Mask.* Cleveland: American Weave Press, 1962.
*Awaken, Bells Falling.* Columbia: University of Missouri Press, 1968.
*The Inhabitant.* Northampton, Mass.: Despa Press, 1970.

**Viereck, Peter**
*Terror and Decorum.* New York: Scribner, 1948.
*Strike Through the Mask.* New York: Scribner, 1950.
*The First Morning.* New York: Scribner, 1952.
*The Persimmon Tree.* New York: Scribner, 1956.
*The Tree Witch.* New York: Scribner, 1961.
*New and Selected Poems.* Indianapolis, Ind.: Bobbs-Merrill, 1967.

**Wagoner, David**
*Dry Sun, Dry Wind.* Bloomington: Indiana University Press, 1953.
*A Place to Stand.* Bloomington: Indiana University Press, 1958.
*The Nesting Ground.* Bloomington: Indiana University Press, 1963.
*Staying Alive.* Bloomington: Indiana University Press, 1966.
*New and Selected Poems.* Bloomington: Indiana University Press, 1969.

*Working Against Time.* London: Rapp and Whiting, 1970.
*Riverbed.* Bloomington: Indiana University Press, 1972.

**Wakoski, Diane**
*Coins and Coffins.* New York: Hawk's Well Press, 1962.
and others. *Four Young Lady Poets.* New York: Totem-Corinth, 1962.
*Discrepancies and Apparitions.* New York: Doubleday, 1966.
*The George Washington Poems.* New York: Riverrun Press, 1967.
*The Diamond Merchant.* Cambridge, Mass.: Sans Souci Press, 1968.
*Greed: Parts I and II.* Los Angeles: Black Sparrow Press, 1968.
*Inside the Blood Factory.* New York: Doubleday, 1968.
*Some Poems for the Buddha's Birthday.* New York: Pierrepont Press, 1969.
*The Magellanic Clouds.* Los Angeles: Black Sparrow Press, 1970.
*The Motorcycle Betrayal Poems.* New York: Doubleday, 1971.
*Smudging.* Los Angeles: Black Sparrow Press, 1972.

**Wallace, Robert**
*This Various World and Other Poems.* New York: Scribner, 1957.
*Views From a Ferris Wheel.* New York: Dutton, 1965.
*Ungainly Things.* New York: Dutton, 1968.

**Warren, Robert Penn**
*Thirty-Six Poems.* New York: Alcestis Press, 1936.
*Eleven Poems on the Same Theme.* New York: New Directions, 1942.
*Selected Poems, 1923-1943.* New York: Harcourt Brace Jovanovich, 1944.
*Brother to Dragons.* New York: Random House, 1953.
*Promises: Poems, 1954-1956.* New York: Random House, 1957.
*You, Emperors and Others: Poems, 1957-1960.* New York: Random House, 1960.
*Selected Poems: New and Old, 1923-1966.* New York: Random House, 1966.
*Incarnations.* New York: Random House, 1968.
*Audubon: A Vision.* New York: Random House, 1969.

**Whitehead, James**
*Domains.* Baton Rouge: Louisiana State University Press, 1966.

**Wilbur, Richard**
*Poems of Richard Wilbur.* New York: Harcourt Brace Jovanovich, 1963.

*Walking to Sleep: New Poems and Translations.* New York: Harcourt Brace Jovanovich, 1969.

**Williams, John**
*The Broken Landscape.* Denver, Colo.: Alan Swallow, 1949.
*The Necessary Lie.* Denver, Colo.: Verb Publications, 1965.

**Williams, Miller**
*A Circle of Stone.* Baton Rouge: Louisiana State University Press, 1964.
*Recital* (English and Spanish). Valparaiso, Chile: Ediciones Océano, 1964.
*So Long at the Fair.* New York: Dutton, 1968.
*The Only World There Is.* New York: Dutton, 1971.

**Wright, Charles**
*The Dream Animal.* Toronto: The House of Anansi Press, 1968.
*The Grave of the Right Hand.* Middletown, Conn.: Wesleyan University Press, 1970.

**Wright, James**
*Collected Poems.* Middletown, Conn.: Wesleyan University Press, 1971.

**Young, Al**
*Dancing.* New York: Corinth Books, 1969.

## RECORDS OF THE POETS READING FROM THEIR OWN WORKS

BLY, ROBERT (with others). *Today's Poets: Their Poems, Their Voices.* Folkways/Scholastic, Vol. 5 (LC R-68-3668).

BROOKS, GWENDOLYN. *GB Reading Her Poetry.* Caedmon (TC 1244).

CIARDI, JOHN (with others). *Anthology of Contemporary American Poetry.* Folkways/Scholastic (LC R-62-135).

CIARDI, JOHN (with others). *As If.* Folkways/Scholastic (FL 9780).

CIARDI, JOHN (with others). *This Strangest Everything.* Spoken Arts, 2 vols. (957).

CREELEY, ROBERT (with others). *Today's Poets: Their Poems, Their Voices.* Folkways/Scholastic, Vol. 3 (LC R-68-3002).

DICKEY, JAMES. *The Poems of James Dickey.* Spoken Arts (SA 984).

DICKEY, WILLIAM. *The Poetry of William Dickey.* McGraw-Hill Seminars in Sound (75 994).

EBERHART, RICHARD. *RE Reading His Poetry.* Caedmon (TC 1243).

HALL, DONALD (with others). *Today's Poets: Their Poems, Their Voices.* Folkways/Scholastic, Vol. 1 (LC R-66-2642).

HAYDEN, ROBERT (with others). *Today's Poets: Their Poems, Their Voices.* Folkways/Scholastic, Vol. 4 (LC R-68-3275).

HOWES, BARBARA. *The Poetry of Barbara Howes.* McGraw-Hill Seminars in Sound (78113).

HUFF, ROBERT. *The Poetry of Robert Huff.* McGraw-Hill Seminars in Sound (78131).

HUGHES, LANGSTON. *The Best of Simple.* Folkways/Scholastic (FL 9789).
———. *The Dream Keeper.* Folkways/Scholastic (LC R-55644).
———. *The Poetry of LH.* Caedmon (TC 1272).

KINNELL, GALWAY (with others). *Today's Poets: Their Poems, Their Voices.* Folkways/Scholastic, Vol. 5 (LC R-68-3668).

LEVERTOV, DENISE (with others). *Today's Poets: Their Poems, Their Voices.* Folkways/Scholastic, Vol. 3 (LC R-68-3002).

LOGAN, JOHN (with others). *Today's Poets: Their Poems, Their Voices.* Folkways/Scholastic, Vol. 5 (LC R-68-3668).

LOWELL, ROBERT. *The Poetry of Robert Lowell.* McGraw-Hill Seminars in Sound (78112).

MILES, JOSEPHINE (with others). *Today's Poets: Their Poems, Their Voices.* Folkways/Scholastic, Vol. 2 (LC R-66-342).

PATCHEN, KENNETH. *KP Reads His Love Poems.* Folkways/Scholastic (FL 9719).
_____. *KP Reads with Jazz.* Folkways/Scholastic (FL 9718).
_____. *Selected Poems.* Folkways/Scholastic (FL 9717).

RICH, ADRIENNE. *The Poetry of Adrienne Rich.* McGraw-Hill Seminars in Sound (78114).

RICH, ADRIENNE (with others). *Today's Poets: Their Poems, Their Voices.* Folkways/Scholastic, Vol. 4 (LC R-68-3275).

ROETHKE, THEODORE (with others). *Anthology of Contemporary American Poetry.* Folkways/Scholastic (LC R-62-135).

ROETHKE, THEODORE (with others). *Words for the Wind.* Folkways/Scholastic. (LC R-62-851).

SEXTON, ANNE. *The Poetry of Anne Sexton.* McGraw-Hill Seminars in Sound (75999).

SHAPIRO, KARL. *Anthology of Contemporary American Poetry.* Folkways/Scholastic (LC R-62-135).

SIMPSON, LOUIS (with others). *Today's Poets: Their Poems, Their Voices.* Folkways/Scholastic, Vol. 1 (LC R-66-3642).

SMITH, WILLIAM JAY. *The Poetry of William Jay Smith.* McGraw-Hill Seminars in Sound (78103).

SNYDER, GARY (with others). *Today's Poets: Their Poems, Their Voices.* Folkways/Scholastic, Vol. 4 (LC R-68-3275).

STAFFORD, WILLIAM (with others). *Today's Poets: Their Poems, Their Voices.* Folkways/Scholastic, Vol. 2 (LC R-66-342).

WAGONER, DAVID (with others). *Today's Poets: Their Poems, Their Voices.* Folkways/Scholastic, Vol. 2 (LC R-66-342).

WILBUR, RICHARD. *RW Reading His Poetry.* Caedmon (TC 1248).

WILLIAMS, MILLER. *The Poetry of Miller Williams.* McGraw-Hill Seminars in Sound (81624).

WRIGHT, JAMES (with others). *Today's Poets: Their Poems, Their Voices.* Folkways/Scholastic, Vol. 3 (LC R-68-3002).

*The Caedmon Treasury of Modern Poets Reading Their Poetry* (TC 2006) has one or two poems each read by twenty poets, including from this collection Elizabeth Bishop, Richard Eberhart, and Richard Wilbur.

# Index of Poems

# Index of Poets